Learning Resources Centre

...or before the
...te stamped below.

Kingston College
Kingston Hall Road
Kingston upon Thames
KT1 2AQ

BRADMAN'S BEST

THE WORLD'S GREATEST CRICKETER SELECTS HIS ALL-TIME BEST TEAM

ROLAND PERRY

BANTAM PRESS

LONDON · NEW YORK · TORONTO · SYDNEY · AUCKLAND

TRANSWORLD PUBLISHERS
61–63 Uxbridge Road, London W5 5SA
a division of The Random House Group Ltd

RANDOM HOUSE AUSTRALIA (PTY) LTD
20 Alfred Street, Milsons Point, Sydney,
New South Wales 2061, Australia

RANDOM HOUSE NEW ZEALAND LTD
18 Poland Road, Glenfield, Auckland 10, New Zealand

RANDOM HOUSE SOUTH AFRICA (PTY) LTD
Endulini, 5a Jubilee Road, Parktown 2193, South Africa

Published 2001 by Bantam Press
a division of Transworld Publishers

A catalogue record for this book is available from the British Library.
ISBN 0593 049012

Printed in Great Britain
by Clays Ltd, Bungay, Suffolk

1 3 5 7 9 10 8 6 4 2

To the memory of

John Winkleman
Harvey Atkinson
& Andrew Merry

Three fine men and cricketers

Contents

Acknowledgments

My thanks go to Sir Donald Bradman who, over the last six years of his life, indulged my keen interest—he called it 'obsession'—in knowing his best-ever world team and the reasons for his choices.

My appreciation goes to all those who helped in my research and the creation of this book. They include some players and their families, the Bradman Museum, the MCC library, Roger Page, Alan Young, Deborah Callaghan, Martin Ashenden, Thos Hodgson, Philip Wood, James Bell and all at Random House, in particular Managing Editor, Vanessa Mickan, and Head of Publishing, Jane Palfreyman.

Some of the royalties from the sale of this book will go to the Bradman Memorial Fund administered by the Bradman Museum. The fund was set up by Richard Mulvaney and John Bradman to honour Sir Donald's last public wish that support be given to the development of indigenous and other cricketers from less privileged backgrounds.

Roland Perry
August 2001

BRADMAN'S
BEST

THE
SELECTOR

Sir Donald Bradman saw more big cricket than anyone else in the 20th Century, watching the best
cricketers from all major playing nations—with
just a handful of exceptions—from the very early
years of the century onwards. This, plus the fact
that he played with or selected Test sides from 1928 to 1971,
forged in him an unparalleled appreciation of the game. He
was second to none in judging a cricketer's capacities and
talents, and had a deep comprehension of the game. He was
the buff's buff, with command over the laws, the facts and the
stats. Easily one of the game's finest observers, Bradman
remembered all the details, from the trivial and the humorous,
to the greatest incidents—and the darkest. He never lost the
ability to distil it all with astuteness, and the vision that was
sometimes a half-century ahead of its time.

Bradman's love affair with cricket began when, at the age of
12, he saw his first Test—the Fifth of the 1920-21 Ashes
contest between Australia and England—at the Sydney Cricket
Ground. Bradman knew that his father George was catching
the train from Bowral to watch the first two days and nagged
him into taking him along. On Friday, 25 February 1921, the
young Don stepped into the fabled arena for the first time and
developed a passion for the game—a passion that would last
for the rest of the 20th Century.

Like countless small boys, Bradman dreamt of playing for
his country. Now the dream took shape at the SCG, with its

quaint English-style Members' Stand and the famed 'Hill', 20,000 spectators, and Ashes players out on the ground. Bradman played on a rough strip at his local state school, on the Bowral Oval with the local senior team, with friends and family in the street, and alone, hitting a ball against the water tank at the back of his house. From that moment on, when he played, in his mind he would be in the big time where the gods of the game strode the rich green surface. They were no longer just names in his head in those endless solo games in the back-yard at Mum's, but on the field in fierce competition. Among the English players he saw in those two days were greats such as Hobbs, Rhodes, Hendren, Woolley and Parkin. The Australian side included Armstrong, Bardsley, Macartney, Taylor (Bradman's hero), Gregory, Ryder and McDonald.

'Woolley's beautiful stroke-making, the smooth rhythm of Ted McDonald and the glorious catching of Parkin by Johnny Taylor come back to me as though they happened yesterday,' Bradman recalled to me 75 years later.

'I have seen as an observer, player or administrator,' he said, 'all the great players of the century. I can claim to span almost every decade of it because many of the great 1920-21 (English and Australian) players also played before the great war. I was always fascinated to watch and compare players of the different generations.'

Bradman was a spectator at several Test matches in the 1920s, then at the age of 20, in the 1928-29 Ashes series, walked into the game as a player at the highest level. It wasn't to be the auspicious debut against England that he wanted. He made 18 and 1 in the First Test at Brisbane, and there was disagreement among selectors over whether he should be retained or dumped. The four selectors met a few days before the Second Test at Sydney. New South Wales' Warren Bardsley wanted to give Bradman a second chance. So did South Australia's Dr Dolling. However E E Bean from Victoria and

J S Hutcheon from Queensland wanted him out. There was discussion, debate, then fervent argument. Late that night the selectors reached an impasse and decided to reconvene the next morning. Bean hammered the point that Bradman had dropped two catches in the Test. Hutcheon reminded the others that former Australian captain Warwick Armstrong had said Bradman was 'too raw and flawed' to be a Test player yet. After further heated argument, Dolling relented and left Bardsley as the only selector supporting the young, potential champion. Bradman was made 12th man. So acrimonious and divided was the meeting that Aubrey Oxlade, the chairman of the Board of Control, the then governing body of cricket in Australia, publicly called for an odd number of selectors to always be appointed so that a majority decision could be reached.

The omission was one of the worst decisions ever made in the history of Australian cricket and a personal blow for Bradman, but he had the character and the ability to put it behind him. It was the second poor selection decision made against Bradman. The other was made two years earlier by several Test, state and club selectors and administrators when Bradman travelled to Sydney for a nets tryout. Only one, Harold 'Mudgee' Cranney, thought him a serious batting prospect. The others wrote him off. Cranney tried and failed to secure him a place in the Petersham club team in Sydney. But according to the collective genius of the selectors, the return train fare from Bowral to Sydney—about 85 cents in today's money—was too much.

Bradman took both poor selection decisions and proved them all wrong.

After his Test setback in 1928-29, Bradman returned for the Third Test of the 1928-29 season, made 79 and 112 in a beaten side and never was dropped again in his 20-year career. Through 52 Tests against England, the West Indies, India and

South Africa, Bradman established himself as the greatest batsman of all time. His average of 100 (rounded off from 99.94) over a Test career of 80 innings is about twice the average of the next best bunch of batsmen in history. In his 234 first-class matches and 338 innings he averaged 95.14. Even at club level in Sydney and Adelaide he averaged around 87. Over time he played against and with the best of his era and, as a captain of Australia and South Australia, developed an acute appreciation of the skills and weaknesses of others.

Bradman was an Australian selector on the Ashes tour of England in 1934 as Bill Woodfull's deputy. He was a state selector in 1935-36, when he transferred from Sydney to Adelaide to live. From then on, he became a key assessor of Australian and world talent.

In 1936, Bradman was appointed as a Test selector, just a few days after his 28th birthday. The vacancy had arisen when Dr Dolling, the South Australian representative, died in June that year. Bradman took his place officially on 10 September alongside E A Dwyer (New South Wales) and Bill Johnson (Victoria).

There had never been a younger selector. Bradman accepted the place 'with some reservations'. It gave him increased power over and above his position—soon to be announced—as Australian captain.

To many, such as former Test captain Richie Benaud, he was the finest selector of all.

'Sir Donald was easily the best selector I came across in the game anywhere in the world, not just Australia,' said Benaud.

Bradman could be blunt in his assessment, and rarely let sentiment touch his judgment. This upset some along the way. In 1934, opening bat Jack Fingleton blamed Bradman for being left out of the tour. Bradman was not a selector *for* the tour (only on it), and resented being put on the spot by selectors about whom he thought would be the better opener in

England: Fingleton or Bill Brown. Bradman had no hesitation in saying Brown, and the selectors agreed with him. No-one could argue that Fingleton would have done better than Brown in England, yet Fingleton never forgave Bradman.

In 1938, when Bradman was skipper and a selector, there was another selection furore. The great leg-spinner Clarrie Grimmett, then 46 years old, was left out of the England tour. In his place was Frank Ward, 29, who was far fitter and a better field. During the preceding first-class season, 1937-38, Ward had done far better than everyone, including Grimmett, in a Test trial match. During the season Ward had taken 25 wickets at 27.88 compared with Grimmett's better figures of 30 at 22.86. Bill O'Reilly was always going to be the first spinner chosen and Leslie Fleetwood-Smith had earned the second spot after his effort in the 1936-37 series. Australia was short of quality speedsters and therefore forced to take a third spinner, Ward.

'It was the collective judgment (of the three selectors) at the time that Grimmett was past his best,' Bradman commented. 'He wasn't using his leg-break as much as he used to because he couldn't turn it as much as he once could. Certainly between 1927-28 when I first faced him and 1937-38 there was a marked difference in his capacity with the leg-break. He was using the flipper a lot more in the twilight of his career, and had been since 1932-33.'

Bill O'Reilly made much of the Grimmett omission from then until O'Reilly's death in 1992, and indeed afterwards. In tapes left with the National Library of Australia's Oral History Archive and made public posthumously, O'Reilly claimed that a dressing-room confrontation in 1937-38 between Grimmett and Bradman caused the spinner to miss the 1938 tour. Bradman denied this.

'That's totally untrue,' he said. 'It was just part of the long-running vendetta by O'Reilly and Fingleton.'

'There was no particular argument between you two?' I asked.

'No.'

Nevertheless, when asked what his feelings were for Grimmett at that time, for the first time ever Bradman spoke of a problem with the old bowler.

'He was difficult to handle at times in the latter part of his career,' Bradman admitted. Was it a factor in the decision to leave Grimmett at home in 1938? Knowing Bradman as I did, I doubt it. He was hard-headed enough to put aside differences when Australia's interests were at stake. It's likely, though not a known fact, that Bradman voted against Grimmett.

Yet, as he remarked: 'I was castigated more than once for the omission of a certain man when in fact I fought for his inclusion. But those details couldn't be published.'

It should be noted that Bradman was often outvoted, especially in his early years, by Dwyer and Johnson, who regarded him as a novice despite his awesome playing record.

If Bradman were in part responsible for Grimmett's omission, it could be argued that it was an error, especially as Australia struggled in 1938 and Grimmett had been so successful in England on three previous tours. Given that Bradman had been involved in half of all the Australian Test sides that took the field from 1877 to 1971, when he stepped down as a national selector, he should be allowed a few mistakes at least.

He found another selection decision in 1938 much tougher. It concerned young Ross Gregory who was vying for a place with Arthur Chipperfield.

'There was practically nothing between them as all-rounders in batting and bowling skills,' Bradman recalled. Gregory had a better future as a batsman and he was younger, but Chipperfield was a better field in a key position that needed filling. This gave Chipperfield the place in the squad.

Gregory was 'a great personal friend' of Bradman's.

'He had outstanding skills and was a fine character, and would have made a fine (sporting) ambassador (for Australia),' Bradman said. 'I wanted to select him but my conscience dictated that I vote against him.'

'How did you cope when faced with tough decisions like that?,' I asked. 'Did you cast your vote and then put it behind you?'

'Not in that case. I couldn't sleep for two nights after it.'

'You had to tell him?'

'No, the board would have informed him. But of course I saw him again. Ross was naturally disappointed but took it with the courage one expected of him.'

'Did you tell him how you felt?'

'I wasn't allowed to. I told him he was young, talented and there would be other tours.'

'But there weren't ...'

'No. World War II intervened. He was in the Air Force and lost his life serving the country.'

After Bradman retired as a player, he maintained the same uncompromising approach to selecting teams. He leant towards attacking players rather than those he called 'stodgy', but sought a balance between the two. In the 1965-66 Ashes he dropped the talented left-hander Bob Cowper, who had batted well in the first three Tests of the series. Bradman wanted new, attacking bats. Keith Stackpole and Ian Chappell came into the side for the Fourth Test, and with left-hander Bill Lawry, who was regarded as a less attacking player, on the team there was no room for Brian Booth and Cowper, who occupied the middle ground between the slow and the slick. Cowper was justifiably angry at his omission. He was brought back for the Fifth Test in Melbourne and clobbered 307, thus breaking a Bradman record (299 v South Africa) for the highest Test score ever made in Australia.

There has been a questionable tradition in Australian cricket forbidding selectors from explaining their decisions. Only recently has this changed, with national selector Allan Border remarking on the progress or otherwise of players—a practice that could yet cause problems.

Bradman only once broke the rule of silence concerning the dumping of players. After the Third Test in the 1965-66 Ashes series, Brian Booth, who had captained the Australian team in two matches of the series, was dropped. Bradman wrote to him:

> Dear Brian,
> Never before have I written to a player to express my regret at his omission from the Australian XI. In your case I am making an exception because I want you to know how much my colleagues and I disliked having to make this move.
>
> Captain one match and out of the side the next looks like ingratitude, but you understand the circumstances and will be the first to admit that your form has not been good.
>
> I sincerely hope that your form will return quickly and in any event assure you of the highest personal regard in which you are held by us all and our appreciation of the way you have always tried to do everything in your power to uphold the good name and prestige of Australia.
> Yours Sincerely
> Don Bradman

Bill Lawry and others received no such written consolation, which was the 1960s equivalent of player counselling. Lawry was dropped as player and captain after the Sixth Test in Adelaide of the 1970-71 Ashes series of seven Tests, and Ian Chappell took over. Lawry learned of his sacking from team-mate Keith Stackpole, who heard it on the radio in a taxi to Adelaide airport the morning after the Test.

When asked about it, Bradman said: 'That was unfortunate. Bill Lawry had given excellent service to the country for a decade. As for the reasons for dropping him, the final Test in the series was an opportunity for blooding a new captain. It would have been untenable to have Lawry play under Chappell, a situation unfair to both players.'

It ushered in a 'new order' under Chappell and, as the 1970s unfolded, proved to be the correct decision. Yet I feel it's a pity that Lawry could not have toured England in 1972. Stackpole was a success, but the three other openers who were tried all failed, only one of them scoring more than 20 in nine attempts. The series ended two wins all, thus leaving the Ashes in England's possession. Lawry's inclusion may well have led to Australia winning back the Ashes. His performances had been better on previous England tours in 1961 and 1964 when he wasn't captain, than in 1968 when he was the skipper.

'You can never win as a selector,' Bradman remarked. 'There are always going to be disappointments. The main thing is to attain the right balance for the conditions in which a Test is played. But there are many "balances", between left- and right-handers, both bowlers and batsmen, attacking players and defenders, bowlers suited to certain wickets and not others. No-one has ever found the perfect balance.'

Once retired, Bradman was happy to shed the thankless burden of Test selector—a job without remuneration—and watch Test cricket for pleasure. When, in his late 80s, he stopped attending games, he viewed countless hours on TV at his Kensington Park home. The introduction of cable TV in the 1990s allowed him to watch much more than he otherwise would have expected, and he enjoyed it.

Apart from playing, captaining and selecting with the highest level of skill ever in cricket history, Bradman demonstrated formidable expertise in comprehending cricket's laws and writing about technique in all aspects of the game, and he had an impressive command of statistics thanks to his collection of *Wisden* yearbooks and wide reading.

Bradman sat and passed the New South Wales state umpire's exam at the age of 24, and soon afterwards, in 1934, wrote a short instructional book, *How to Play Cricket*. On retirement he wrote a more complete manual, *The Art of Cricket*, first published in 1958. After more than 40 years it is still the finest such work on cricket ever published. Innumerable first-class cricketers worldwide have used it as a technical bible.

Over countless interviews Bradman and I discussed the greatest players of the game from Grace and Trumper at the beginning of the 20th Century through to Warne and Tendulkar at the end of it. I was intrigued to know his ideal team of all time.

Bradman first set a blueprint for his ideal team, to achieve the perfect balance under normal playing conditions:

Two recognised opening batsmen of whom one is a left-hander;

Three other batsmen of whom one is a left-hander;

One all-rounder;

One wicket-keeper who is also a good bat;

One fast bowler to open into the wind;

One fast- or medium-pace to open into the wind;

One right-hand off-spinner or a right-hand leg-spinner; and

One left-hand orthodox first-finger spinner.

This differed from the ideal team Bradman had formulated in the 1950s, which didn't include a leg-spinner. Back then, his decision was based on 'normal' conditions, where a wicket was not usually, or early in a game, conducive to big turn—in other words, not a Sydney 'turner' where the ball might take spin on day two and turn square on the final day. In going for left- and right-hand off-spinners, he had enough variety of spin on an average first-class wicket in most countries. But after another half-century's involvement in the game, he had modified his ideas. During his career, he had played with two exceptional leggies—Bill O'Reilly and Clarrie Grimmett—and he loved watching Shane Warne. I expected that his best-ever side would include a leg-spinner.

In selecting the best players since the beginning of Test cricket in 1877, I suspected—and hoped—that Bradman would ignore his own blueprint. He might prefer to select five right-handers in the top order, or two all-rounders or two leg-spinners.

Setting aside Bradman's hypothetical best-ever team for the moment, what was the most near-to-perfect balanced combination he had ever seen in real life?

Bradman had been retired for eight years when he returned to England for the 1956 Ashes battle as a journalist. England won 2:1 and had the superior team, with right-hand off-spinner Jim Laker in blistering form, especially in the Fourth Test at Manchester when he took 19 wickets for 90 runs on a dust bowl, a world record. Bradman thought highly of the England combination and he noted the make-up of the team for the Fifth Test at The Oval, which was drawn because of poor weather. The home team was in control. It was composed of, in batting order: Richardson, Cowdrey, Sheppard, May, Compton, Washbrook, Evans (keeper), Laker, Lock, Tyson and Statham.

'This went very close to perfect (balance),' Bradman said. 'England had a left- and right-hander to open, but there was neither a left-hand batsman nor an all-rounder in the next four.'

The Australian 1921 team also went close to perfect. It was: Collins, Bardsley, Macartney, Andrews, Taylor, Pellew, Armstrong, Gregory, Oldfield, McDonald and Mailey. It also had a left-hand (Collins), right-hand (Bardsley) opening batting combination, and all-rounder Charlie Macartney was a right-hand bat and slow left-arm first-finger bowler. There wasn't a left-hand bat from number two to six in the line-up. Bradman thought Gregory, who batted at number eight behind Armstrong and was a good Test batsman, covered this to a degree. In 21 Ashes Tests, Gregory had 30 innings, scored 941 runs with a top score of 100, and averaged 34.85, which was better than Trumper's Ashes average (32.79).

The opening bowling attack of Gregory and McDonald was formidable. In place of Bradman's theoretical right-hand off-spinner and left-hand spinner, there was 133 kg skipper Warwick Armstrong, who was a leg-spinner (74 wickets at 30.91 in Ashes Tests) and a good bat (average of 35.03 in Ashes Tests), and 'genuine googly bowler' Arthur Mailey.

Bradman also liked his 1948 Invincibles, the unique squad that went through an entire Ashes tour of 34 games without losing a single contest. Its Fifth Test team was: Barnes, Morris, Bradman, Hassett, Miller, Harvey, Loxton, Tallon, Lindwall, Ring and Johnston. This was arguably the nearest to Bradman's perfect balance. Arthur Morris was a left-hand opener and the 19-year-old Neil Harvey was the other 'leftie' in the top six. Lindwall and Miller made up one of the game's greatest opening fast-bowling duets, with a first change of Bill Johnston, who doubled as a left-arm fast-medium swinger *and* slow spinner. In the 1950s, Bradman thought there was one player missing from that 'ideal' team: a right-hand off-spinner. That place was taken by Doug Ring, a leg-spinner, the type of bowler Bradman came to later see as capable of achieving near-perfect balance.

Not only was this team beautifully weighted on paper in almost every respect, it was arguably the best combination of all time. Apart from the five bowlers mentioned (if Johnston was counted twice), there was the all-rounder Sam Loxton, a right-arm fast-medium bowler and aggressive bat.

Bradman admired Loxton's hard-hitting style, especially his lofted drive, and his stamina when bowling fast-medium. He noted that his fielding was outstanding, especially when throwing off balance.

Thus Bradman had six top-class options with the ball. Then there were the batsmen. The first six made up one of the finest top orders ever, with the first three—Sid Barnes, Morris and Bradman—having exceptional Test averages. Harvey, at number six, was establishing himself as one of the best left-handers in history. The team batted with authority down to Lindwall, at number nine, who scored two Test centuries. Don Tallon was a brilliant keeper by any standard in any era, and he could bat. His performances with the willow in Shield seasons before World War II were, by all accounts, sensational.

Then there was the captain. There will always be arguments about who was the best leader of the century, but Bradman would figure prominently, if not at the top, in all discussions. While he was in charge Australia lost only three out of 24 Tests. He lost his first two Tests as skipper in 1936-37 against England, when he seemed to struggle to come to grips with the new job while maintaining his batting dominance. It didn't take him long to rectify the problem. Australia won the next three Tests, and the series, with Bradman accumulating scores of 270, 212 and 169. His only other loss as captain was the Fifth Test at The Oval in 1938. England batted on and on with Len Hutton hitting 364 in fear of Bradman's response. It stopped at 7 for 903 soon after Bradman injured his ankle and was removed from the competition. What were the chances he would have scored at least a double century in one of the two innings and thrown down a greater challenge to England? (His previous scores at The Oval had been 252 not out and 5 in 1930 v Surrey; 232 in the Fifth Test v England; 77, 27 and 61 not out v Surrey in 1934; 244 and 77 in the Fifth Test of the

1934 Ashes; and 143 v Surrey in 1938. In addition, during the 1938 Ashes he was in brilliant and consistent form, scoring centuries in each of the three Tests played—144 not out, 102 not out and 103—along with three big double centuries and six other first-class centuries on tour.)

When he led his outstanding 1948 squad in England, Bradman was a seasoned skipper, who knew all the tricks about managing a diverse group of men on tour, and winning on the field. His command of strategy, tactics, preparation, and his leadership by example, elevated him to the status of an exceptional skipper. Lindsay Hassett ably backed him up.

I asked Bradman if the 1948 team was the best since cricket's inception.

'It's difficult comparing teams from era to era,' he replied with some diffidence, but conceded that it was 'the best team I was ever involved with as a player'.

But was it the best in history?

'I suppose that could be argued,' Bradman replied. 'Its biggest challenger would probably be Armstrong's 1921 side or the West Indies teams of the 1980s (under Clive Lloyd and Viv Richards).' He paused, smiled wryly and added, 'A match between any two of these teams would have been worth seeing.'

Bradman was touched for life by watching Armstrong's 1921 team, the first Australian side he saw play. I believe Bradman's 1948 side would win a five-Test series against Armstrong's 1921 team, because it had Bradman in it. He was past his best and nearly 40 years old in 1948, but he still made two big Test centuries at critical moments, topped the tour aggregate and averages (2,428, 89.93, 11 centuries) and led the side faultlessly.

No doubt some enterprising artificial-intelligence expert will create a virtual Super-Test series between all the top teams in history—including Steve Waugh's record-breakers—to decide which is best. Such a thing is already being done in the World Cup of robotic soccer.

During our many interviews and discussions it was not difficult to gain a feel for Bradman's likes and dislikes. He admired fast-scoring stroke-makers, and liked aggression with the ball from pacemen and spinners. He would not have as much respect for a slow batsman who accumulated runs as he would for one who went for his shots, even if flawed. Intelligent bowlers who out-thought their opponents were Bradman's favourites, rather than those who tried to intimidate or impress with speed or even turn. He had enormous admiration for Lindwall after witnessing his controlled brilliance in England in 1948. Lillee and Hadlee could turn on the pace if they wished, but Bradman enjoyed the way they used the conditions, summed up opposition weaknesses and exploited them. He thought much of the West Indies, great speedsters of the 1970s, 1980s and 1990s—Michael Holding, Andy Roberts, Joel Garner, Malcolm Marshall, Curtly Ambrose and Courtney Walsh—and ranked them among the best pace bowlers, alongside Richard Hadlee, Dennis Lillee, Ted McDonald, Ray Lindwall, Glenn McGrath, Alec Bedser, Wasim Akram, Tim Wall and Sydney Francis Barnes. (Bradman never saw Barnes play but learned much about him on his first tour of England in 1930.) Yet he was not happy with the way the West Indies speedsters slowed up the game with six-minute overs, and how they often bowled too short for shot-making, leaving batsmen with only the option to make adventurous strokes square of the wicket.

The over-arching feature that Bradman looked for in a player or team was entertainment. He was always concerned about the spectators and the adverse effect negative play had on the game. That is why Shane Warne's emergence in the early 1990s pleased him so much. Warne sparked the new era of spin and the end of the long reign of the West Indies speed quartets, who had enabled the West Indies to dominate, but were killing the game as a spectacle. With Warne's arrival, national teams began to drop a speedster for a spinner much more often. India and Australia regularly used two and sometimes three. And the Windies batsmen, fed on a continual diet of speed at home, were vulnerable in the face of spin.

'Nothing was more boring than watching a speedster trudge back to his mark, bowl short enough to disavow other than a defensive shot, and have no run scored ball after ball, over after over,' Bradman commented. 'If a team had four such pacemen it could be intolerable. Just one spinner out of the four, who might get through an over in two minutes, was preferable to this.'

In the 1980s, Bradman worried that all-pace attacks were killing Test cricket. Crowd numbers were down worldwide, and he acknowledged that one-day cricket was the game's saviour in this period.

'But Test cricket is where the game's great artists with bat and ball are allowed free expression,' he remarked. He wasn't sure whether the damage done in the 1980s was reversible.

When I asked Bradman to name his world best-ever team, I felt it was important that it be the best team—not a list of the 12 best players of all time. There was more than a subtle difference here, given how certain players would perform in combination.

I didn't want him to be restricted to players he had seen, but to be free to select greats whom he had not seen but had read or heard about. These included Australia's Victor Trumper, England's W G Grace, and the great English medium-pacer Sydney Francis Barnes. Bradman had done his homework in the 1930s and had come to the conclusion that Barnes was one of the greatest bowlers who ever lived. In Tests against Australia, statistically he stood with the best of all time, taking 106 wickets at 21.58.

I began to formulate a team of my own to prod Bradman into thinking about it, and soon realised what a tough task it was. I ended up choosing 10 players I had seen perform in the flesh and just two—Bradman and Jack Hobbs—I had not. (I had viewed many hours of Bradman in film archives and had a fair idea of his style and impact. Hobbs' record, especially his 12 hundreds against Australia and 197 first-class hundreds, along with many observers' comments, influenced me to select him.) In batting order, my best-ever team was Jack Hobbs (England), Barry Richards (South Africa), Don Bradman (Australia), Viv Richards (West Indies), Sachin Tendulkar (India), Greg Chappell (Australia), Garry Sobers (West Indies), Keith Miller (Australia), Ian Healy (Australia), Shane Warne (Australia) and Dennis Lillee (Australia) with Richard Hadlee (New Zealand) as 12th man.

I knew Bradman would certainly choose O'Reilly, Sobers and probably Lindwall, and he would have to select himself. After that I was merely guessing. (I later found I had managed to match only five of Bradman's names.)

Bradman's only response to my team was to say 'interesting top order'. At first he was reticent about disclosing his own such list and wrote to me saying:

> ... as regards to the question of a best XI, I am not pre-pared to do this. From experience it would only lead to a massive increase in my mail, which, despite my 89 years, is almost driving me insane ...

On average Bradman received 400 letters *a day*. When his name hit the front pages on his 90th birthday in 1998, the volume quadrupled. After Mark Taylor scored 334 not out against Pakistan, equalling Bradman's record of 334 in 1930, the number of letters soared again. Bradman felt that it was his duty to the nation and the world to reply to what he called 'the sensible ones'. He bashed out about 80 letters a day on his battered portable typewriter in four or five hours each morning. He wouldn't have countenanced a standard thank-you letter—the only time he did this was in the days following Lady Bradman's death in 1997.

Bradman's mail would go through the roof if his 'World Best Ever' or 'Dream Team' were made public. I felt that as a professional selector, he may have liked thinking through such a team on paper. But any private sense of enjoyment would be eclipsed by the huge mailbags of complaint and opinion arriving on his doorstep, and the subsequent criticism and speculation in the media.

Bradman hated being in the news—and his fame—with a passion. This was driven home to me when I discussed with him the possibility of making a feature film or TV series on his life. I had received two offers from English producers and I was in early negotiations with a Sydney-based film group to write and produce such a project based on my book *The Don*. Bradman met with his son John and the director of the Bradman Museum, Richard Mulvaney, to discuss the matter. Mulvaney liked the idea. Bradman was more circumspect. I had a long phone discussion with him and at the end of it he agreed to 'think about it'. He was haunted by the thought of all the publicity and mail, and also wanted to protect his relationship with his son John, who, in his 60s, seemed to have overcome the problem of some people regarding him—as he said himself—as a 'social souvenir', not an individual in his own right. In 1972 John changed his surname to Bradsen after being introduced at Adelaide University to a visiting British legal dignitary as 'the son of Sir Donald Bradman'. John recently changed his surname back to Bradman.

After Lady Bradman died, John drew closer to his father, who needed his support. Losing Jessie was a devastating blow to Bradman, who had become frail, especially since a minor stroke late in 1995. He didn't wish to do anything to strain his relationship with his son. Bradman was further fearful of protecting the privacy of his grandchildren, Gretta, Tom and Nicholas. A film, he felt, might somehow put the spotlight on them.

Bradman wrote to me:

> I hope you don't go ahead with the film idea. In my brief time remaining on earth I was hoping for a period of rest and privacy.

Those poignant words were enough for me. I rang the Sydney film group and told them I was pulling out of the project. Bradman was relieved. He had not been impressed with earlier attempts to portray him in the TV series *Bodyline*. Dramatic reconstruction, with its necessary departures from reality, would never impress The Don. Then there was the attendant limelight, which he hated. As English cricket writer E W Swanton wrote in his review of *The Don*, Bradman 'has been, if any man ever was, a victim of his fame'.

His understandable reticence to stir up more publicity made a book on his best team untenable, so I suggested that the team only be made public posthumously. I sent him a pool of players to choose from:

Openers (one a left-hander): Gavaskar, Greenidge, Haynes, Hobbs, Hutton, Ponsford, Barnes, Lawry, Simpson, Morris, Sutcliffe, Barry Richards, Slater;

Three other bats (ideally one a left-hander): Bradman (an automatic selection), Lara, Tendulkar, Viv Richards, Mark Waugh, Steve Waugh, Graeme Pollock, Headley, Weekes, Hammond, McCabe, Harvey, Macartney, Greg Chappell, Compton, May, Trumper;

One all-rounder: Sobers, Miller, Davidson, Benaud, Procter, Kapil Dev, Botham, Hammond, Grace;

One wicket-keeper who is also a good bat: Tallon, Healy, Knott, Dujon, Marsh, Evans;

One fast-bowler to open with the wind and one fast- or medium-pacer to open into the wind: Ambrose, Hadlee, Lillee, McGrath, Lindwall, Donald, Marshall, Holding, Roberts, Walsh, Bedser, Tyson, Larwood, Wasim Akram, Davidson, Johnston, Barnes;

One right-hand off-spinner: Laker, Gibbs;

One left-hand orthodox first-finger spinner or an orthodox leg-spinner: Verity, Rhodes, O'Reilly, Grimmett, Mailey, Warne.

I received a letter from Bradman soon afterwards. It contained his world best-ever cricket team.

CHAPTER 2

THE TEAM

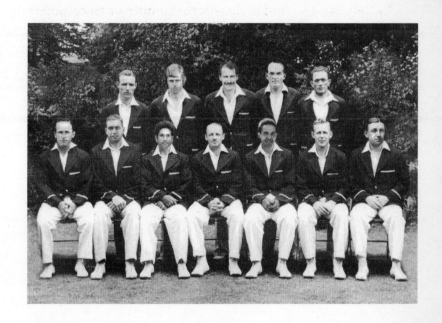

In batting order, Bradman's best-ever team was:

BARRY RICHARDS (South Africa)

ARTHUR MORRIS (Australia)

DON BRADMAN (Australia)

SACHIN TENDULKAR (India)

GARRY SOBERS (West Indies)

DON TALLON (Australia)

RAY LINDWALL (Australia)

DENNIS LILLEE (Australia)

ALEC BEDSER (England)

BILL O'REILLY (Australia)

CLARRIE GRIMMETT (Australia)

WALLY HAMMOND (England) (12th man)

Several points distinguished Bradman's team:

❋ Seven of the 12 were Australian, but all 12 or none would have been from his home country if he felt it formed the best combination in the history of cricket.

❋ Four of the team played in Bradman's all-conquering 1948 Ashes team—himself, Morris, Tallon and Lindwall.

❋ Six of the 12 captained their country: Morris, Bradman, Tendulkar, Sobers, Lindwall and Hammond.

❋ Bradman played with or against eight of the 12.

❋ Nine of the team played Test cricket *after* World War II.

❋ Only Bradman and Hammond played both before and after World War II.

❋ Only Sachin Tendulkar was playing at the time Bradman made his selection.

❋ No player performed in Tests before World War I.

❋ Three played Test cricket after 1970—Tendulkar, Sobers and Lillee. (Richards did not play official Tests after 1970, but played on at first-class level until the early 1980s.)

❋ Seven players had scored Test centuries. Five had scored double centuries. Three—Bradman, Sobers and Hammond—had scored Test triple hundreds.

❋ Bradman chose just four for batting alone—Richards, Morris, himself and Tendulkar, although he would have chosen all-rounder Sobers just for his bladesmanship.

❋ South Australia (Bradman, Grimmett, Sobers and Richards) and New South Wales (Bradman, O'Reilly, Morris and Lindwall) were the best first-class sources for the team. Sydney's St George club provided Bradman, O'Reilly, Lindwall and Morris.

Bradman said he 'didn't want any argument' regarding his selection. Yet there were many questions to be answered. With so many openers of almost equal skill to choose from, Bradman selected the best left-hander in his eyes—Arthur Morris—first.

'What I saw in 1948 was enough for me,' Bradman said. 'Towards the end of that tour he was playing the best cricket of any left-hander I'd seen. Since then I've had to modify my view considering performances of Harvey, Sobers and Lara. Yet Arthur was still the best left-hand option to open an innings.'

'What were his finest attributes and qualities?' I asked.

'He had powerful wrists and forearms. The most outstanding quality—a factor common to good players—was plenty of time to make his shots. He could glance, drive, hook and cut. All were executed with the same facility. Arthur was a wonderful player to watch from the beginning of an innings. He often set the tone for a game.'

'He wasn't always orthodox?'

'Arthur wasn't always straight in defence. But this was merely a sign of genius. I think you'll find that he rarely, if ever, got out from this.'

'And his temperament?'

'Ideal. He was always forceful and aggressive in outlook. Like everyone, he could get bogged down, but it would not be by design.'

'He started out as a bowler ...'

'He could bowl a good left-hand googly, and often did in the nets. But he decided early that his batting would take him further. He could field anywhere and was a brilliant catch close to the wicket. Arthur was a great team man—someone who studied the game well and always made intelligent observations.'

Morris' partner in the mythical World XI was Barry Richards, whom Bradman considered the best right-hand opener ever.

'He was one of the best players of the short ball, opener or otherwise, ever,' Bradman noted. 'He was always aggressive and fearless and had all the shots. I thought he played spin and speed with equal ability. Barry could concentrate for long periods when he had a mind to do it. His limited opportunities at Test level were a pity and one of the biggest disappointments for exceptional talent unfulfilled in Test history.'

Bradman found both Len Hutton and Sunil Gavaskar fine 'technicians' but thought their chief 'fault' was lack of aggression.

'It is not sufficient to keep the ball out of the stumps and not give a catch,' Bradman noted. 'There is a need to attack, take the initiative from the bowlers and set up conditions for the batsmen to follow.'

Bradman's attitude was that a batsman should score runs as quickly as possible in order to dismiss an opponent twice. He wanted batsmen who would go for a win from the start and not concern themselves with staying at the wicket and maintaining averages. He was criticised by some English commentators for his approach to big scores. Bradman *always* scored big and fast in search of victory. There is no instance in his entire career—unless defending to save a game—where he didn't play to win. Even his big double and triple centuries usually led to his team's victory. Bradman would never occupy the crease to shut the opposition out of a contest when more aggressive batting could win it. Morris' and Richards' approach was similar.

———◆◆◆———

The next three spots—three, four and five in the batting order—were easy for Bradman. He was at number three. The arrival of Tendulkar in the 1990s made easier what otherwise may have been an agonising selection for number four.

Bradman ranked Tendulkar for the number four spot, which we shall soon see was the only one available—above Brian Lara, Graeme Pollock, George Headley, Wally Hammond, Mark Waugh, Steve Waugh, Viv Richards, Everton Weekes, Stan McCabe, Charlie Macartney, Neil Harvey, Greg Chappell, Denis Compton, Peter May and Victor Trumper.

'When you look at the statistics, and it's fair to say they mean something if sustained over time,' Bradman remarked, 'most of these batsmen were close in performance. You could choose any one of them to come in at number four and he would do well. They are all greats of the game. At that level it's hard to say that one is better than another or the rest.'

Nevertheless, from further discussions, I got the impression that Bradman ranked Tendulkar and Lara as marginally above the rest.

'Lara and Tendulkar have proved to be the two best batsmen in the 1990s,' Bradman remarked. 'Tendulkar has a very strong defence. He's very tight. But he can be very aggressive, as he showed in that one-day series against Australia early in 1998, and in the Tests (in India). On balance, however, Lara has probably proved more aggressive, though more mercurial. Tendulkar is proving more consistent.'

Bradman had already picked two left-handers in his top five batsmen. To select a third—Lara—would have been unusual. In the end, he selected Tendulkar, which seemed as much based on his similarity to Bradman than his superiority to Lara and the others.

Bradman felt he was looking at a mirror-image of himself when he watched the little Indian. Their techniques were very much the same, except for their grip on the bat. Their 'compactness' and 'shot production' were also close. They both liked to attack and take control of bowlers. A minor difference was that Tendulkar lofted the ball more frequently early in his career, whereas Bradman was 24 years of age—during the

Bodyline Ashes series—before he began regularly hitting over the field. Like Bradman, Tendulkar has everything. He is the near-perfect batsman. Yet Bradman's average in Test cricket remains at close to twice that of both Tendulkar and Lara.

While branding Tendulkar and Lara as the best of the modern-day players, he was at pains to praise both the Waughs, saying there was very little difference between them and Lara and Tendulkar. In technique, he ranked Mark with the best stroke-makers of all time, including Greg Chappell, and had a high regard for Steve's 'tremendous' application in tough situations. When Bradman watched Steve's 120 not out in the 1999 World Cup game against South Africa he said he had 'never seen a better one-day innings, given the circumstances'.

Another player of recent times for whom Bradman would like to have found a place was Viv Richards. He liked his style and aggression, and never missed a Richards innings in Adelaide, or on TV anywhere if he could help it, in the 1970s and 1980s.

'Until I saw Viv Richards,' he commented, 'I didn't think I'd see anyone who could hit the ball as hard as Garry Sobers and Wally Hammond. Viv, like Wally, seemed to be caressing the ball when he really thumped it.'

Of the rest considered for selection, the only player Bradman had not seen play was Trumper. His thoughts had been influenced by all the laudatory comments that had been made about this champion. He conceded that it was tough to compare Trumper, who played his last Test in 1912, with the top players of the next 90 years. Trumper played 74 Test innings, with 5 not outs, and scored 3,163 runs at an average of just 39.04. In Ashes Tests—the most competitive of his era—he scored 2,263 at 32.79.

He was not prepared to assess the merits of W G Grace (36 Ashes Test innings at a similar average of 32.29) or Victor

Trumper, but noted that they would have been great players in any era. He said that their batting averages could not be used as a reliable guide. Wickets have changed. The psychology and technique of cricket have been altered. The stumps have been made larger, the ball smaller. Also the LBW law had been amended in the bowler's favour.

South Africa's great left-hander of the 1960s, Graeme Pollock, was also considered for a batting spot. He had 41 Test innings and averaged 60.97, the next best after Bradman. He hit 7 centuries including 2 doubles, both against Australia. Pollock first came to Bradman's attention in 1963-64 when he scored 127 not out in Perth against an Australian combined XI before a five-Test series. Bradman went into the Springbok dressing room and congratulated the 19-year-old, saying, 'If you ever score a century like that again, I hope I am there to see it.'

He did, twice. Pollock hit 122 out of 186 in the Third Test at Sydney, and 175 (his century coming in 126 minutes) in the next Test in Adelaide. At 19 years and 333 days of age, he became the third player after Neil Harvey and Mushtaq Mohammad to score 2 Test centuries before his 20th birthday. Bradman liked his aggression and exceptional concentration.

George Headley played against Bradman in 1930-31 when the West Indies toured Australia. He scored two centuries in a beaten side.

'He was the West Indies' best bat of that era,' Bradman said. 'He was small in stature, compact and nimble on his feet. He was essentially a back-foot player with few if any weaknesses. He had a very good shot production.'

Headley had 40 Test innings for an excellent average of 60.83. Despite this, Bradman ranked Everton Weekes (80 innings at 58.62) as the best West Indian batsman he ever saw.

'Everton knew how and when to destroy an opposition. He was the most marvellous player of the pull shot I ever saw and used it as his main weapon of destruction. He was always quick on his feet against pace and spin.'

Bradman considered Greg Chappell 'one of the 20th Century's great stroke-makers and stylists', but simply could not fit this champion, and several others, in. His decision to choose only four specialist batsmen left him with just one option, given that the openers took up two spots and himself another. It was Tendulkar or someone else, and he opted for the Indian.

Garry Sobers, the left-hander, was to bat at number five. Bradman's thinking was that he 'would have to be chosen above the other left-handers because he was not only in their class with the bat, he could bowl on a par with the best ever as well'.

Sobers was also Bradman's first choice as all-rounder, ahead of a fine list.

'The others (Keith Miller, Alan Davidson, Richie Benaud, Kapil Dev, Mike Procter, Ian Botham, Wally Hammond and W G Grace) would be assets in such a side, but Sobers is superior to them all,' Bradman remarked. 'After him, they are difficult to rank. Miller and Botham, for instance, were similar. Both were highly volatile. They drove the ball with tremendous power and were always on the lookout for a six. They could be prodigious hitters, but both would have been better had they curbed their desire and shown more judgment in shot selection. Their batting averages (in the mid-30s) did not do justice to their skills. Better concentration would have seen better results.'

'Miller was faster and more dangerous with the new ball, swinging it both ways. He liked using the bouncer and was nearly as fast as Lindwall. Botham was not as quick, but used conditions brilliantly and intelligently to swing the ball.

Ideally, he was a first change bowler. Botham played many more Tests than Keith and was consistent with the ball over a long period. Keith was more of a rangy, athletic type, whereas Botham was powerfully built. They both played football— Keith Aussie rules, Ian soccer. Both were excellent fielders. Miller was the best slipper in the world at one point in his career, beginning in 1948. Botham was also very good in slips. Overall they were both entertainers. They had crowd-pleasing personalities like Jack Gregory before them.'

Bradman was also impressed with South Africa's Mike Procter, who, despite limited opportunities compared to the others, showed he was a top-class all-rounder. He was more a bowling all-rounder, a 'brutally efficient' fast bowler and hard-hitting middle-order bat.

'Davidson, Benaud and Kapil Dev were also more bowling all-rounders, who could produce with the bat when quick runs were required or when their teams were under pressure. You could place any of these players in the team and they would do a fine job. But I could only select one all-rounder.'

Bradman didn't choose a recognised batsman at number six. His choice of just five (four specialist) key batsmen was an inspired move. When I expressed surprise that he had chosen just five batsmen, he remarked: 'If they couldn't make 500 then who could?'

There could be little disagreement with that. Bradman's Test average of about 100 meant he was the equivalent of two batsmen, considering that some of the game's greats averaged around 50. In effect, he had selected five batsmen worth six. Statistically, these five would reach a very respectable score. Their averages in Tests were: Morris—46 Tests at 46.49, Richards—four Tests at 72.57, Bradman—52 Tests at 99.94, Tendulkar—82 Tests at 56.94, and Sobers—93 Tests at 57.78. An average innings for this bunch would collect 333.70 runs. Throw in average scores from Tallon and Lindwall, in addition to runs from the longish tail of Lillee, Bedser, O'Reilly and Grimmett, and this team would usually top 400, or 800 if it batted right through twice. Given the team's breathtaking bowling attack, this probably would be enough runs to win against any other combination of players in history. Yet only on closer inspection of this team did the depth of the selections become apparent.

———◆◆◆———

I wondered about the batting prowess of Don Tallon at number six compared with Ian Healy. Bradman thought highly of Tallon's skill despite his Test Ashes record of 340 runs at 18.88 with a top score of 92. According to many good judges besides Bradman, Tallon's performances with the bat before World War II were exceptional. More importantly, Bradman and many Test players of Tallon's era ranked him as among the finest, if not the greatest-ever keeper.

'He was tall (at 180 cm or 5 ft 10½ in), and the most agile keeper I've ever seen,' Bradman noted. 'He was at his best when keeping to speed. He could keep up to the medium-pacers and was a natural athlete.'

Bradman agreed that Ian Healy proved incredibly durable and had improved with age, both behind the stumps and with the bat.

'Healy had had the benefit of keeping for years to Warne,' Bradman said, 'and this developed his skills, the way it did Bert Oldfield—the greatest keeper of his day—when he kept to Grimmett and O'Reilly. Healy was the best of the keepers of the 1990s.'

Bradman also admired the leg-side work of England's George Duckworth to medium-pacers because he covered so much ground, which meant that to avoid being caught Australia's bats could not play the leg-glance. Duckworth was only displaced by Les Ames because Ames was a top-class bat.

In his book, *Farewell to Cricket*, Bradman commented on Godfrey Evans' great work during the 1946-47 Ashes tour of Australia. Evans didn't concede a sundry until after Australia had scored 1,000 runs.

Bradman was also impressed with Adam Gilchrist, who made the Australian Test side late in 1999. Bradman observed that 'if he maintained his batting average about 50 and his form behind the stumps, he would be the most valuable keeper–batsman in history.' Bradman did not rank Gilchrist as a better keeper than Tallon.

<hr />

Five places—spots seven to 11—were filled by bowlers, giving the team the most awesome bowling firepower imaginable. Five specialist bowlers *and* Sobers—three bowlers in one with his left-arm medium-fast, left-hand orthodox finger-spin and left-hand wrist-spin—made at least *eight* top-line options. Bradman believed he had nine options, as Tendulkar was showing so much potential as a leg-spinner with creative variations that he could be used as a 'surprise' for the opposing batsmen.

Bradman's lateral thinking was once more apparent. Instead of selecting just two bowlers (which he would have to have if he'd stayed with his ideal blueprint team) from this grand pool of speedsters, he went for three. And, in effect, he would have four with Sobers, *and* variety since he was a left-arm medium-pacer. Sobers, in fact, was a key to the team. He was the luxury who allowed a chain reaction of dazzling alternatives with bat, ball and even field placements.

Most selectors would have sleepless nights over who to choose in seventh place after Tallon, but it did not seem difficult for Bradman.

'With such a list of talent (the pool of speedsters) you have no choice but to look for a breaking point, a characteristic that allows you to select one fellow over the others,' said Bradman. 'There are several exceptional right-arm speedsters. None could bat as well as Lindwall. He had scored Test centuries. He took the number seven spot.'

The number eight and nine spots appeared to be tougher to fill. One of them would go to a right-arm quick—one who wouldn't mind bowling into the wind. The players left to choose from were Curtly Ambrose, Richard Hadlee, Dennis Lillee, Glenn McGrath, Malcolm Marshall, Michael Holding, Andy Roberts, Courtney Walsh, Alec Bedser and Sydney Francis Barnes.

In this tricky situation, Bradman was forced to eliminate Barnes, the outstanding English bowler of the late 19th and early 20th Centuries. He had earmarked Bedser for the ninth spot, so he had to choose from six.

Lillee was Bradman's selection at number eight.

'They are all fast, accurate and outstanding,' Bradman noted. 'Lillee, in my opinion, was marginally better in delivering most aspects of the speedster's armoury. He had a superb leg-cutter. He taught Marshall how to bowl it, and very well. Lillee also relied less on the short ball than some of the others. Remember, we are talking at the margins here. These are all great players, who would perform in any era. They are or were capable of destroying an opposition, but Lillee was capable of the most devastation, at least from what I saw, and against the best batsmen in the world.'

In December 1971 in Perth, Bradman witnessed Lillee, who was fighting off a virus at the time, playing for Australia, taking 8 for 29 in 57 balls against a powerful World XI. Paul Sheahan, who was playing for Australia, noted that some of the world's best batsmen seemed so terrified that they capitulated.

'He was formidable,' Bradman recalled. 'The sheer pace he generated opened up weaknesses you wouldn't normally see in such good techniques as on display in the World XI.'

After he stopped South Africa from touring Australia in 1971-72, Bradman had set up alternative Tests. The world squad included captain Garry Sobers, Sunil Gavaskar, F M (Rooky) Engineer, Rohan Kanhai, Zaheer Abbas, Clive Lloyd and Tony Greig. In effect, Bradman had a yardstick for judging Lillee's place in his hypothetical world best-ever XI. Lillee had carved up a *real* world XI consisting of this powerful batting line-up. Surprisingly, Bradman also took into account Lillee's efforts in the 'Packer Circus' of 15 Supertests between March 1977 and December 1979. In that concentrated, at times brutal, competition among the world's finest players, the paceman took 79 mainly high-quality wickets at 23.91, including Viv Richards seven times. He had far better figures than his two great rivals Andy Roberts and Michael Holding.

Alec Bedser's place at number nine could have been taken by several other brilliant speedsters, but Bradman always liked the idea of adding variety to his fast attack, a luxury he had rarely until after World War II. Bedser, a medium-pacer who could swing and cut the ball, was as lethal as anyone into the wind. Bradman thought it made good sense to have a third paceman of a different style, rather than three speed merchants.

'Medium-pacers must so often be prepared to bowl with the wind or against it,' Bradman noted in *The Art of Cricket*. 'They must be willing to take the new ball or be denied it. They must be prepared to attack or hold the fort as directed.'

'Bedser was particularly accurate,' Bradman remarked. 'He could swing the ball either way and had a prodigious leg-cutter. Alec had a nice, quite deceptive change of pace, but never sacrificed accuracy when applying it. He also had heart and determination. He never gave up.'

Bradman preferred a talented, intelligent medium-pacer, who could turn workhorse when asked. Bedser was his choice, even at the expense of world-class left-arm bowlers such as Wasim Akram (the best in Bradman's opinion) and Alan Davidson, whom he also admired. But Bradman already had his left-arm medium-fast bowler in the side: Garry Sobers, one of the best of all time.

———◆◆◆◆———

Bradman had no equivocation in selecting Bill O'Reilly at number 10.

'He was the best bowler I ever saw or played against,' he said.

This left the last spot in the team for either Clarrie Grimmett or Shane Warne. Bradman knew I preferred Warne to Grimmett, whom I'd never seen play, and attempted to pre-empt any debate by repeating that he bracketed Warne with O'Reilly and Grimmett as the three best spinners he had ever seen.

Bradman noted that the performance figures of Warne and other great conventional leg-spinners of the 20th Century, Dr H V Horden, Arthur Mailey and Clarrie Grimmett, were remarkably similar.

'Mailey had the best strike rate of all. He got a wicket about every seven overs. Horden took about nine overs, whereas Grimmett and Warne come in at about every 12 overs.'

I pointed out that Warne had sustained his great Test performances over a longer period.

'He's the best young leg-spinner (under 30), and the best in the past 50 years,' Bradman remarked, 'and history might place him above the others. But I can't go past O'Reilly and Grimmett.' (This comment was made in 1999. Warne's marginal decline from his best in 1999 and 2000 made it unlikely that Bradman would have changed his mind.)

When forced to make a choice Bradman opted for the devil he knew. He had captained O'Reilly and Grimmett, who in

tandem bowled with enormous success and delivered comple-
mentary styles of leg-spin. O'Reilly liked bowling with the
wind, and Grimmett into it, using resistance to create minor
changes in direction. The partnership lasted four years and 15
Tests. It yielded 169 wickets.

Bradman had also faced both men in competition. When
discussing leg-spinners, he always put O'Reilly in a category of
his own.

'O'Reilly relied on pace and bounce,' Bradman said,
'whereas Grimmett at his best spun his leg-break further. He
always had a very good flipper and top-spinner. Neither
Grimmett nor Warne bothered much about the wrong'un.
Both had the amazing ability to come on at any time and drop
onto a perfect length. Like Arthur Mailey, Warne had more
vicious spin than Grimmett. Yet Warne and Grimmett were
more accurate than Mailey, who sacrificed accuracy to obtain
big turn,' said Bradman.

'Mailey was often called the "millionaire",' I commented.

'He didn't care how many runs were scored off him as long
as he took wickets.'

'And Grimmett was the miser?'

'Clarrie never liked to give a run away. I think he liked to
bowl a maiden as much as take a wicket.'

'Warne's not exactly a miser, but he's been economic with
few exceptions in his Test career.'

'He has been prepared to experiment more than Grimmett,
but has maintained his accuracy and length.'

'Grimmett was known as the fox. He was cunning?'

'He was deadly against new batsmen (who had not played
him before) who played back to him. He secured many LBW's
that way.'

'If Grimmett is the fox, Warne is the wolf,' I suggested, 'He
loves to create a crisis and stalk the batsman who freezes or
decides to defend.'

'It is always a mistake to let a spinner dictate terms.'

'Do you agree then, that there is very little between Warne and Grimmett?'

'Again, as with choosing the pacemen, the differences are marginal and very much in the beholder's subjective eye and experience.'

Grimmett's figures (so far) have been more impressive than Warne's. In 37 Tests, Grimmett took 216 wickets at 24.21 runs per wicket. His strike rate per Test was 5.84 wickets. After 87 Tests Warne has 376 wickets at 26.92. On average, he takes 4.32 wickets a Test.

What were Bradman's views on the two top right-hand off-spinners, Lance Gibbs (79 Tests, 309 wickets at 29.09) and Jim Laker (46 Tests, 193 wickets at 21.24)?

'I faced Laker in 1948 when he hadn't fully developed,' Bradman said, 'By the mid-fifties, he was very good on either dry or rain-affected pitches. He was devastating in the 1956 Ashes (in England) when the pitches suited him. Gibbs could spin the ball hard and was as good as Laker on dry pitches. He didn't have the experience on wet wickets, but he was always thinking. Like Laker, he was aggressive—fiercely competitive.'

Bradman was never tempted to select one orthodox leg-spinner and one off-spinner, or the orthodox left-hand first-finger spinner as set out in his criteria for the 'ideal' team. The reason, once more, was Sobers, who could bowl orthodox left-hand finger-spin and wrist-spin.

❖━◆◈◆━❖

Bradman chose Wally Hammond as 12th man. The athletic, fleet of foot Hammond was a classic batsman. If a player in the XI was injured before the game, it would be better to have as a back-up a 'batting all-rounder'—a batsman who could bowl—since the team had only five recognised batsmen. Hammond had scored 5 double centuries and a triple in Test cricket. He was also a useful medium-pacer and fine fielder.

'Wally had the best-ever cover drive,' Bradman said, 'off the front or back foot. He had tremendous power on the off, but one of his weaknesses was a lack of shots between square leg and mid-on. Another weakness was that he didn't like using the hook, especially if forced into it. These were not problems that would necessarily cause his downfall. Wally was difficult to dismiss because he had no defensive weaknesses. O'Reilly and Grimmett could curb him by bowling leg stump. But he had patience and didn't often surrender to frustration.'

I finally asked Bradman who was his first choice when he sat down to consider the team.

'Sobers,' he said without hesitation. 'He offers balance and variety with bat and ball. He is, in my opinion, the greatest cricketer of all time.'

CHAPTER 3

THE TIMES, THEY WERE AGAINST HIM

BARRY ANDERSON
RICHARDS

I

(South Africa)

21 July 1945—

*'He brought pleasure to all who
watched him ... it was a privilege to
see him play, even in club cricket.'*

SIR DONALD BRADMAN

The schoolboys spotted the imposing figure of
Muhammad Ali outside the Sportman's Club on
Tottenham Court Road, London. They ran to
join the crowd clamouring to have something
signed by the great man, who was in town to fight
Henry Cooper. One of the schoolboys called out to Ali to get
his attention and thrust a piece of paper at him. Ali squinted
and looked around at the boys as he began signing.

'Where you boys all from?' Ali asked.

'South Africa,' they said.

Ali looked up from the paper and glared. He then finished
signing, thrust the paper back to the boy and turned his back
to greet others.

That look stayed with one of the boys—Barry Anderson
Richards—forever. It was July 1963, the month Richards
turned 18, and he was in England on a South African
Schoolboys' tour. Ali's reaction embarrassed the boys. Didn't
this hero know about how South Africa really was? Didn't he
realise that blacks in their country were too ignorant to 'get on'
the way whites did, or the way someone as sensational as Ali
did in the United States? Didn't he understand that it was not
the fault of middle-class schoolboys?

It was a foretaste of a problem that would grow in parallel

to Richards' development as a right-hand opening batsman of enormous ability. Richards' team played mainly against county second XI's that season, and usually won. One of the highlights was a game against the Lord's Taverners at The Oval captained by Peter May and including Richie Benaud, who set Richards up for a flipper that bowled him after he had made an impressive 37. Richards, along with his close friend Mike Procter, did well enough to suggest they had first-class futures.

They were niggled by press items suggesting their tour should be banned because of the South African policy that only whites were to represent their country. The reports resonated with the wide-eyed look of suspicion the boys had seen on the face of Muhammad Ali. In discussions they had with their polite English hosts on tour Richards and the other boys defended their country in a way that was to be expected from apolitical privileged young souls benefiting from a system that prevented the black population from participating in democracy. When questioned, Richards would say that Western-style democracy in his country was impossible because black people were 'educationally inferior'—they couldn't read or write. Rarely did anyone challenge him about *why* blacks were illiterate, and who was responsible for the repression.

Richards kept on doing what he loved—playing cricket. In the following year, 1964, he made his first-class debut for Natal against Transvaal, at Kingsmead, Durban, but didn't get a hit. One of his boyhood heroes, Roy McLean, made a double-century stand with Derek Varnels, so the young Richards, batting down the list, wasn't needed. In the next Natal match at Kingsmead against Mike Smith's touring MCC side, he went in at number 5 and scored 15 in Natal's first innings of 9 for 360 declared. The MCC replied with 445. Richards came in early as Natal crumbled to seamers. He put his head down and defended in classic style, achieving a top score of 29 out of 102. He was run out for 11 against Rhodesia in Salisbury in his only other first-class innings in that 1964-65 season. He and Mike Procter took off for England to play for the Gloucestershire second XI. The youngsters did not qualify for the firsts in the County Championship, but were both given their chance against Peter van der Merwe's touring South Africans at Bristol.

Richards came in at 2 for 28, and was joined by Procter at 4 for 62. In 93 minutes Procter crashed 69 and Richards 59 in a 116 partnership that enabled the county to reach 279 before the last two days were washed out.

At the end of his third year in county cricket in 1966, Richards didn't have enough money to watch a Test between England and the West Indies. At age 21, he cleaned out the West Indies dressing rooms and did jobs for the players, including Wes Hall, Rohan Kanhai, Garry Sobers and Lance Gibbs, so he could see the game.

In his autobiography, *The Barry Richards Story*, Richards wrote that he couldn't imagine what his father would think of this, but knew that the irony appealed to many. One of them may have been big West Indian speedster Wes Hall, who walked up to him, handed him his pads and told him to give them a clean. Wes had runs to make that day.

Richards returned to his home city of Durban to prepare for the 1966-67 season and Bob Simpson's touring Australians.

Currie Cup and County Capers

The Currie Cup domestic season began inauspiciously for Richards, but he was included in a South African XI to play the Australians in East London. He scored a scintillating 107 in 150 minutes. It was his first century in first-class cricket. The soundness of his defence and the range of his attacking shots—including 2 sixes and 15 fours—meant he was a near certainty for Test selection. But one night during the game Richards was involved in a scuffle with bouncers who wouldn't allow him into a nightclub. He kicked over a metre-high vase, spillling soil into a pool. The South African cricket hierarchy reacted by telling the South African XI captain, Trevor Goddard, to drop Richards down the list when batting in the second innings. He came in at number eight, and slipped out of contention for the Tests, despite further scores of 38, 75, 88 and 65 against the Australians (for a total of 385 and an average of 77). He was selected as 12th man in the Fifth Test at Port Elizabeth. It was a bitter blow for the young man. He had lost opportunities because of one hot-headed, insignificant action. It made Richards more determined to reach the top. He spent the winter of 1967 playing squash well enough to represent Durban and ensure an unprecedented level of fitness for the 1967-68 domestic season playing for Natal. He hit 4 centuries, and at the age of 22 decided to be a professional cricketer, much against the wishes of his parents, who hoped he would find more prestigious work. Richards, feeling that he was unqualified for any other vocation and disinclined to find out, signed his first county contract—with Hampshire—for the 1968 season. That year Procter went to Gloucestershire, Richards' schoolboy cricketing friend Lee Irvine to Essex, and Tony Greig to Sussex.

Richards' £1,300 salary was resented by some. His off-the-cuff remark in a TV interview that he expected to make 2,000 runs for the season didn't diminish the ill feeling. His image was further tarnished by drunken brawling in a room at the Imperial Hotel, Brighton. But he settled down and hit his straps early with 70 on a wet wicket against Yorkshire with great English speedster Fred Trueman in full cry. Richards reached his 2,000 target with ease by early September, thus silencing the nay-sayers for future county seasons. His final 1968 aggregate was 2,395, the highest of any player. This included a double century against Nottinghamshire, 4 other centuries and 17 half-centuries, at an average of 47.90. This tally was second only to that of Geoff Boycott, who had far greater experience of county cricket and the extra-wet conditions of this English summer. Richards even took a career best 7 for 63 bowling off-breaks against a World XI. His victims were Eddie Barlow, Graeme Pollock, Seymour Nurse, Barry Butcher, Clive Lloyd, Wes Hall and Saeed Ahmed. Hampshire could hardly have made a better investment.

Wisden noted that Richards was second only to Garry Sobers in impact among the overseas players in England that year. It named him among the top five players of 1968:

> It was the composed manner and assurance, and the mature technique for one so young, which impressed the critics, friends and foe alike. His off-drive and cover driving were frequently compared with the great Walter Hammond and Sir Leonard Hutton. And, as many a bowler found to his cost, a shorter length ball, designed to avoid punishment, produced a savage square-cut ... Few, if any batsmen in the world, have his possibilities.

Richards returned home for the 1968-69 season and to prepare for the scheduled five-Test series against England. On 17 September, his dreams were smashed when South African, Basil D'Oliveira, a Cape Coloured, was selected to tour with the England squad. The South African Prime Minister, John Vorster, said his country was not prepared to receive a team with 'certain political aims'. A week later England cancelled its tour.

Richards, whose moody streak emerged when events ran against him, became depressed. His aim of playing for his country had been thwarted, this time by political events. He was photographed the morning after the announcement sitting alone in the Wanderers Stadium, Johannesburg, where he was due to play in an early pre-season friendly. It was a sad, poignant portrait. Richards still didn't understand South Africa's political predicament.

Richards had now missed the chance to play in 10 Tests. But he was not upset for long. He simply looked ahead to the 1969-70 tour by Bill Lawry's Australians and concentrated on his new role as opener, which meant he had to defend more. The style of the times was to be dour at the top of the innings as exemplified by Jackie McGlew and Trevor Goddard for South Africa and Bill Lawry for Australia.

Bad weather, an arthritic ankle and other injuries restricted Richards in the 1969 season for Hampshire, where he scored 1,440, nearly a thousand runs less than his first season. Yet he was ready to lift his rating. After six years of Currie Cup cricket and two years with Hampshire, the 24-year-old prepared for the big step up to Test cricket. He demonstrated his prepared-ness by spanking 3 centuries for Natal in four games in which he amassed 515 at an average of 103.

A Test at Last

At Newlands, Cape Town, on 22 January 1970, a nervous Barry Richards marched out in his first Test with an even more edgy Trevor Goddard, performing in his 39th. Richards batted stoutly, despite some sledging from Paul Sheahan, until Alan Connolly bowled him off an inside edge for 29 after a 127-minute stay. Eddie Barlow snailed his way to 127, which helped South Africa to reach 382, while off-spinner Ashley Mallett took 5 for 126. Australia responded with 164. Doug Walters managed 74 and speedster Peter Pollock, at 4 for 20, did the most damage.

Connolly had Richards caught behind for 32 in the second innings as South Africa struggled to 232, thanks to the speed and swing of Connolly (5 for 47) and the mixed leg-spin/off-spin of John Gleeson (4 for 70). Lawry (83) and Ian Redpath (47 not out) were the only batsmen to resist as Australia gathered 280 (with Mike Procter at 4 for 47) and were beaten by 170 runs.

The Second Test at Kingsmead began on 5 February. The normally plush green ground had been burnt yellow by a relentless summer sun. Just 14,500 people were in attendance but none of them would forget one of the great days in the history of South African cricket. Richards crunched his way to 86 in 114 minutes. With six minutes left until lunch, he powerfully off-drove Alan Connolly to the fence. He was into the 90s and a chance for a century before first interval, which had only ever been achieved on the first day of a Test by three batsmen, Australia's Victor Trumper, Charlie Macartney and Don Bradman. Connolly's next ball was wide of the off stump. Richards square cut it with force through point for another boundary to reach 94. Lawry was aware that someone other than an Australian could achieve the tonne before lunch for the first time in Test history. The Aussie skipper strung out Graham McKenzie's following over by doing up his shoelace and talking to the bowler about a field placement. Ali Bacher took a single on the first ball and McKenzie bowled tight enough for Richards to shut up shop. He wanted that century and would not take any risks. Yet he was unaware of the immortality that would have been his if he'd achieved three figures before lunch. He said later that had he known he would have gone all out for the extra runs. But he didn't. The clock ticked over to 12.30—lunch—as the umpires reached their positions. They ruled that another over could be bowled. Bacher wanted to give Richards the opportunity of the elusive milestone. He tried and failed to score off Connolly's first ball. Bacher attempted to push the second ball to leg for a single but was bowled round his legs. With the clock showing 12.32 the umpires called lunch. Richards had missed his chance. Nevertheless, he made the century easily enough seven minutes after the break in just 116 balls and 127 minutes. He had not given anyone a chance. Nor could anyone remember a serious appeal for his wicket.

Graeme Pollock joined him and they added 103 in 61 minutes before Richards on 140 lifted his head playing a careless drive at Eric Freeman and was bowled. He retired to the pavilion to watch Graeme Pollock smash 160 not out and the home side reach an entertaining 5 for 368 at stumps. Pollock went on to a magnificent 274 out of 9 for 622 declared.

The demoralised Aussies crumbled for 157 (Eddie Barlow taking 3 for 24) with only the stylish Sheahan (62) fighting creditably, in the face of South African sledging led by Richards. Australia was ordered to follow on and Stackpole (71), Walters (74) and Redpath (74 not out) gave the tourists some backbone by gathering 336. Yet South Africa won by an innings and 129 runs.

The farce continued in the Third Test with South Africa again winning the toss and batting first on a green pitch. Richards rattled up 42 runs from the first 6 overs. When Goddard was out for 6, the total was 56 and Richards was on 49. He was in a square-cutting and hooking mood but his belligerence couldn't last. At 65 off 74 balls with 12 fours and a six, he was well caught by keeper Brian Taber off Connolly. This stunning effort, along with 79 from Lee Irvine, propelled the home side to a modest 279. The Australians were woeful in the field as they had been all tour, dropping catches and fielding sloppily. Their reply was an even more modest 202 brought about primarily by fine bowling by the very quick Peter Pollock (5 for 39) and Mike Procter (3 for 48).

Richards (35) was out of sorts in the second innings and his timing was awry, yet he stayed nearly two hours to frustrate his opponents and set up Pollock (a dashing 87) and Barlow (110), who nudged the score to 408. Only Gleeson (5 for 125) was penetrating among the Australian bowlers. The tourists' reply was a feeble 166 with the consistent Redpath (66) the only batsman to keep out Procter, Barlow and Pollock, who took three wickets each.

Richards demonstrated some contradictions in his make-up in the final Test at St George's Park at Port Elizabeth when he scored runs in quick time in a 157 opening partnership with Barlow (73). The Australian malaise on the field continued. Richards was dropped off an easy chance and then went after the bowling in a cavalier fashion until Connolly dismissed him for the fourth time in the series—caught behind for 81. At times Richards had an almost park-cricket mentality to batting. He felt that if a bowler beat him and deserved his wicket, then he would throw the bat, increase the risks and give the unlucky bowler another chance. This was in contrast to his image as a mercenary who made runs for money. Only later in his county career would he graft for runs and make the opposition pay for errors in the field.

Connolly's brilliant spell (6 for 47 in all) on the second morning of the final Test reduced South Africa to 311. Only Redpath (55) and Sheahan (67) could reply well as Australia again crumbled to 212 in the face of Pollock (3 for 46) and Procter (3 for 30).

South Africa's skipper Ali Bacher called for quick runs in the second innings and Richards responded with a dashing display, making 126. He was dropped three times by the butter-fingered Australians. He attacked Gleeson, Walters, McKenzie and Connolly, dispatching them all to the boundary with ease.

Irvine (102), Bacher (73), and J D Lindsay (60) continued the onslaught until Bacher called a halt at 8 for 470, setting Australia 569 to win. Lawry (43) and Sheahan (46) put up token efforts as the tourists capitulated to Procter (6 for 73) for the last time in reaching 246, some 323 short. The South Africans had given Australia one of its worst hidings in winning 4:0, thanks in large measure to Richards who scored 508 runs with 2 centuries at an average of 72.57. Test cricket had been worth waiting for even more than he had dared to dream. He finished the season with 106 (in 128 minutes) and 69 for Natal against Rhodesia and a record South African aggregate of 1,172 runs—including 6 centuries and 3 half-centuries in 18 innings.

There was only one sour memory from that wonderful season. In the dressing room after the Third Test, Richards watched in despair as Trevor Goddard was told to 'retire gracefully' rather than be dropped and never picked again. It brought back bitter memories of his father's forced departure from the company he worked for after a corporate takeover. Richards saw it as a case of being offered the scrapheap when it was undeserved. He was determined never to be treated that way. Richards wanted to have something to show for his efforts over the next decade, especially as he had no training in anything else. After four years of continuous first-class cricket he was exhausted. He was just 24 and feeling enough strain to make a holiday to Bangkok and Japan (for Expo 70) seem like a good idea. The now-established star needed mental and physical refreshment before the next big challenge in 1970, which was shaping up to be a pivotal year in his career and life.

Hain Pain

Soon after the Australian series, Richards was kitted out for the South African tour of England. Meanwhile, in London, rebel student–politico Peter Hain was busy organising the disruption of South Africa v England rugby matches, which sent a shudder through MCC management. Games at Lord's had to be fenced off with barbed wire. Sir Donald Bradman,

Australia's cricket supremo, looked on with interest. He thought that sport and politics should not be confused. Yet he also felt that sport could be used, to a degree, in diplomacy. He saw cricket as a metaphor for life and how people should behave towards each other. But if *his* sport became a vehicle for violent political protest, that was another matter. As an Australian representative on the International Cricket Council (ICC), he would monitor events closely, shuttling between South Africa and England.

Richards and his team-mates became nervous as the first month of the tour schedule was wiped. While the squad attended net practice in Durban, they were lifted by news that the ICC endorsed the tour. However, the ICC was a toothless tiger on this issue—it couldn't dictate to the MCC or the South African Cricket Board, nor could it stop Peter Hain, who had set up the 'Stop the Seventy Tour' committee.

Richards flew to London in early May 1970 and witnessed the protests first-hand before the rest of the squad arrived. His attitude was turning now from ignorance into resentment. He felt Hain and company were attacking the wrong sport. He argued that in South Africa, cricket was the pastime primarily of people of English extraction. Rugby was the sport of the Afrikaaners, who were of Dutch background and who mostly supported the apartheid government. He believed that South Africans of English descent were more liberal in outlook, but they were outnumbered by the Afrikaaners and relatively powerless. Richards felt that the South African government was sacrificing cricket because it didn't threaten its support base, the Afrikaaners, who were kept content by South Africa playing international rugby.

Richards no longer believed that non-whites didn't deserve the vote because they were illiterate. He was in the throes of a very tough inner battle, and his attitude to this tricky and deep issue was changing by degrees. In those heady weeks in May,

Richards remained silent in public but privately endorsed the words of his skipper Ali Bacher, who said protest was 'totally acceptable' provided it was not violent and didn't interrupt play. Hearing this, the protesters felt they were getting somewhere. They stepped up their activity.

The British Home Secretary stepped in and asked the Cricket Council to call off the tour. On 23 May it was cancelled. The political protesters had won a round. Apartheid and cricket were the losers, as were Richards and his stunned team-mates back in South Africa. The consolation for Richards, Peter and Graeme Pollock and Mike Procter, was their selection in a 'Rest of the World' squad that was put together in a rush to play the five Tests against England. The contests—*Wisden* called them 'Tests'—would not have the same emotional feel of an international, yet Richards was uplifted by the experience of playing with an elite troupe. Apart from his South African team-mates, he was lining up next to some big names, including Garry Sobers, Clive Lloyd, Intikhab Alam, Rohan Kanhai, Mushtaq Mohammad, Graham McKenzie, Lance Gibbs and Rooky Engineer.

When the squad members were introduced to each other at a London function, Richards asked Sobers, Kanhai and Gibbs if they recalled a young South African cleaning their pads at The Oval four years earlier in 1966. They couldn't recall the itinerant help, but were amused to discover they were now on the same team.

The England team could be no match for the talent in the 'ROW' contingent and was beaten 4:1, but not disgraced. It was not short of top-liners itself, including Ray Illingworth, Colin Cowdrey, Alan Knott, John Edrich, John Snow, Derek Underwood, and Basil D'Oliveira and Tony Greig, both South African exiles.

Richards did not distinguish himself the way he did against the Australians, scoring 35, 64, 30, 47, 32, 21 not out, 14 and

14—for an aggregate of 257 and a modest average of 36.71. He claimed he could not take these games as seriously as proper country v country Tests, and that there was not the same fierce competitive atmosphere. However, other players thought and performed to the contrary. The clear superstar among Richards' stellar company was Sobers, who scored 588 runs at an average of 73.50, with two glorious centuries, a dominant 183 at Lord's and 114 at Edgbaston. He took the most wickets (21) at an excellent 21.52. Eddie Barlow was next best with 142 at Trent Bridge and 119 at Lord's, an aggregate of 353 and an average of 39.22. He topped the bowling averages with 20 wickets at 19.50, while Procter took 15 wickets at 23.93. Boycott also took it seriously, scoring 157 at The Oval, while Tony Greig (the best bowler for England with 11 wickets at 26.18) and D'Oliveira (110 at Edgbaston, aggregate 308, average 44, and with the ball, 9 wickets at 30.88) made it very much a South African affair.

Good Prospect

Fortunately, Richards did not carry his mediocre 'Test' performance into his games for Hampshire. He topped the county averages and collected 100 before lunch against Derbyshire. On turning 25 years of age in mid-1970, Richards' dilemma was: where to next? He didn't wish to go back to his former non-cricketing job of insurance clerk, and no Durban business stepped forward to employ him so he could play Currie Cup at home in 1970-71. Then the Prospect Club in Adelaide offered him a deal. Coca-Cola Australia would provide him with a car and a salary, and pay him a dollar a run and $10 a wicket for the season. The sponsor didn't have to worry about a major pay-out for wickets. Prospect had two Test spinners, leggie Terry Jenner, and off-spinner Ashley Mallett, and fast-medium bowler Jeff Hammond. Richards liked the idea of playing a season in Australia in preparation for the South African Test tour, scheduled to take place in 1971-72.

Prospect was very happy to have Richards as he gave their batting a boost. Yet it was the South Australian state side, and cricketing fans across the nation, who benefited even more. Richards had been given no guarantee of state selection, but when his name was put forward the local selectors, including Don Bradman, were eager to slot him into the same team as the Chappell brothers.

Richards began for South Australia against Western Australia at Adelaide in November, watched by Bradman, then Australia's Chairman of Selectors and a more than interested spectator at the back of the Members' Stand. Richards collected 7 and 44 not out, and Ian Chappell asked him to bowl. He took 3 for 29, including the wicket of Rod Marsh caught at slip, and collected an $81 bonus from Coca-Cola.

Richards' next game was against the touring MCC side. It was the type of situation that challenged him, and he wanted to impress. He noted in his autobiography that he was aware it was a big chance to make runs in a prestigious match that would gain international publicity. He concentrated on making a responsible, professional performance.

He scored 224 in six-and-a-quarter hours and outshone Ian and Greg Chappell in two long partnerships, as South Australia reached 9 for 649.

Bradman remembered Richards' innings as 'full of upright grace and controlled power. It was a near-faultless display, and when he was not looking to drive, hook or cut, he showed an immaculate defence.'

Bradman made a point of congratulating the young star at the end of the day's play, and it was this innings that first sprang to his mind three decades later when he selected him as his ideal right-hand opening bat. The Don even turned up to watch Richards play for Prospect, for whom he scored 558 runs at 55.8 with a top score of 151 not out.

Another innings that will stay in the minds of everyone who witnessed it occurred in Perth in the return match against Western Australia on Friday 21 November 1970. Ian Chappell won the toss for South Australia and Richards opened with John Causby, facing Graham McKenzie and Dennis Lillee, the young tearaway, who was a hot tip to make the Australian Test side against England in the 1970-71 Ashes series. Tony Lock, the former England star off-spinner, was captaining the Western Australian side, and was more than useful in tandem with leg-spinner Ian Brayshaw. The attack was strong and of a standard that would challenge the South African.

Richards pushed uncertainly at McKenzie's first ball, a warm-up outswinger, and missed.

'Geez,' called Rod Marsh behind the stumps as he tossed the ball to John Inverarity at first slip, 'I thought this bloke was supposed to be able to bat a bit.'

Richards was used to much more abusive sledging. He put his head down, and took 15 minutes to get off the mark with a delicious back-foot square drive that flashed past point to the boundary. By lunch, Richards had reached 79 in 90 minutes, and after the break sailed into the spinners to reach his century in 125 minutes. He went from 100 to 200 in just 84 minutes, tormenting Lock at the crease or in the field. In one over from Brayshaw, he smashed three fours at catchable height past the diving, frustrated Western Australian skipper at mid-off. After Richards reached 150, he began to slog, and the fielding side thought it was only a matter of time before he offered up a catch, as he was wont to do once he had done his job. On 169, he gave an easy chance to Brayshaw at mid-on off McKenzie, but it was grassed. After tea he rose from 200 to 300 in 108 minutes, giving just one more chance as he ran for the triple century. A cross-bat shot towards cover miscued and flew off the edge to third man, where the super-fit Bob Meuleman just got a hand to the ball without holding it.

Richards' 300 had taken only 317 minutes and he reached 325 not out in 330 minutes for the day, with an insouciant 'walk' down the wicket towards bowler Lillee, who was driven straight to the sight-screen for four. Richards kept moving to the pavilion.

'I suppose he can play a bit,' Inverarity said to Marsh as they trudged off the ground behind the star performer, who raised his bat to the tiny band of witnesses to one of the greatest-ever innings in first-class cricket. Richards batted another 42 minutes to reach 356 on day two. He had batted 372 minutes in all when he received a full toss down leg-side from Tony Mann, which he attempted to 'paddle' round to fine leg, where there was a gap in the field. Richards missed and was hit on the pad. The ball looked to all observers to be missing leg stump. Mann went up vociferously and umpire Warren Carter gave the batsman out. Richards hit 48 fours and 1 six.

Throughout 1970-71 Richards continued to be an exciting run-making machine, hitting 146 against the MCC in a return match; 35 and 155 v Queensland; 6 and 178 v New South Wales; and 105 and 72 v Victoria. His season aggregate of 1,538 (at 109.86) was close to Bradman's 1,552 for South Australia (at 86.2) in 1936-37, and was not far short of Bradman's 1,690 (at 93.88) for New South Wales in 1928-29 and 1,586 (at 113.28) in 1929-30. Richards' efforts helped South Australia to win the Shield competition, and an Adelaide paper wrote him an open letter thanking him for the Shield. Richards was pleased to have been a big part of it, and grateful for the opportunity to form a friendship with Bradman, who had been one of his heroes ever since receiving *The Art of Cricket* as a gift from his parents when he was boy. It became his most treasured possession and he used the photos of Bradman playing shots as his model for honing his technique. When he wasn't playing street games with other youngsters, he would hit a ball in a sock hanging on a rope from a beam in the family garage. Richards memorised Bradman's method for playing all the strokes and practised them until they were automatic responses to that ball swinging at him. Richards was always a powerful, proficient hooker against the speed bowlers of his era. His confidence was rooted in those endless hours alone batting against the ball in the sock. When Richards learned of Bradman's method of using a stump to hit a golf ball against the brick base of a water tank, he tried it against a brick wall and was soon ducking and weaving against the flying, unpredictable golf ball. His eye improved to a point where using a bat against a flying cricket ball was easy, and second nature.

After that sensational 1970-71 season, Richards became one of The Don's favourite cricketers.

'You could never tire of watching him,' Bradman said. 'Barry was a player that brought the crowds back to the game. It was a tragedy that he was not allowed to play a hundred Tests. Yet he brought great pleasure to all who watched him at every level of the game over nearly two decades. It was a privilege to see him play, even in club cricket.'

At the end of the season, at a Coca-Cola function in his honour, Bradman spoke generously of Richards as a cricketer—and a character. He was 25 years old and looking forward to revisiting Australia with the South African Test team the following year, 1971-72. The trip was controversial given the cancellation of the Springbok tour to England in 1970, but Bradman and his board wanted them. They were the best team in the world and would have been powerful opposition to Ian Chappell's new team of mainly untested potential stars.

Bradman's Ban

Richards left Australia buoyed by the feeling that he and his fellow South Africans would be supported on their tour. En route to England for the county season he stopped off at home for a festive match between Transvaal and the Rest of South Africa, which was to be a trial game for the Australian tour five months later. He and Procter were being paid 2 rand per run by a sponsoring clothing company, and cries of 'mercenary' were heard again. But Richards was used to that, and not concerned. He was preoccupied by the atmosphere in his country, which had soured after the South African government rejected the South African Cricket Association's proposal to allow two non-white cricketers, on merit, to be members of the squad for the upcoming Australian tour.

Half a dozen players, including Richards, organised teams to protest the government's intransigence. When the game began, Richards (batting for Transvaal for the only time in his career) took a single off Procter and then the players walked from the field and presented cricket officials with a letter of protest:

> We fully support the South African Cricket Association's application to invite non-whites to tour Australia, if they are good enough, and further subscribe to merit being the only criterion on the cricket field.

This, of course, was only scratching the surface of the problem. Unless non-whites were given an equal opportunity to develop in every way in a truly democratic system there would be little hope of them reaching the top in anything, including sport. Yet Richards' involvement demonstrated that he now understood his country's deeper problem. He was no longer the callow youth asking for Muhammad Ali's autograph.

After the mild protest, the game resumed. But the government indulged in a protest of its own. The Minister of Sport, Frank Waring, cancelled a barbecue for the two teams that night at his home.

Richards carried on with his magnificent Australian summer by scoring 140 and 67, thus maintaining his century-plus average for the prolonged season. He then flew on to England and another season with Hampshire from which he had exacted a better contract. As usual he justified it and raced to 1,000 by mid-June, collecting 1,938 at 47.26 with 2 centuries and 17 half-centuries by the end of the season.

Meanwhile, the apartheid problem had crossed the Indian Ocean to Australia. South African rugby teams touring the country met with hostile receptions, and protests were even staged against a squad of Springbok surf lifesavers.

Australia's consciousness had been awakened on the issue. Bradman, treated like an uncrowned monarch in Australia, was in his last year as the country's cricket supremo. If he gave the upcoming South African cricket tour the thumbs up, nothing could stop it. Some politicians, church leaders, academics and other concerned citizens appealed to him to stop the visit. Bradman savoured public opinion and took keen interest in the polls showing that 65 to 70 per cent of Australians were *for* the visit. Behind the scenes, he spoke to cricket administrators, presidents and prime ministers in Australia, England and South Africa.

'My conscience was beginning to dictate the right thing to do once I had fully briefed myself,' he told me, 'There was always a dilemma. Should I let the political problem in a foreign country override Australian cricket lovers' rights to be entertained by these fine sportsmen, who were, as far as I could ascertain, themselves against the ugly divisions and politics of apartheid?'

This was Bradman's toughest issue in his many years as a

cricket administrator and he would have preferred that the decision fell to someone else. He was particularly fond of South African cricketers and administrators he had met, and was aware of the high regard in which he was held in a country that had never even seen him play.

Bradman found the breaking point that would decide the issue for him when he attended a rugby Test in Sydney with the South African Ambassador in the Australian winter of 1971. It had a profound effect on him.

'The ground was protected by barbed-wire barricades,' he said, 'and the police were ready for things such as smoke bombs and flares. But the barricades didn't stop the protesters. They invaded the arena.'

He went away convinced that it would be impossible to police a cricket match. There would be violence. Any game would be ruined and cricket would be the worse for it; it would be dangerous and embarrassing to the nation. The Australian Cricket Board met on 9 September 1971 and decided to cancel the tour. Bradman informed the press. It was difficult for him. He disliked being dragged into politics—especially when a majority of Australians wished the tour to go ahead. He hated letting down the innocent South African cricketers, and loathed disappointing fans in Australia.

The decision left the ACB with a big financial hole to fill in the 1971-72 season. As ever, Bradman used his ingenuity and organised a multi-racial Rest of the World XI to play Australia in a five-Test series. Three South Africans were in the side, excluding a disappointed Barry Richards, who for the third time was being denied an international Test series. When he heard Bradman's decision, Richards signed a three-year contract arranged by a group of Durban businessmen to coach in Natal, and play for the province in the Currie Cup and also club cricket.

Instead of tense, high-quality competition playing for South

Africa against Australia and other nations, Richards now faced the bitter truth that he was unlikely to represent his country ever again. The repressive system and attendant political problems in South Africa were entrenched. Cricket would be the scapegoat. He feared he might remain in a milieu of mediocrity, never to be challenged by top-class competition or stirred by the tension of international rivalry.

Packer to the Rescue

Richards dominated Currie Cup and county cricket from 1971-72 to 1977 and from time to time turned on performances that made games a farce. In 1973 his top score was 240 against Warwickshire at Coventry; the next best score was 56. He scored 189 out of a score of 6 for 249 for Hampshire v MCC at Lord's in 1974. In the same year he clobbered 225 not out in a first-class match at Trent Bridge, when only two other batsmen passed 30. Season after season in two countries he sailed past a thousand, collected 3 or 4 centuries and averaged from 42 to 80. He was the best batsman in county cricket until 1976 when Viv Richards challenged his supremacy.

Barry was forced to watch others enjoy Test cricket while he had no choice but to demonstrate his exceptional talents against county trundlers. It irked him and he envied those of lesser ability who made names for themselves as Test stars in the 1970s.

Little wonder that Richards jumped at the chance to sign on with Kerry Packer in 1977 when Packer set up his World Series to challenge the establishment forces running cricket. It meant he would be competing at the top level, perhaps for the last time.

Richards played first in the Fourth Supertest between Australia and a World XI at the Sydney Showground beginning on 14 January 1978 in front of a crowd of 14,883 spilling onto the arena between the fence and roped-off square boundaries. Later in front of a similar crowd he found himself opening the batting with West Indian Roy Fredericks (4) who was caught by Marsh off Gary Gilmour when the score was 7. He was joined by his opening partner at Hampshire, Gordon Greenidge, for a promising stand of 52 before Max Walker had the West Indian caught behind for 23. For a brief time the spectators and TV audience were teased by the brilliance of the two Richards, Barry and Viv, together in a stand of 46. With the score at 95, Gilmour bowled Barry for 57 and Viv went on to 119 before Walker had him caught. Walker also dismissed Barry caught behind in the second innings for 48 as the World XI struggled to a 4-wicket win.

Richards' next Supertest was at Gloucester Park in Perth, which began on 27 January. The challenge there was even greater. Lillee was back from an ankle injury to take on the World XI. Richards was out to reaffirm a point he first made in Perth in 1970 when he accumulated 356 and humiliated the young speed demon, who took 0 for 117 from 18 overs. Since then, Lillee had become the premier world fast man. It may not have been an international Test, yet Richards built himself up for it as if it were one. He wanted to destroy Lillee again and also bat better than his fellow players in the World XI.

He opened with Greenidge and at lunch was 60 not out in 87 balls, while his partner had 51 from 98 balls. Richards reached his century in 30 fewer deliveries. Greenidge, on 114, hobbled off with a hamstring injury, bringing Viv Richards to the wicket. Barry stepped up his efforts a notch, aware that people would be making a judgment on who was the best batsman in the world—the black Richards or the white one. Barry won the vote this day by outscoring a younger and unconcerned Viv 93 to 41. Barry miscued Ray Bright and was well caught by Greg Chappell at deep mid-off for 207. Greenidge came back to reach 140 and Viv Richards notched

177. Lillee (4 for 149) took a hammering early but came back to dismiss Viv Richards, Clive Lloyd, Asif Iqbal and Tony Greig.

Barry Richards also played in the Sixth Supertest at VFL Park, Melbourne, which began on 9 February, and scored 76 and 0. Viv this time outshone him with 170 and 18. Barry's aggregate in these three games was 388 with an average of 77.60 and was second only to Viv, who played in six games, compiled 862 and averaged 86.20.

By 1978-79 the Supertests extended to three teams representing Australia, the West Indies and a World XI. Richards returned to play two games at the Sydney Cricket Ground—a venue that represented a serious breakthrough for Packer. The South African had 3 innings—37, 28 and a match-winning 101 not out in the Grand Final against Australia, which was won by the World XI. Richards easily topped the averages with 166 runs at 83.00.

It naturally pleased him to be nominated by most observers as the 'world's best bat' at the time, just ahead of others prominent in the 1970s, such as Greg Chappell, Viv Richards and Geoff Boycott. His brief encounters at this unique top level would never match his experience in those four Tests against Australia in 1970. Yet it gave him a measure of satisfaction before he returned to the relative mundanity of county and Currie Cup cricket through 1979 and into the 1979-80 season. In 1981, Richards married Anne Harries and they have since had two boys, Mark and Steven.

There was not a remote hope then that he would ever again represent South Africa, except in Tests against rebel squads of cricketers in the early 1980s, when he was in his late thirties and past his best.

Richards, with years of experience outside South Africa, had come to terms with his country's dilemma, even if South Africa's regime was still more than a decade away from major change. He wrote courageously in his 1978 autobiography that apartheid should be abolished regardless of the risks involved. Richards then had a full appreciation of Muhammad Ali's look, which had taken away his political and social innocence as a schoolboy.

Now with apartheid consigned to history and South Africa playing internationally again, Richards' frustrations have fallen away, and according to those who have known him over the decades, he has mellowed. He and his family are Perth-based and since retiring in 1983 he has had stints of coaching in South Australia and Queensland. He now has a media career, writing and commentating on TV. He is also President of the International Players' Association.

Nothing could make up for the loss of a fabulous career in international cricket. Yet Don Bradman's selection of him at the top of his batting order, as the best right-hand opening bat ever, gave him something back. This placement looked beyond the record books and acknowledged greatness for its own sake. Bradman could have been forgiven for sticking to proven Test players, who had played, for example, a minimum of 20 matches. Yet he didn't pick the great Jack Hobbs, Len Hutton, Gordon Greenidge or Bill Ponsford, as potent as these players were. He chose Richards without equivocation. This confers on the South African the status of a legend, when his meagre Test record alone could not justify it. Bradman has assured Barry Anderson Richards his rightful place in history as one of the game's truly outstanding players.

CHAPTER 4

IMPRESSIONS OF AN ARTIST WITH A BLADE

ARTHUR ROBERT
MORRIS

2

(Australia)

19 January 1922—

Arthur Morris—Bradman's first choice of a left-hander to open the batting—is most often described as an artist. In fact, he seems very like another artist called Arthur—Arthur Boyd—who was talented, generous and humble, and had an ironic wit that was revealed to people close to him. Over the decades Morris, a stylist and a handsome stroke-maker, has been amused by the number of people who have asked him if he was playing at The Oval in 1948 when Bradman was dismissed for a duck, thus robbing him of a hundred Test average.

'I was up the other end when he was bowled by Hollies,' Morris has replied countless times.

And then the inevitable question: 'How many did you make?'

'196,' Morris responds, always deadpan.

That innings was the highlight of a terrific tour for the New South Welshman who topped the Test aggregates and averages with 696 at 87. His 29 innings for the entire tour netted 1,922 runs at 71.79 and he hit 7 centuries and another 7 fifties. Only Bradman with 31 innings for 2,428 runs at 89.93 (11 centuries and another 8 fifties) did better.

'I made a slow rise to 1948 and a slow slide down from there,' Morris said. There was a five-year gap between his debut first-class season in 1940-41 until the end of World War II when he was able to work his way back to the top. His 'slow slide' refers to the seven years from 1948 to his premature retirement, forced upon him in 1955 by the illness of his first wife and his need to make a living. Had Morris been playing today he may have enjoyed up to another decade of first-class cricket. His exceptional gifts would have seen him well rewarded and set up for life. Yet he has never been bitter or resentful. On the contrary, Morris was grateful for the chance to achieve at the top of his chosen sport.

Ever the pessimist and claiming to be low on self-confidence, Morris said he was always surprised not to be out for a duck.

'I wish I had the confidence of some of the players today,' he lamented in a cable TV interview in 2000. They would wish they had Morris' ability.

His country schoolteacher father encouraged young Arthur to play sport—cricket, rugby and tennis. The boy excelled at all of them with a certain nonchalance, as if surprised that others would find such ball games difficult. His earliest influences were the finest cricket players of the 1930s, whom he saw performing for and against New South Wales in Sydney, after travelling from his home town of Dungog, and later Newcastle. Bradman, McCabe, Kippax and O'Reilly were his heroes, along with interstaters Ponsford, Woodfull, Grimmett and Richardson. That golden era touched him. He dreamt of playing like them, and for Australia.

Morris commenced playing for Newcastle High School's first XI at just 12 years of age. He started as a bowler of left-arm slow Chinamen which spun from the off, not a common skill and one that bamboozled most opposition schoolboy bats. His early school coaches didn't think much of his batting and put him in last. On Saturday afternoons he played with Blackwall, a local C-grade team. The more experienced park cricketers were interested in what he offered them as a batsman, and only occasionally did they give him a bowl.

By this time his parents had split, and this may account for his professed lack of self-confidence. Family friends said that Arthur tended to be shy. His father took a posting at Beverly Hills (formerly Dumbleton) in Sydney and competitive games became Morris' stage for coming out of himself. Arthur went to Canterbury High from 1936 to 1939, where he excelled at sport and proved a good student. His strong character, hitherto hidden, blossomed as teachers and peers became aware of his exceptional integrity. He slipped with ease into the school first XI and was chosen for the Combined High Schools' cricket side in 1937, 1938 and 1939. He took to rugby in the winter and demonstrated a toughness not so obvious on the cricket field. He made the school's first XV in 1938 and 1939. In his final year he was the only student surprised that he was appointed school captain. Morris' self-esteem improved as he took to his leadership duties. His cricketing confidence was growing too thanks to his experience at the St George Cricket Club. At 15, in 1937-38, he was in the seconds. During the holidays he played in a club under-16 competition, the A W Green Shield, and excelled as a bowler, taking 55 wickets at 5.23, which more than six decades later still stands as a record.

O'Reilly's Influence

At 16, from the commencement of the 1938-39 season, Morris was in St George's firsts. Its skipper, one Bill O'Reilly, studied his slow left-armers in the nets and on the field and quickly disabused him of continuing his career as a bowler. O'Reilly found Morris 'moderately skilled' and advised him to concentrate on his batting.

He was not required to bowl much at St George where six players—Ray Lindwall, O'Reilly, Stapleton, Cristofani,

Longbottom and Green—would always be tossed the ball before him. The captain was drawn to his sincerity and quiet, honest application. As a teenager he was capable of hitting the ball hard. Yet his defence was outstanding. He could pick the right ball to hit and was developing all the shots against pace and spin. He was brave enough to hook Lindwall in the nets. Nothing seemed to faze him.

Morris was generally batting at number six, until one day, without notice, O'Reilly asked him to open. The sturdy teenager of medium height took up the challenge and was from then on selected at the top of every order he played in.

At the end of 1939, Morris became a clerk in the Prosecutions Branch at Sydney Town Hall and continued his progress as a batsman at St George. The 18-year-old cracked the state side the next year, 1940-41, and promptly made a name for himself by becoming the first Australian ever to score a century in both innings (148 and 111) of his initial first-class game which was against Queensland. Cricket selectors, experts and commentators took note. A dual performance such as this stamped him as a player with an unusual, if not outstanding, temperament. It demonstrated exceptional powers of concentration and determination. Morris remembered having much luck in both innings, being dropped early in each. Observers noted that he was not unsettled, but saddled up again and rode on towards his century. In that first season he encountered South Australia's Clarrie Grimmett, who was 48 years old, and past his prime. The former Test star did not have a big leg-break by then, but fooled the tyro by delivering a string of straight balls that sent him back onto his stumps. When nicely pinned down like a specimen in a butterfly collection, Grimmett made an extra effort, pushed a leg-break (off-break to the left-hander) through faster and bowled Morris, 30 years his junior, for 33. It was a lesson not forgotten by Morris: never let a bowler corner you.

In World War II Shield competition was suspended and Morris, aged 19, enlisted in the AIF and was stationed in Australia and New Guinea. Just at the point when he was about to develop into a Test player, he was forced to abandon cricket for the odd rugby match for the Army and Combined Services. England's Test squad had been due for a visit in 1940-41. Given his amazing start and the fact that he was a left-hander, Morris could even have made the Test side then. He would have been a near certainty to make the squad scheduled to tour England in 1942. Instead he had to be content with receiving accolades not for cricket but his second sport, rugby. In 1943, coach Johnny Wallace thought Morris was the 'best five-eighth in Australia'.

Morris' AIF experience was not as dazzling as his cricket career. He remained a private for five years and was joyous about being demobbed and returning to a normal existence, especially as he would be able to take up his cricket career once more. He returned to his unprepossessing clerical job at the Town Hall, but found that the local civic bureaucracy was inflexible about him taking time off for four-day cricket matches. This was too much for this disgruntled talent, whose opportunities to develop his rare skills had been thwarted for half a decade. Like many returned servicemen, Morris experienced the pressure to make up for time lost. He looked for other work, this time in sales which was notable in some industries for its flexible hours. In 1946, motor vehicle distributor, Stack & Company, saw the benefits of having the personable 24-year-old on the payroll. Its management gave him time off for training and playing and wished him well in his quest for national selection.

Second Beginning

Morris' Army service stopped him from making the brief

Australian tour to New Zealand in March 1946 for one Test but he pushed for selection early in the Ashes season of 1946-47 with scores of 27 and 98 for New South Wales against Queensland in Brisbane. The latter innings drew such praise that he was selected to play for an Australian XI against England in Melbourne early in November. Bradman was leading the home side. It was a key game in his comeback after five years of severe fibrositis from 1940 to 1945.

'I was in awe of Bradman then,' Morris recalled in the 2000 cable TV interview. 'He had been a hero of mine right through the 1930s and now I found it hard to believe I was in the same side, playing under him.'

How did he find him as a skipper and team-mate?

'He was marvellous. If you had a problem, you could go to him and sort it out. I found him relaxed and straightforward.'

Bradman, as ever, treated players at that level professionally. There was no patronising remark or eager pepping up. Morris found himself in a partnership with The Don for the first time in that Melbourne match. Early in the innings, Bradman wandered towards him for a chat in the middle. An expectant Morris wondered what pearls of wisdom or encouragement would spill from the great man's lips.

'Would you mind calling when you're going for a run?' Bradman said quietly and without rancour. Morris obliged. It was just the right comment for the moment. A remark such as 'don't be tense, you can do it' could make a beginner more on edge. Instead, Bradman treated his new partner as an equal by getting right down to basics. He didn't want a run out.

It focused Morris and the two built a cautious, solid part-nership of 196 for the second wicket. Bradman tore a muscle and limped up to 106, while Morris reached 115 in 297 minutes. Their efforts had lasting impacts for the summer, and post-war cricket. Bradman would play in the Tests. Arthur Morris had shown enough, with a sound defence—all middle and no edges—to be selected to open for his country in the First Test at the Gabba, Brisbane on 29 November 1946.

Bradman won the toss at Brisbane. Morris was first out for 2, caught by England's skipper Wally Hammond in slips off fast-medium swinger, Alec Bedser. A towering 193 cm (6 ft 4 in), with huge hands, he was something new and problematic. His late swing, coupled with pace off the wicket and a superb leg-cutter, put the Englishman in a class of his own. Bedser was England's secret weapon and a difficult bowler to score off.

His dismissal brought Bradman to the wicket in a tense atmosphere. The England team knew he had been ill and that his form was middling. If they could remove him early they could take the series. The team included six experienced pre-war Test players: Hammond, Hutton, Edrich, Compton, Voce and Wright, to Australia's three: Bradman, Hassett and Barnes. Bradman scratched around until he was 28, when he hit a ball from Voce to Ikin at slip. Bradman, Hassett up the other end, and the two umpires thought without equivocation it was a bump ball. There was a belated appeal. The batsman was given not out. The English team, indulging in some wishful thinking, were upset at the decision, and the press made much of the incident. Bradman went on to 187 and recovered his pre-war form in a grand innings. Australia ended up with a big win, and an even bigger psychological advantage.

Morris, still unsure of himself, failed again (bowled by Edrich for 5) in his only knock at Sydney in the Second Test in mid-December. He was having an agonising time after the elation of being selected. The home team's capacity to compile huge scores meant Morris was playing only one innings a Test. Australia won easily again, with Bradman and Barnes both making 234.

There was some muttering in the press about dropping Morris, but he shut up his critics in the traditional big Christmas Shield game between New South Wales and

Victoria at the MCG by scoring 83 and 110—the top score in both innings. As the Third Test would follow within days, it made sense to keep the opener. The game began on 1 January 1947 and Morris batted far better before being LBW to Bedser for 21. Yet he needed a 50 at least. If he missed a fourth time, his place could be in jeopardy as 1930s opener Bill Brown was keen to return to the Test arena. Morris lifted and justified the selectors' faith in him by hoisting a score of 155 in six hours— a good return in a Test. Early, his defence was impenetrable and later he displayed all the strokes, especially against Bedser (3 for 176 off 34.3 overs), who went for plenty before gaining a small measure of revenge by bowling him.

Arthur's 'establishing' innings at the top of cricket was the first century by an Australian left-hander since Jack Gregory's 100 in 1921. Neville Cardus, the English critic, who was often a phantom player for England, in that his observations were sometimes meant to create doubt, noted that of Morris there was a 'suspicion of looseness of technique'.

Bradman was more circumspect about criticism for perceived flaws, something he had himself endured in 1928-29 when he first appeared on the scene. He countered Cardus by telling Morris: 'I don't know what you're doing, but just keep doing it.'

'Arthur was unorthodox at times,' Bradman noted, 'but so is any batsman of exceptional ability.'

Morris' departure from copybook technique manifested in his bat not always being straight in defence. But as Bradman commented, 'It was merely a case of genius and it did not let him down.'

Morris 'kept doing it' in the Fourth Test in Adelaide which began on 31 January 1947. England won the toss and tallied 460 (Compton 147) by near the close on day two, and Australia was left a nasty 40-minute session before stumps. Mervyn Harvey, the Victorian opener, replaced the injured

Barnes but was soon on his way for 12 at 18 bowled by Bedser. Bradman came in and received the best ball he ever faced. The delivery began on line with the off stump, swung and hit the deck on leg stump. Bradman played inside the ball—the best leg-cutter ever seen in a Test—and it slipped past his bat, taking middle and off. A comparison would be Warne's ball that bowled Gatting in 1993. But Bedser's was perhaps even deadlier because of the pace of delivery and the batsman he dismissed.

Up the other end, Morris watched and made a mental note to take Bedser as much as possible, feeling he was less vulnerable to this formidable bowler than the right-handers on this particular wicket. He steered Australia to 2 for 24 on Saturday night and then embarked on a cautious recovery on the Monday with Hassett (78). Bedser had Morris caught behind for 122—the fourth time in five innings the gallant bowler had dismissed him. Yet the batsman would have been happy to donate his wicket to anyone in return for the scores he was posting. Some English scribes began mumbling about Morris being Bedser's 'bunny', yet this did not stand up then or for the rest of his career. In all, Bedser got Morris out 22 times from 48 starts. But Morris' average in the games where Bedser removed him was 61. Given his overall Test average was 46.49 and first-class average was 53.67, the batsman actually played *better* in these encounters than in other innings and against other teams.

Compton made another brilliant century in his second innings and this prompted Morris to apply himself to the task as well. Mindful of his sensational start to first-class cricket in 1940, he set out to achieve the feat again. He reached 124 not out in a much more enterprising knock than in his first innings, and put on an unconquered 99 with Bradman (56 not out). The match was drawn.

In the Fifth Test, Morris continued his fine form with 57

(LBW to Bedser) and 17 run out. His Test average was 71.86 from an aggregate of 503. It cemented him at the top of the Australian order. Only a desperate loss of form would see him dislodged as the nation's premier opener. The other spot would be fought over by the surfeit of class right-handers, including Barnes and Bill Brown.

Morris was not quite so deft against the Indians in 1947-48, scoring just 209 at an average of 52.25 and only one century. Yet he was never in danger of not going to England for the 1948 tour, the first by Australia since the war and one much anticipated by the English.

Morris shared the New South Wales captaincy with Sid Barnes in 1947-48 and thus he was the third selector with captain Bradman and vice captain Lindsay Hassett for the eight-month enterprise in 1948.

That Campaign

Bradman harboured an ambition that he kept to himself: to go through the entire tour without losing a game. But Morris and Hassett were closer to him than the others in the squad and were privy to his meticulous planning, which commentator John Arlott once said 'would match any General's military campaign'.

The traditional opening match under the Cathedral at Worcester was to set the tone for the rest of the tour. The county was put back in the pavilion for a modest 233. When Australia batted, Bradman and Morris proceeded to destroy the Worcestershire attack. Everyone at the ground wondered whether Bradman would go on to his fourth successive double hundred. He shocked the spectators and media stuffed into the small ground by throwing his wicket away at 107. The Don, nearly 40 years and mindful of his recurring fibrositis, was fearful of doing himself muscle damage. The long innings was a thing of the past for him. Not so for the very fit 26-year-old Morris, who had 34 runs when joined by his skipper. He pipped Bradman to the century by one run and then went on to 138 in four hours. It was a sensible beginning as Morris adapted to the different pace of the English wickets, where the ball swung more and kept lower.

His next several efforts were yeoman-like as he felt his way in the different conditions and scored 17, 3, 65, 26, 64, 5, 22, 5 and 16. He began to peak just before the First Test, scoring 184 against Sussex. He struggled again in the First Test at Trent Bridge, hitting 31 in the first innings and falling in the second to his now familiar old foe Bedser, bowled for 9.

Morris came in for some criticism for these returns and his technique was put under the microscope. Australian journalist and former Test opener Jack Fingleton offered gratuitous advice. He thought Morris was shuffling across the crease when playing back rather than putting his left foot back. Again, Bradman preferred that his top batsman ignore the armchair experts. Morris stepped his performance up a notch as he slashed 60 against Northamptonshire. He lifted for his first-ever Test at Lord's with a masterly 105 and a follow-up 62 in the second innings. He was capable of making a big impression on a special occasion, such as scoring a century in each innings in his initial game in first-class cricket, or in his debut at the spiritual home of the game.

In his next match, against Gloucestershire at Bristol, Morris came up against accomplished off-spinner Tom Goddard. He was the hot tip to replace Jim Laker in the Third Test. Goddard had been in fine form skittling the counties and was being billed as the bowler to topple the tourists. Morris played him with skill, either going out to kill his spin if he were full, or stepping back to drive and cut if he were short. Goddard tried bowling down the off. Morris pulled him through the on-side field. When the bowler stacked the leg-side and bowled that line, Morris, on a high, used his feet and launched his deliveries into the off, often over the top. By lunch Morris had a century and Goddard and his Gloucester partners were struggling. By tea they were in tatters as Morris crashed through 200. He went on to 290 in 300 minutes. His sensational innings included 40 fours and 1 six. Goddard had been demolished. Laker kept his place in the England Test team.

In the Third Test at Old Trafford, the opener managed 51 and 54 not out in a drawn match, followed by 108 against Middlesex. He even looked like challenging Bradman as the biggest scorer on tour.

The Fourth Test at Leeds, commencing at the height of the summer on 22 July, was one of the greatest Morris ever played in. England, gradually finding form after two losses and a good showing in the draw, amassed 496 with its big guns—Hutton (81), Washbrook (143) and Edrich (111)—firing.

When Australia replied, Bedser had Morris caught for 6. Harvey, in his first Ashes Test, made 112 and was supported by Miller (58), Loxton (93) and Lindwall (77) as the tourists posted 458. Second time around, England declared at 8 for 365, giving them a lead of 403, easily enough runs to win based on the results of all Tests played in the history of Test cricket.

Australia was set 404 to win in 345 minutes (England batted on for two overs into the last morning).

The English press wrote the visitors off, saying the game would be over somewhere around lunchtime on the last day. The wicket was expected to take spin.

Bradman privately agreed that England would go for a win and probably succeed. Down 0:2, skipper Yardley had no choice. Morris felt the same, but was incensed at being written off. He resolved to fight. He began with Hassett as if planning to stonewall a draw. Six runs came from the first six overs. Laker came on and went for 13 in his first over. In the first hour, just 44 runs were gorged out, leaving 360 to get from 90 overs in around 285 minutes.

At 1.00 pm, Compton caught and bowled Hassett (13). The score was 1 for 57. Morris looked to the pavilion as a terrific roar went up. In the words of English commentator, H S Altham, Bradman's 'small, serenely moving figure with its big-peaked green cap' emerged from between the line of worshippers. Bradman may have been touched if nothing were at stake, but he could not afford to be emotional. Like Morris, his mind was set on not losing. A Test and the outcome of a series were on the line. There were 347 runs to get in 257 minutes, or 257 minutes to survive.

Morris watched for the skipper's approach to the first ball he faced. Would he defend, play himself in or attack? The delivery was from Laker, pitched well up on off stump, spinning in. Bradman clobbered it against the spin for 4 through the off-field. Morris had his answer. The Don was keeping all options open, including the outside chance of victory. These two allegedly arch-pessimists made at first a gentle raid on the clock—enough to stay just in reach of a win.

Part-time leg-spinner Hutton was given the ball. Morris hammered three successive fours from him and reached 50. The Yorkshire crowd gave a lukewarm response to their hero being dispatched with such disdain. Bradman took 2 more fours off Hutton in the next over. The tempo of the game had changed. Bradman raced to 35 in 30 minutes. Morris stayed with him. Nothing was said between the two batsmen. But Morris knew what the plan was now. Bradman was going for a win.

Australia went to lunch on 1 for 121. They were ahead of the clock. After the break they blasted Compton, the left-arm Chinaman spinner, out of the attack. Australia reached 202—they were halfway there—with 165 minutes left. A mini crisis occurred when Bradman reached 79. He was in pain from a fibrositis attack. Morris took the strike until the spasm passed. Bradman celebrated by taking 10 off Bedser in three balls. Morris reached his century and the pair went to tea less pessimistic. Australia was 1 for 288, Bradman on 108 and Morris 150. They had their share of luck, yet this was always the case in a big partnership, especially one that yielded 167 in the two-hour session between lunch and tea. With the score on 1 for 358 and the partnership worth 301 in 217 minutes, Morris was caught by Pollard off Yardley for 182—an exceptional innings under pressure. Bradman went on to 173 not out and Australia reached the target with 3 for 404.

With the series lost by England, critic Cardus now accepted Morris into the fold of the greatest players he had ever witnessed. He observed:

> Morris once more was beyond praise—masterful, stylish, imperturbable, sure in defence, quick and handsome in stroke play. His batting is true to himself, charming and good mannered but reliant and thoughtful. Seldom does he spare a ball of suspicious character, yet he is never palpably acquisitive, never brutal. He plunders bowlers tastefully and changes rubbish into cultured art.

This sort of praise made Morris blush rather than preen. This game established him as the best bat of either side in the 1948 Tests, such was his mastery of pace and spin. He confirmed it in the Fifth Test commencing 14 August (after a lean trot between the Tests of 32, 20, 49 and 16) with his magnificent 196 run out, when he did battle with Hollies, who snared 5 wickets. Morris held the innings together with more than half the score of 389. This was in reply to England's dismal 52, thanks to Lindwall, who took 6 for 20. Australia went on to win the Fifth Test by a huge margin, and thus avenge the horrible loss of 1938, much to Bradman's satisfaction.

With scores of 43 and 62 against Kent and Levenson-Gower's strong XI, Morris did more than anyone for the entire tour, except for Bradman himself, to deliver his skipper's long-held dream of going through a campaign of 34 engagements without a loss. This has not been done by another touring Test team on a full tour.

Only Mark Taylor—also a left-hand opener from New South Wales—could be compared in statistical terms to Morris on any Ashes tour in the 50 years since. In 1989 Taylor had 11 Test knocks in accumulating 839 runs at 83.90. This included a top score of 219, 5 fifties and 2 centuries. Morris had 9 innings for his 696 at 87 with 3 hundreds and 3 fifties.

The astonishing sporting feat of Bradman's 1948 team brought every member of the squad—known henceforth as 'the Invincibles'—immortality.

The team scarcely had time to savour the effort before they were back in action in an Australian summer that marked the end of the Bradman era. He played in three testimonials and bowed out. The pressure was on Morris now to live up to his big reputation as the country's top bat.

To the Top

In January 1949, on the last day of a low-scoring, tight game, New South Wales needed 142 to win against Queensland. Morris, facing 80 deliveries in 82 minutes, made 108 not out and New South Wales won before lunch. Journalists and scorers reached for the record books to find that Morris' feat placed him in the best of company. Until then only Bradman had managed to hit a century before lunch in a Shield game. (He'd done it four times.)

Morris maintained an impressive 1948-49 season with an aggregate of 1,069 runs at 66.81. In 12 months he played 30 games for 46 innings (3 not outs), and accumulated 2,991 runs at 69.56 an innings. Even more formidable was his success rate, with 13 centuries and 9 fifties, which meant that on average he got his team off to a good to excellent start every second time he batted. Few openers in history could claim such quality, consistency and run accumulation in a year at the top.

Did Morris, as he said himself, take a slow slide down from that amazing peak year, April 1948 to March 1949? The figures suggest more of a plateau in form and output from 1949 to 1952 than a noticeable decline, but a slide was evident from 1953 to 1955. On the Australian tour of South Africa in 1949-50 (won by Australia 4:0) he rattled on 1,411 from 27 innings (3 not outs) at 58.79. After a mediocre start in the Tests he lifted with centuries in the fourth and fifth games of the series and ended up averaging 52.75 from 422. Neil Harvey took the mantle of top Australian batsman with 660 runs at 132.

Australia continued its post-war dominance in 1950-51 against the visiting Englishmen, beating them 4:1. Morris' form for the first time in his Test career could be called 'ordinary', although in the Fourth Test at Adelaide he made a fine 206 in his first innings while the other 10 Australian batsmen between them could only manage 159.

Bradman thought that Morris' innings was 'faultless—a terrific Test double hundred'. It would be bracketed with his 182 and 196 versus England in 1948 and was his seventh century against the old enemy. He then ranked second only to Bradman (19 hundreds) in Australian centurions in Ashes Tests, surpassing Bill Woodfull and Victor Trumper, which put his less heralded career into a realistic perspective. It showed he still had all the skills for top-level batting acts, despite his relatively impoverished aggregate for the series of 321 at an average 35.67. His first-class figures nonetheless seemed to reflect the true Morris. In 22 innings (1 not out) he collected

1,221 at 58.14 and managed 6 centuries and 3 fifties on the 1950-51 journey. Those tonnes again reflected his sense of the big occasion. He had 3 fine innings (of 100, 168 and 105) also against the touring MCC, and another against Victoria (182) in a state match.

Morris was still in fine form through 1950-51, despite some hectoring press analysis about his problems with Bedser, who got him five times in 9 innings. In the first game of 1951-52, Morris took out his frustration about Bedser on the Queensland state bowlers when he walloped 253. Over the winter he had worked on his stance, that mythical or otherwise across-the-crease shuffle, and his strokes. This helped him to open up his off-side shots more. He notched 210 in the game against Victoria in November between the Second and Third Tests. These thumpers lifted his first-class average to 53.69 from an aggregate of 698, despite his worrying form in a series against the West Indies. His Test scores were 33, 48, 11, 30, 1, 45, 6 and 12 for a total of 186 at an average of 23.25 in a series won 3:1 by Australia.

This time it was not pace and swing that troubled him but the wiles of the spin twins, orthodox left-hand finger-spinner Alf Valentine, and the diminutive Sonny Ramadhin, who bowled a mix bag of offies and leggies while wearing a cap and with buttoned-down sleeves. They snared him five times from eight encounters and caused him to be dropped for the first time since he began in Test cricket in 1946. He had captained the side in the Third Test at Adelaide over Christmas when Hassett was injured. Morris won the toss and decided to bat on a rain-affected pitch. Twenty wickets—Australia 82 and the West Indies 105—fell on the first day. Morris made 1 and in the second innings 45, which was second-top score, but not enough to save Australia, who were beaten by 6 wickets.

Life After Cricket

Morris, now 30, knuckled down again in the winter months and worked on his technique. Any supposed flaws were less evident than ever, and in 1952-53 he had an uncanny run of unspectacular but consistent innings. For New South Wales (as captain, shared with Keith Miller) and for Australia (as vice captain to Hassett in the Tests against South Africa) he made: 95, 58, 55, 39, 69, 10, 15, 29, 58, 43, 12, 1, 18, 1, 77, 99, 44, 40, 34, 11 and 105. There were seven 'failures' in 21 innings. Morris' aggregate was 913 at 45.65. When viewed alone, these two statistics hid his ability to get a team off to a strong start, which he managed in nearly 70 per cent of his innings. Though his average had slipped from that amazing year of 1948-49, the evenness of his efforts meant he was nearly as effective for his teams during the 1952-53 season. The 1952-53 Tests v South Africa saw him score 370 from nine innings at 41.10, his best effort in three series. This series—drawn two-all—was the first sign of a decline in Australia's dominance since the war.

On the 1953 Ashes tour, Australia's decline continued, coinciding with a more cavalier, and less effective, approach to batting by Morris, then 31 years old. Perhaps it was a natural diminution of his outstanding batting skills, or maybe it was because his mind was on other joys in life. Arthur had fallen in love on the tour with an English showgirl, Valerie Hudson. They met when she was appearing in the Crazy Gang vaudeville show at London's Victoria Palace. It was a relationship destined to overcome geographical boundaries.

On the cricket field, Morris started the Test series promisingly enough, with scores in the first two encounters of 67, 60, 30 and 89. His performance fell away after that with knocks of 1, 0, 10, 38, 16 and 26. A combination of Bedser's guile and Laker's spin was his downfall. For the first time since he broke into top-class cricket in 1940-41, his Test performances (337 from 10 innings with an average of 33.7) and his entire first-class season performances (1,302 from 37 innings at 38.29) were not up to his capabilities. His return of 1 century from 37 starts in England, and just 2 from 58 starts between November 1952 and August 1953 suggested Morris' best days were behind him, at least as far as his sporting endeavours were concerned. The Australian team was beaten 1:0 by England in 1953 after four draws.

If Morris was worried about his cricketing prowess, more important things in life, particularly his blooming relationship with Valerie—a woman who matched his notable personality, character and integrity—took his mind off it. Valerie joined him in Australia after the 1953 tour and they married soon afterwards.

Morris had a good, if slight, domestic season in 1953-54, scoring 487 at 54.11 with 2 centuries and 2 fifties from six matches. He had a break from international cricket until a powerful England team returned for the Ashes battle of 1954-55. Its squad included Hutton, May, Bailey, Bedser, Loader, Compton, Edrich, Tyson, Cowdrey, Evans, Graveney and Statham.

The Australian side, including Morris, perhaps gained a false sense of superiority in the First Test at Brisbane when Len Hutton won the toss and fielded. Morris and Les Favell opened and faced Statham and the fearsome Frank Tyson, whom Bradman said was the fastest bowler he had ever seen. Tyson relied on pace and bounce, but the Brisbane wicket this time held fewer terrors as Australia battled to 2 for 208 at stumps with Morris, in a dogged mood against the speed men and Bedser, on 82 not out. Harvey was unbeaten on 41. The pitch's lack of ferocity did not prevent Tyson giving the two gutsy left-handers a body battering. Both were sore at the end of play.

Hutton's slowing-up tactics and his bowlers had delivered

an appalling 58 overs in five hours of cricket, yet Australia's rate of nearly four an over was good for Test cricket. Such a dilatory approach from the bowling side was becoming more prevalent, threatening to kill cricket as a spectator sport.

The next morning, Morris, the dasher of the 1953 Ashes tour, returned and added another 56 before lunch to be 138, while Harvey dawdled to 76. Morris was caught launching into Trevor Bailey after lunch for 153, which took seven hours. He and the stubborn Harvey (eventually out to Bedser for 162) added 202 and this set up Australia for a declaration at 9 for 601.

England was then rolled for 190 and 257, giving Australia a win by an innings and 154 runs. The visitors, with Colin Cowdrey and Peter May batting strongly and Tyson firing, then won the next three Tests and the series (3:1). Morris— along with the rest of Australia's batting line-up—succumbed to the 155 km per hour express of Tyson, who took 7 for 27 on a cracked pitch in the second innings of the Melbourne Test. Morris' scores of 12, 10, 3, 4, 25 and 16 were enough to make him a scapegoat for the line-up's failure. He and Jim Burke were dropped for the Fifth Test.

Yet his career was not spent. In March 1955, he was selected for the back-to-back tour of the West Indies following the Ashes disaster. As he hit 157 against Jamaica, Morris was thrilled to have his fine touch return after the shellshocks of Tyson and Statham. It showed he could still deliver on an important occasion, this one being his initial first-class game in the West Indies. He had now achieved this feat four times—in Australia, England, South Africa and the West Indies. Making this kind of a score first up on a tour was Morris' way of impressing the opposition, the spectators and the selectors with his huge talent. This time it helped selectors make up their mind on who should open the batting with the young Victorian Colin McDonald. Morris ran this form into the

Tests with 65 in the Sabina Park, Kingston Test (he was out-ranked by Harvey's 133 and Miller's 147), and then 111 in the Test at Port of Spain, Trinidad. His form held well enough in the Third Test at Georgetown, where he hit 44 and 38. A severe attack of dysentery prevented him playing in the Fourth Test at Barbados. Les Favell (72 and 53) joined McDonald at the top of the order, whose good form held throughout the series. Morris, 34 years old, and a relatively old lion of the game, missed the Fifth Test because of lingering illness.

His Test aggregate was 266 at a respectable average of 44.33 but he was well behind Harvey, Miller and McDonald. Nevertheless, it was close enough to his overall Test average in 46 Tests of 46.49 (from 79 innings, 3 not outs and an aggregate of 3,533). The realisation that he was likely to be squeezed out of opening contention during the next series—to be held a year later in England—forced Morris to contemplate retire-ment. Even though his Test career was short for one so gifted, he was running out of incentives. He had scored a century in each innings of a Test; he had been the best bat in perhaps the best team of all time (the 1948 Invincibles); he'd scored several double centuries in first-class cricket and one in a Test; and he'd captained his state and his country.

The list was long enough for Morris to wonder if there was anything he had not already achieved. Perhaps it was time for life after cricket. This option was forced on him on his return to Sydney, where he learned that his wife Valerie had a life-threatening illness. Her health deteriorated over the next year. The deeply saddened Arthur was determined to get her home to England to see her family. He got a job reporting for London's *Daily Express* during the 1956 Ashes series. This, plus help from his former skipper Lindsay Hassett, meant he could carry out his compassionate plan. Valerie saw her family, returned to Australia and died soon afterwards, aged 33. She and Arthur had been married just 18 months.

Morris' natural charm, sincerity and personality had endeared him to many. In the aftermath of this tragedy, his friends offered Morris all the comfort and help they could. One of them, J G (Ginty) Lush, asked Morris to help promote ten-pin bowling in Australia. However, the enterprise was slow to take off and did not live up to their hopes and expectations. Later, England cricketer Doug Insole persuaded Morris to work with British engineer, George Wimpey. After a few years there he took a position at Wormald's Ltd, the Sydney-based security group, where he remained until retirement in the late 1980s. Morris put much back into the game as a Trustee of the Sydney Cricket Ground for 22 years, eight of them as deputy chairman. During his time the old ground was modernised and the Don Bradman stand was built. With Arthur as a guardian, the ground's dignity, history and beauty were maintained.

In 1968, 12 years after Valerie's death, he met and married Judith Menmuir, a Western Australian. Two decades later, she and Arthur retired to live in Cessnock, a mining town near Newcastle in the Hunter Valley. He was still playing tennis in his late seventies, and enjoying watching Test cricket, although he has never had time for the one-day game.

In 1998, Arthur, Judith and the other remaining members of the 1948 'Invincibles' and their wives, were feted with special dinners, functions and appearances across Australia to mark the 50th anniversary of their now legendary achievement.

Bradman's quiet obsession and grand leadership gave every member of that team sporting immortality. Morris, the dominant player of the Ashes series in 1948, will go down as one of the best left-hand batsmen ever to play cricket. Bradman's choice of him as opener for the best team ever is an acknowledgment and recognition of this.

CHAPTER 5

MORE THAN

A MASTER

DONALD GEORGE
BRADMAN

3

(Australia)

27 August 1908—25 February 2001

*'He was never uninteresting,
he merely abstained from
vanity and rhetoric.'*

NEVILLE CARDUS

Donald George Bradman placed himself at number three—first wicket down—in his best-ever world team. Not to select himself would render the concept of the 'best' team meaningless. It would also have changed the whole pattern of the side. Two batsmen would have to be selected to replace him, which would mean dropping a bowler, but who? A spinner or a speedster? If you take away Grimmett from his combination with O'Reilly, you rob the side of a certain dimension. If you drop Bedser, you lose balance and variety. The team would not have the added bowling firepower to dismiss any opposition XI twice. And how could you measure the psychological advantage of a team boasting Bradman in its number?

By any measure, he was the greatest batsman the world has ever seen. Bradman batted 338 times in first-class cricket over 22 years from 1927 to 1949, scoring 28,067 and averaging 95.14. He hit 117 centuries at better than one every three innings, a rate that no other batsman has even hoped to approach. He also scored 6 first-class triple centuries, including a quadruple (452 not out v Queensland in 1930), a 299 not out, and 37 first-class double centuries. He maintained a rate of 42 runs an hour (84 runs a session or 252 runs in a day) and at a strike rate of 75 runs per hundred balls, which would be respectable even in modern *one-day* cricket.

Analysis of Bradman's first-class innings shows that 75 of his centuries were chanceless, while 95 were chanceless up to 100. On top of that he threw his wicket away in at least 46 innings. He made only 16 ducks, six of them first ball and three second ball, and had only seven ducks in 80 Test innings. In 52 Tests he managed 6,996 runs at 99.94—or rounded off, a century every time he went out to bat. He hit 29 Test centuries, including 12 doubles, 2 triples and a score of 299 not out. Even in grade cricket and what were once called 'second-class' matches, he kept up this relentless run accumulation and average, which were unmatched by anyone else.

The next best batsmen in Test history—17 players who had at least 30 Test innings—fall into a close bracket of averages between 50 and 60. For South Africa, Graeme Pollock had 41 innings at 60.97. The West Indies produced George Headley (40 innings at 60.83), Everton Weekes (80 at 58.62), Garry Sobers (160 at 57.78) and Viv Richards (182 at 50.24). England boasted Herbert Sutcliffe (84 at 60.73), Eddie Paynter (31 at 59.23), Ken Barrington (131 at 58.67), Wally Hammond (140 at 58.46) and Len Hutton (79 at 56.67). Australia's batch include Greg Chappell (151 at 53.86), Allan Border (265 at 50.56) and Jack Ryder (32 at 51.63). India's representative is Sunil Gavaskar (214 at 51.12). Pakistan's stand-out was Javed Miandad (189 at 52.57). (Sachin Tendulkar and Steve Waugh were also both averaging more than 50 at the time of writing.)

On average Bradman made 40–50 runs more per innings than this group. If you take the range of averages for the next fine batch of batsmen—including Gooch, Gower, Boycott, Cowdrey, Greenidge, Mark Waugh, Lloyd, Haynes, Boon, Vengsarkar, Kanhai, Harvey, McCabe, Walters and Mark Taylor—and add them to any of the top 17 you have a total of around 100, Bradman's average. In effect, statistically he is worth two of the best of the rest batsmen since the inception of Test cricket. 'Worth' is the key word here, for it would be misleading to claim he was twice as good, other than in statistical terms. Nevertheless, if you picked any great team in history—actual or hypothetical—Bradman would be equal in value to any two other batsmen. Any team containing Bradman would win a series if the rest of the two squads were more or less of the same standard. Indeed, this was the case when Bradman played in full Test series from 1928 to 1948. Australia never lost except for the bodyline series in which his average was pulled back to 56.57—which was still in the range of the next 17 best batsmen in history.

Would any other sport have a player at the top worth the value of the next two performers together? In tennis, would Laver be worth Newcombe plus McEnroe, or McEnroe be equal to Becker and Rafter? No. In boxing, would Muhammad Ali ever be considered the equivalent of Rocky Marciano and Mike Tyson together? Hardly. Or in golf, could Tiger Woods be the equal to Jack Nicklaus plus Greg Norman? Never.

South Australian biochemist Charles Davies analysed this further by creating a bell curve, which weighted Bradman's average against the best of the rest in cricket. Bradman's record is so far from the norm that we would have to wait for another million Test batsmen before someone approaching it would emerge. When the bell curve is applied to other sports we see that the best performers in football, high-jumping, tennis, swimming and running could not get anywhere near the same achievement in comparison to the rest in their sport.

The question is why? How did he manage to be so far ahead of the pack? Concentration, character, courage and determination, technique, knowledge of the game, natural athleticism, competitiveness and intelligence. Woven together they at least partly explain Don Bradman's uniqueness and genius.

Concentration

When Bradman was in his late 80s I conducted many long interviews with him—up to seven hours sometimes—yet he never wavered or seemed to tire. His answers were sometimes long, but never complicated or confusing. It wasn't difficult to imagine what he was like when he was concentrating on his batting from the age of 11 to 40. He differed from other batsmen such as Boycott, Barrington and Lawry who could stay at the crease for long periods minimising mistakes, in that he was also an attacking player. His destructive skills ranked him with all the great belligerents from Hammond and McCabe to the two Richards and Tendulkar. The longer he stayed and accumulated, the faster his rate of accumulation. To do this without 'having a bash' took enormous concentration. His batting would build to a crescendo. Bradman's last 50 runs in all his massive scores above 200—about 50 in all forms of cricket, including 9 triple centuries and 1 quadruple—often came in half an hour.

Bradman never lost control unless he wanted to. He would often throw his wicket away, that is, let loose without concern for losing his wicket. And he did not make those big innings just for the sake of it or for the record. Bradman played big innings—or threw his wicket away—when it was necessary to set up a win. When he made that whopping 452 not out for New South Wales against Queensland in January 1930, his team won easily with more than a day's cricket to spare.

Bradman's aim always was to win, and in the most entertaining way possible. He believed that cricketers must give the paying public the best value possible for their money. He felt that everything must be done to keep crowds coming through the gates, especially in the modern era where there is so much competition—on television or otherwise—from other sports and entertainment.

Character

Neville Cardus, who knew Bradman well, said this of one of Bradman's innings: 'He was never uninteresting, he merely abstained from vanity and rhetoric.'

This succinctly summed up The Don. I came to know Bradman in our interviews, chats and correspondence spanning several years. He always got to the point, without flim-flam. He never beat his own drum. Bradman, to borrow a phrase from the Nike commercials, just did it. The indisputable record was there for all to see. That was enough for him. This wasn't a case of false modesty or manufactured humility. The Don had a strong sense of self, yet he was not egotistic. In conversation, he never unnecessarily dwelled on the 'I' and the 'me'. He listened to and absorbed comments, as he did when he was captaining or running Australian cricket. He would be critical of others, but never with malice. His standards of excellence were on a different plane.

His self-proclaimed pessimism was the one contradiction in his nature. It was his way of preparing for a failure or loss. How many players in cricket history set their sights on a triple or big double century at the most critical point in a Test series and achieved the aim? Bradman's pessimism was his way of softening any possible fall.

In competition, as in conversation, he cut straight to the point. His aim was to make as many runs as possible in time to dismiss the opponent's XI twice. All else was superfluous. Bradman batted and captained with this attitude. Rarely could a bowler con him into a shot he didn't wish to play. Rarer still were rushes of blood to the head after, say, two well-hit fours. Bradman knew all about focus. He was never tempted to play beyond his limitations—in other words, vanity never got the better of him. He remained patient when necessary. There was always a time to tear an attack to pieces, whether from the first ball or after he had reached a century and the opposition was demoralised.

Like his batting, conversations with Bradman were never dull and were often unpredictable. He never hesitated and always gave organised, layered answers to questions. If he didn't have an answer, he would say so, just as if he were playing back in defence. If he had an answer it came quickly and articulately, sometimes with subtlety like a late cut, often surprisingly like a cover drive off a leg-cutter.

After 1996 I stopped writing articles about Bradman because the enormous amount of mail he received whenever anything appeared in the media caused him distress. He couldn't understand, nor did I try to explain to him, why his name came up every day in papers in England and Australia. Public discussion about him had been out of control since the 1927-28 cricket season when he first played for New South Wales. His enduring popularity is partly due to the fact that his record has grown in significance in the more than five decades since his retirement. When he bowed out in 1948, no-one realised that a cricketer with a Test century average over their career would not be seen again for a long time, maybe ever. Great players burst on the scene, were worked out by bowlers and pegged back to averages between 40 and 60. In hope and expectation, some were dubbed the new Bradman. Less than a decade after The Don retired, the public was hungry for a new champion and the media fed that hunger. In 1956, Ian Craig was the 'baby Bradman'. He was promising and stylish but the mantle was too much of a burden for him. Norm O'Neill was next, and he could certainly belt the ball harder than most. Early on, his scoring was heavy, and his Test start in 1958-59 against England had parallels to the Bowral Boy's debut 30 years previously. He levelled out with a strong Test career with an average in the mid-40s. Then in the mid-1960s, easygoing Doug Walters started with two terrific hundreds against

England. He even looked like Bradman in the baggy green. Yet Walters also disappointed, not because he wasn't popular or attacking or first rate. The poor fellow simply averaged in the 40s rather than 100.

A half a century went by and analysts began to acknowledge that the finest batsmen ever born would always fall into this good to excellent 40 to 60 range. Then there was Bradman, way off the graph. This, coupled with his request for privacy after decades of close media attention, created an aura of mystery around him.

When Bradman didn't come to the 90th birthday celebration for him in Adelaide in 1998 some disparaging remarks were made in the media. Those who made the comments seemed to make no concession for the stroke Bradman had in late 1995. The stroke had left him with an almost imperceptible speech impediment, but he felt that he could not live up to the high standard of speeches he had made during his life. He didn't want to face the strain of being the centre of attention for a thousand celebrators who meant well, but could not understand what it was like to be Don Bradman, and 90 years of age. Many fans and the media wanted him to always live up to the image of his playing days. In reality, while still mentally vigorous, he was a frail old man who just wanted 'peace and privacy'.

Courage and Determination

Bradman's determination ranked him with the most courageous and tough-minded individuals ever to play the game. Perhaps his most determined performance came in the Fourth Ashes Test of 1934 at Leeds, one that Australia could not afford to lose. He scored 304 not out despite being weakened by a mystery illness that had left him looking alarmingly gaunt. He still managed a masterful innings, despite cramps and extreme fatigue, reaching 271 not out in a day. Instead of tiring himself by running twos and threes he crashed 43 fours. He collapsed after the day's play and had to be undressed by team-mates. Bradman went on to his second triple Test century. In the next Test, while similarly debilitated, he ensured Australia won the Ashes by hitting 244 and 77 and soon afterwards was rushed to hospital for surgery. He was found to have a lingering case of peritonitis. Bradman was not expected to live, but pulled through.

Five years later he won the South Australian squash championship in a one-hour game that observers said was the most ferocious and fast final ever played in Australia until then. Bradman said it was so tough that he would never play squash again in official competition. He was so determined to win that he would go beyond normal levels of endurance.

In the 1932-33 Ashes series his enemies questioned his courage and criticised his methods against the bodyline tactics of Larwood, Voce and Bowes. The leg-side was stacked with fielders while the fast bowlers bounced the ball on or about the leg-stump line at the level of the ribcage and head, thus forcing a batsman to fend off, get hit or play a risky stroke.

Bodyline was designed by England captain Douglas Jardine to destroy Bradman, by both injuring him and limiting his scoring capacity. Bradman decided the only way to counter this was to move inside the ball and drive it on the off-side where there were no fielders. The tactic—the only one to counteract the speed and accuracy of Larwood—was a success by any other standard than Bradman's. His then Test average of 112.29 was reduced in those four Tests to 56.57. By the end of the 1932-33 bodyline series, his overall Test average was 99.71. In that infamous series, all other Australian batsmen were so badly bruised or shellshocked that their confidence was shattered. Yet Bradman's critics in Australia and England were vocal because he used unorthodox ways, and presumably because he didn't submit to a hammering of leather on flesh. He knew he would be labelled 'frightened' for introducing a few tennis shots as he moved across the wicket.

'I saw no advantage to me or the team whatsoever in standing still and being struck,' he told me. 'If you view film of Larwood bowling to me you'll notice where the ball passes (at 155 km per hour) when I move away. If I had remained where I was I would have been struck in the chest or head. The only sensible way was to move into position to avoid the fast-rising delivery or in order to play scoring strokes.'

Bradman pointed out that his counteraction would in fact increase the chance of being hit:

'The orthodox manner of playing the fast lifting ball is to move across to the off and out of the line of flight. The ball on middle and leg will go by and you're unlikely to get hit. The danger of being hit is if you stand precisely where you are, or if you back away a bit to the leg-side to try to play it on the off, because the ball is then following you. What I planned put me in much greater danger of being hit than if I adopted an orthodox method. But there was no way I was going to get runs playing orthodox cricket.'

Bodyline would have ruined the game. Fortunately, it was outlawed by the next year, 1934, and it faded into history. Bradman survived it, and illness, and went on to dominate another five Ashes series.

Technique

Bradman's batting technique was both orthodox and unorthodox. Early in his career, he was criticised for playing cross-bat shots when pulling balls around from the off-side to the on. Bradman pointed out the absurdity of this criticism by asking: 'How else do you score on the on-side when a ball is well outside off stump?'

If Bradman faced a strong off-side field, he was not going to worry about playing a cross-bat shot through the on-side if that was the only way to score. However, it must be conceded that Bradman could play such shots with impunity because of his extraordinary skills. His batting methods were more effective than anything before or since.

He had no backlift in the technical sense. Bradman used the top hand on the batting handle to lever the bat up when playing a shot. This reduced the time it took him to be ready to play a shot. It also took the strain off the muscles in his arms and shoulders. He stood with his bat between and in front of his feet, which were not far apart. In a marginal sense he sacrificed style and appearance for effectiveness, at least in his stance. But Bradman played every shot in the manual—and some that were not—to perfection.

His grip added to the less attractive appearance of his stroke execution. The right, or lower, hand was turned over so far that the handle pressed against the base of the thumb, instead of resting against it. The left, or upper, hand was turned so that the wrist was behind the handle.

If this grip is tried by someone coached in an orthodox way, or even by an untrained natural batting talent, it is the most uncomfortable, unnatural feeling. Only someone with supple, powerful wrists could even *try* to play shots using this method and not feel awkward. Any conscientious coach would quickly disabuse a child of trying it now. Did anyone attempt this with the young Don?

'No,' he said. 'I was never coached. I did experiment with other methods, but I went back quickly to my own style. It was natural to me. I used it with an axe for my daily chore of chopping wood (at home from about age 8 to 18 years). That's one reason I gained strength (in forearms and wrists).'

This Bradman grip produced three unique outcomes in attack or defence. First, the bat sloped at about 45 degrees to the ground, ensuring the ball was kept down. Second, when the player hooked or cut, the wrists rolled the bat over the ball so that with normal contact the ball was kept down. Third, with a clean straight drive, or to off or on, Bradman didn't automatically loft the ball, because the top, or left-hand, grip acted as a brake. He only lofted when he wanted to. He applied the brake—that is, kept the ball down—for most of his career, particularly early on, and hit only 44 sixes in his 338 innings. Instead, he stroked fours—2,580 of them (and two fives), mostly along the ground.

Bradman once suggested to a young Greg Chappell that he should change his grip to the Bradman grip—with both hands forming a 'V' on the bat handle. He told Chappell that the only other player to whom he had given this advice—and who had not taken it—was no longer in the South Australian team. Chappell took the advice and his technique improved to the point where he could play drives on the off-side as well as the on-side, which he favoured almost exclusively before Bradman's intervention.

Bradman's unorthodoxy didn't end with the way he held the willow. He developed a 'closed face' technique where he would move across to the off-side and turn the front of the bat to the on-side when making contact. On contact he would follow through over the ball. Bradman observed modern players who were coached to keep an open face and play everything square on, which seemed to restrict the capacity to follow through over the ball.

'If the ball leaves they tend to open the blade a little to advance the ball behind point and down to gully or third man,' Bradman noted. 'This exposes the edge of the bat more than I used to. This in turn exposes them more to being caught behind the wicket.'

Bats today were too heavy for Bradman's liking. It was acceptable to play perpendicular shots with a heavy bat, but it was tougher to play horizontal shots. It made batsmen lazier in their defensive patterns.

Bradman usually took block middle to leg, an alignment he thought lessened the likelihood of being trapped LBW. He was more interested in the position of his stumps than most players. He made more use of the crease than perhaps any player before him, sometimes ending with a foot some way *behind* the stumps at the finish of a shot.

At the point of the bowler's delivery, Bradman moved his right (back) foot back and across to the off. At the instant a ball left the bowler's hand, he levered the bottom of the blade up level with the top of the stumps. It was this preparation, coupled with his lightning feet, body movements and good eye (rather than eyesight—his was average) that gave him technical and physical advantages.

His technique left him more unscathed than most. In 20 years of Test and first-class batting—338 innings—he may have been hit on the hands only once. The main reason was that he almost always hit the ball, which is remarkable in itself. There were, of course, occasions when he was hit on the body, when hands and bat were not involved. One instance was at The Oval in 1930, when he made 232. In a tough pre-lunch session, in which Bradman scored 90 on a dangerous wicket, Larwood hit him on the upper arm. In the Fifth Test of the 1932-33 bodyline series, Larwood hit him again on the forearm. Yet for the rest of his career, even on sticky wickets, Bradman got bat to ball. Many keepers, from George Duckworth to Don Tallon, attest to his not letting anything go through to them.

Another result of his technique was his 'wagon-wheel'—the sketch of his shots around the wicket during an innings. The English county court circuit judge B J Wakley wrote a book on Bradman's statistics and found his range of shots 'varied more than any other cricketer' from innings to innings. Bradman had his favourites, but rarely indulged them if the conditions were not right. He reset his mental computer and range of shots for each visit to the crease to meet the needs of the moment, his aim always to attack and score fast, unless in a rearguard action.

Knowledge of the Game

Bradman made himself a master of the game by reading about its history and how it developed, and by sitting the New South Wales state umpire's exam in 1932 at the age of 24. His study gave him ideas—an annoying thing for the slow-to-change cricket establishment. In 1933 he wrote a humble letter to the MCC suggesting that batsmen using their pads against balls pitched outside the line of the off stump should be judged LBW if, in the umpire's opinion, the delivery were going to hit the wicket. Bradman's suggestion was not in the batsman's interest, but it made for far brighter cricket. It was several decades before his advice was heeded and a new rule introduced. Now, if a player is deemed not to have attempted to hit the ball and is struck on the pad or anywhere on the body outside the line of the off stump, he is given out, if the umpire judges the ball would have hit the wicket.

Bradman wrote books on the game and did a fair amount of journalism over the decades. This and his experiences on the field, as a selector and as a member of Australia's Cricket Board, widened his comprehension of cricket and informed his analysis of such things as the throwing controversy of the 1960s and the South African apartheid problem in the 1970s. It also gave him exceptional vision. Bradman was often decades ahead in his thinking, for instance with suggestions on marketing and the use of video camera technology to help umpires make quick, accurate decisions.

Natural Athleticism

Bradman was a natural athlete and good at all sports. He had a small, compact, lithe frame, and was deceptively powerful. For the first decade of his Test career he was considered one of the best, if not the best, fielder in first-class cricket. He had a deadly, fast throw and moved like Jonty Rhodes and Ricky Ponting of recent times. His strength sprang from his country boy background. He could live off the land by shooting game and fishing, if he wished. Bradman's early life instilled in him an endurance and a strong constitution that would help him survive severe illnesses and live a long, mainly healthy, life. He ate well and enjoyed good wines in his later decades, and was never diet conscious. Even at 90, if he felt like a three-course meal at lunch or dinner he'd have it. (In the interest of trivia, his favourite meals were shepherd's pie or lamb cutlets followed by bread and butter pudding or strawberries and ice cream, along with more than one glass of Henschke Hill of Grace Shiraz, or a Coonawarra Estate. My money would have been on bacon and eggs for breakfast.)

Until 90, his body was taut with noticeably strong forearms, the only concession to his good living being a very slight paunch. At 90, however, his muscle condition deteriorated, and like most people in their old age, he had the odd fall, which left lingering, painful bruises.

He often said 'old age is not funny', and I believed him. His age-related weakness was particularly galling to him because of his long history of sporting prowess and general fitness. In his school years he was a good runner in sprints and long distance, and a top cricketer and tennis player. He was a New South Wales country under-16 tennis champion, but had to decide at that age whether to pursue tennis or cricket. Tennis lost, but in 'friendlies' Bradman beat every Australian Wimbledon player of his era, even though he never played in an official competition after he was 16. Later he played squash for fitness, but could not resist competing in 1939 for the South Australian championship, which he won. He first took up golf, his second sporting love, on the Ashes tour in 1930 and regularly drove the ball more than 260m. His concentration, consistency and precision from tee to the green were impressive. Yet once on the green, his putting, according to former Test player Arthur Mailey, early on 'tended to be erratic'. Nevertheless, Mailey suggested he would have been a champion if he put his mind to it.

'It was incredible to watch Don if he pushed one into a sand bunker,' Mailey said. 'He would never get despondent and drop his game. Instead, he would enjoy stroking his way out of the predicament and the challenge not to drop a shot.'

Mailey criticised that strange grip and stance, and observed that Bradman's batting strokes 'would take a while to iron out of him ... when he's driving, his left foot is well forward, as if he's hammering a straight boundary.' His technique would have needed much work if he were ever to challenge the world's best. Still, in 1935, at the age of 26, he won his first major trophy—the Mount Osmond (Adelaide) club championship—while recuperating from life-threatening peritonitis. By 1940, he had reduced his handicap from 14 to 5. In 1949, after retiring from cricket, he coached those restrictive batting shots out of himself and worked hard on looking like a golfer, not a brilliant batsman who played golf as a leisure-time interest. By 1960, at the age of 52, he had reduced his handicap to scratch and was playing his best golf at pennant level. Bradman aimed at beating the course par rounds wherever he played and achieved this at Kooyonga (par 73) with 69, Peninsula in Victoria (par 73) with 69, Victoria (par 73) with 71, and Kingston Heath in Victoria (par 74) with 70. He retained his scratch rating well into his seventies.

More than 60 years after his first championship win he was

still winning at the club based on an age handicap. Until the age of 88 years he played rounds twice a week at Kooyonga off 23. He would always walk the course and occasionally beat his age.

In mid-1997, I asked Bradman, as I always did, how his golf was going.

'Terrible,' he said.

'Why?'

'I have to use a buggy,' he answered, miffed by the realisation that he would never again be able to stride over 18 holes. The Don was finding it harder than most to bend to the uncompromising forces of old age. He caught a severe flu during a cold 1998 Adelaide winter and tore a calf muscle just before his 90th birthday on 27 August. Any exercise became impossible. He was depressed to think that his golfing days might be over after 70 years of playing.

Competitiveness

Test cricketer Ian Johnson once related a story about his father Bill watching a private billiards game between Bradman and Walter Lindrum, the world's greatest player. It was the winter of 1935 and they were playing at the Adelaide home of Bradman's boss, Harry Hodgetts. Lindrum made a break of 100, which Bradman couldn't match. It riled Bradman's competitive spirit so much that he had a billiards room added to his new home, which was being constructed at the time. Bradman bought a billiard table and, according to Lady Bradman, 'practised every night for the next year' until, like Lindrum, he was able to break a 100 with ease.

Lord Colin Cowdrey told a similar story about asking Bradman to play him at Royal Tennis in the late 1960s in London.

'But I don't know the rules,' Bradman responded.

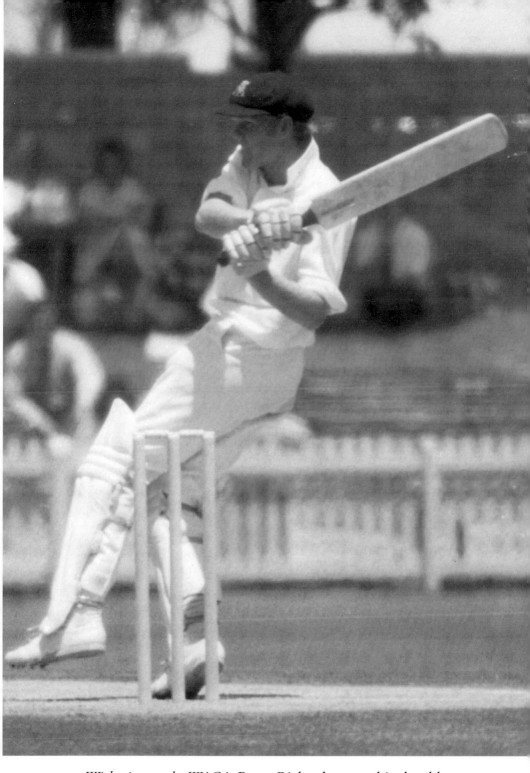

Withering at the WACA. Barry Richards opens his shoulders to belt another 4 en route to that thumping triple hundred in a day versus Western Australia. This innings consolidated his reputation as one of the greatest cricketers in history.

Age Did Not Weary Him.
At 43, Barry Richards
shows all the power of his
youth as he plays off the
back foot in Adelaide.

That Richards Drive.
Barry Richards was
one of the most
attacking cricketers off
the front or back foot.
Here he demonstrates
a front foot drive.

Cracking One Through the Covers. Arthur Morris was one of the game's most elegant stroke-makers. Here he shows his cover drive, a great scorer of boundaries for him.

Morris Horrors. Fleet-footed
Arthur Morris was one of the
most accomplished players of
spin, and was rarely stumped.
This photo is a collector's item.

In For a Big One.
Don Bradman
strides out to bat at
the MCG during
his match-winning
innings of 270
during the Third
Test of the 1936-37
Ashes series.

The Selector. Don Bradman with fellow Australian Test selectors, Dudley Seddon (left) and Jack Ryder in the late 1950s. In his 37 years (1934-1971) as a Test selector, everyone who worked with Bradman judged him the best cricket selector of all.

A Word With the Selector. In 1960, Don Bradman chats with Australian left-armer Alan Davidson, one of the finest opening bowlers of all time. Davidson took 186 Test wickets at 20.53 runs a wicket.

Drive and Follow-through. Don Bradman cover drives with a characteristic bat flourish.

Classic Straight Drive. Sachin Tendulkar executes the straight drive in the Third Test, Trent Bridge, versus England in 1996.

Crashing Cuts. Sachin Tendulkar cuts with precision.

Above: The Ubiquitous Sachin. Sachin Tendulkar's endorsements of several products have made his face one of the most famous in India.

Left: Another Hundred Up. Sachin Tendulkar acknowledges the cheer after reaching a century against Australia at Bangalore in the Third Test of the 1998 series. He scored 177.

Cowdrey gave him a thick rule book about the ancient, elitist game that originally was played for the amusement of France's royal court. Bradman studied it overnight.

'He knew the rules better than I when we played,' Cowdrey remarked.

This was typical of Bradman's tenacity in whatever he did, whether he was playing socially or in a Test match. To him, competition was not worth bothering about unless you were prepared and played to your potential, always aiming to win. He was obsessive and it didn't always please those pitted against him. Keith Miller, for one, thought him too competitive when they played billiards. Yet he always took a loss well. Win or lose, he was never other than generous and honest to his opponents. Though he always performed as if his life depended on it, at the end of the day, he competed for enjoyment. Despite a fierceness that would have made him a formidable performer in professional ranks today, Bradman was forever an amateur at heart.

Intelligence

The Shorter Oxford dictionary meaning of 'genius' is: 'exalted intellectual power, instinctive and extraordinary imaginative, creative or inventive capacity'. The term is overused, but if ever it applied to anyone, it did to Bradman and his approach to cricket. Intellectual strength alone would mean little if a player didn't have the innate and acquired physical skills to play at the top. Intellectual and physical skills were coupled together in Bradman, and the result was an exceptional individual of brilliance, voracity and mental stamina. Add the other features mentioned in this chapter and you have what made Bradman the true master of cricket in the 20th Century. Yet examining his character and intellect to fully explain his genius is a bit like a surgeon dissecting a brain to find a soul. It can't be done.

Bradman on Bradman and
the World's Best

Despite his scholarly comprehension of cricket, Bradman never could explain why his record was so much better than any other player's. He said he had seen plenty of cricketers who looked like better players than him, including two who ended up in grade cricket. One player who Bradman judged 'superior' was Rayford Robinson from Newcastle. He played just one Test, aged 22, at Brisbane in the 1936-37 Ashes series. He was caught by Hammond off Voce in each innings, making 2 and 3. Robinson was dropped and never played Test cricket again. He represented both New South Wales and South Australia, and scored 2,441 at a 31.70 average. Robinson was judged by many to rank in stroke-play and timing with Trumper, Jackson and Kippax.

Bradman couldn't explain why Robinson and others like him didn't make it. Perhaps Robinson's real flaws were in his character. Off the field he worked on the wharves and preferred the company of gangsters and criminals to fellow cricketers. He was once charged with stealing. He had a sad end sleeping rough in parks and under bridges in his native Newcastle, dying there in 1965 at the age of 51.

Others, Bradman said, lacked concentration or had never learned to pace an innings. Even players with the finest style who kept being dismissed early would soon disappear. Indiscretion, lack of discipline, over-flamboyance and lack of concentration. You see it all the time at park or even second-grade or club level. Players look like champions, until they get out. It's not a matter of luck. These types will display all the strokes for a bright 30 or 40 and then play a hopeless shot that will end their innings.

'Great players learned to avoid errors,' Bradman said, 'or they had innate intuition, which allowed them to preserve their wickets without necessarily playing defensively.'

One such great is India's Sachin Tendulkar. Bradman found him: 'Exhilarating. It was inspirational to watch such a champion in his prime.'

CHAPTER 6

THE STAR

OF INDIA

SACHIN RAMESH
TENDULKAR

(India)

24 April 1973—

In the nets, Sachin Tendulkar scratched up a good length of turf outside his leg stump and asked the three leg-spinners to bowl there. They obliged. For the next hour he thrust out his left leg, skipped down the wicket or bent on one knee to belt the ball through or over the arc between square leg and mid-on. He lunged, swept and hammered until he felt confident about playing such a leg-break in the dangerous rough area no matter what the turn or the capacity of the bowler. It was Mumbai in late January 1998, several weeks before the Australians, including Shane Warne, were to arrive to play India from February to April. After a frenzy of shots, Tendulkar asked two of the bowlers to attempt flippers until he felt sure he was playing the delivery properly, while the third served up wrong'uns and top-spinners. He was bowled once, tickled another onto his stumps, and miscued the sweep about three times. After several hours he walked away tired but satisfied that he could handle Warne with skill and confidence. The outstanding world spin-ner was his target. Tendulkar watched him on cable TV destroying South Africa in the Tests of the 1997-98 season in Australia and knew that he had to organise and prepare him-self. The Australian had conquered or controlled every other leading batsman in the world and had his sights set on Tendulkar who, with Brian Lara, was ranked the best, most devastating bat of the 1990s.

Tendulkar practised with the same zeal and application for the next three weeks before the first game of the Australian tour, Australia v Mumbai. In media conferences before the game, Tendulkar played down the heavyweight battle between him and Warne saying it was not a struggle between them, but between India and Australia. Tendulkar wasn't kidding anyone, especially himself. He had been thinking and dwelling on the Australian for months. Warne, for his part, had not been overly concerned with the coming confrontation. He had enormous respect for the Indian, but was not the type to overdo his preparation for any particular batsman. He saw himself as part of a team ambush and believed in concentrating on a big challenge when it was right in front of him. This seemed to be the attitude of the whole Australian squad. They had not watched any recent videos of the Indians and had not seen or even heard of several of the players.

The visitors, particularly Warne, were in for a rude shock when the 163 cm (5 ft 4 in), stocky, 25-year-old Tendulkar strode out to bat, first wicket down in the Mumbai game. He was nervous. His intense focusing on one opponent may have taken a toll. Now was the moment of truth. He began well. Taylor brought Warne on and Tendulkar braced himself, then lifted his second ball over mid-on for 6. He smashed into the leg-spinner and the other Australians with all the gusto of those practic sessions, except this time there were no nets to stop the ball as it sailed over or to the boundary. Tendulkar went on to a magnificent 204 not out in Mumbai's score of 6 for 410 declared. It was his first double century. Warne returned 0 for 111 off 16 overs, his worst figures in years. What's more, Mumbai went on to win by 10 wickets. The Australians—the best Test team of the 1990s—had rarely been humbled like this in a game outside the Tests.

In a tight tour this was a big psychological advantage. At

Mumbai in the First Test soon afterwards, India won the toss, batted in extreme heat and lost 2 for 126. Tendulkar came to the wicket after Mark Waugh had run out Sidhu. Despite his terrific beginning for Mumbai, this was a different day and there was much more at stake. There were five balls left in an over from Warne. The Indian drove the first ball straight, though uppishly, for four. He blocked the second ball. The third spun past the bat. So did the fourth. Tendulkar, desperate to take control before he had settled in, tried to cover drive the fifth ball that was a fraction short and spinning across him. He edged head-high to Taylor at slip. The batsman trudged off upset with himself. Tendulkar was angry, not at his impatience, but at the shot. He felt he had not been quick enough into it, driving at the ball too late. With the dedication of a Geoffrey Boycott, he went into the nets several times before his second knock and had leg-spinners land the ball on or outside off stump. He drove and cut and drove until he felt he had the shot right and that ball covered. In the second innings he did not make the same error and led the way to an Indian victory with 155 not out. This great knock showed his wonderful technique, superb eye-and-hand coordination and sense of balance. Tendulkar displayed all the shots and some specialties. He usually met the ball with the full face of the bat. His straight drive looked in the Gavaskar class. His on-side flicks and drives were a reminder of the taller, elegant Mark Waugh. But the cover drive smashed off the back foot belonged to him alone.

Warne, although being dispatched for just 4 an over in his spell of 30 overs with 7 maidens (one for 122), was this time beaten. Tendulkar had now won two out of three encounters and his team had thrashed the Australians in both games. In the Second Test at Calcutta Tendulkar slammed 79 in just 109 minutes, with 12 fours and 2 thumping sixes, helping India to 5 for 633 (captain Azharuddin scoring a fine 163 not out).

This was enough to defeat Australia by a whopping innings and 219 runs.

The series was won, largely due to the superior skill and preparation of Tendulkar and his fellow batsmen. The slaughter didn't end there, with Tendulkar excelling himself in the Third Test at Bangalore by hitting 177 before Adam Dale bowled him. This was his highest and best Test innings to that point. He faced just 207 balls—an amazing Test run rate for such a score of 85.5—in just short of five scintillating hours at the crease. He crashed 29 fours and 3 sixes, a remarkable 134 runs—75 per cent—from boundaries. Only a few batsmen, Bradman and Wally Hammond included, had similar rates in Test scores over 150.

India lost the Third Test, but won the series 2:1, thanks to Tendulkar, who made 446 runs at an average of 111.25. When he made runs, India scored more than 400. When he failed, India managed 257 and 169.

A one-day competition followed the Tests with Zimbabwe flown in as the third team in the competition. In the first one-day game against Australia, Tendulkar, the most exciting batsman ever to play this form of cricket, failed with the bat. Yet such was his confidence that he made up for it with the ball, winning the game for India by taking 5 for 32 with his odd assortment of offies and leggies.

In the next game against Australia he hit a typically superb one-day century—his 13th. In the final, Australians Fleming and Kasprowicz, with short, well-directed deliveries, troubled the Indians, and Tendulkar was dismissed early. India lost. But Tendulkar made up for this shock in the Coca-Cola one-day series soon afterwards in Sharjah. He made scores of 143 and 134 (on his 25th birthday on 24 April 1998), securing that mini series for his team. Sachin Tendulkar had reached his peak form in Test and one-day cricket, 12 years after he was recognised in Mumbai sporting circles as a cricket prodigy.

Early Announcements

The youngest of four children, Tendulkar was raised near Shivaji Park, a congested middle-class suburb in central Mumbai. His father, Ramesh, was a professor of Marathi, Sachin's native tongue (he also speaks Hindi, English and Sanskrit). His mother, Rajani, worked in a life insurance corporation.

Sachin's older half-brother Ajit was first to spot his brother's exceptional cricketing talent.

'My brother saw me playing with a tennis ball and said, "Why don't you join a club and play with a proper cricket ball?",' Tendulkar told an Indian newspaper. 'In our colony there were eight buildings and all the kids would get together and play all the time. I was three when I first held a bat, but I was 11½ when I first played with a seasoned ball.'

Tendulkar gives great credit for his development as a cricketer to Ajit: 'Ajit was the one who guided me throughout until today. Without him I do not know what I would be. I came to cricket quite late, so I practised quite hard. I practised my backswing with a ball hanging in a sock.'

He scored his first century for his school at the age of 12. A year later Tendulkar's potential was apparent when he captained his Mumbai school team—Shardashram English—to a win in the Giles Shield tournament in 1986-87. He led with panache and hit a match-winning 159 not out. One interested spectator was his idol, India's highest-achieving batsman Sunil Gavaskar. At the end of that season, when the young Sachin failed to win the Mumbai Cricket Association's Best Junior Cricketer Award, Gavaskar anticipated his disappointment and sent him a letter:

Dear Sachin,
I wanted to write earlier, but something or other came in

the way. Then I thought it better to write at the beginning of the new season (1987-88) rather than at the end of the last season.

Congratulations on your performance last season. What was most impressive was the way you batted alone when the others around you were not contributing much. Keep it up.

Also please do not neglect your studies. My experience is that education helps you through bad patches in whichever career you choose.

So go ahead and God bless.

Regards,

Sunil Gavaskar

PS: Don't be disappointed at not getting the Best Junior Cricketer Award from the BCA. If you look at the best award winners, you will find one name missing and that person has not done too badly in Test cricket!!

At his school he had an intelligent coach in Ramakant Achrekar, who examined his natural style. Only occasionally did he suggest subtle changes in technique. Tendulkar had a few 'defects', including playing across the line and waving his bat at bouncers. But as the years rolled on, he developed a nigh-impregnable defence. From time to time he made errors such as leaving the back foot outside leg stump so that he played across straight deliveries, and was corrected.

He was obsessive about practice from the age of 13, being a tireless worker in the nets. At home he hung a ball from the ceiling and struck it with a bat for hours, pretending he was Gavaskar or another of his heroes, Viv Richards, playing in a Test.

In the 1987-88 season at the age of 14, Tendulkar made a name for himself and his school, not just in Mumbai but India-wide. He partnered future Test batsman, and his closest friend then and now, the 15-year-old Vinod Kambli in a game against St Mary's High School in the Mumbai inter-schools competition. At the end of the first day, Sachin was 192 not out and Kambli 182 not out. They received loud applause from their coach, Achrekar, who the next day had an important appointment and couldn't get to the ground. He sent a message to captain Tendulkar to declare early on the second day, but because of a mix-up Tendulkar never received the message and instead went on batting and batting. The result was a world record 664-run partnership with Kambli reaching 329 not out and Tendulkar 326 not out.

Achrekar heard of the batting marathon, found a phone booth and rang the ground. The coach reminded the impish Tendulkar firmly that the game could not be won until the other side was dismissed twice. But the damage—and the rewriting of history—had been done. *Wisden Cricketer's Almanac* recognised the Tendulkar and Kambli performance as the 'biggest partnership recorded'. For the next several games Indian cricket fans seemed more interested in Tendulkar's school's performances than Indian first-class matches.

Tendulkar was invited to net practice by Mumbai's skipper Vengsarkar at the beginning of the 1988-89 season. The 15-year-old boy's performance was so impressive that he was picked for the team a couple of months later when Vengsarkar and Ravi Shastri were touring with the Indian Test side in New Zealand. He was set to join such greats as W G Grace, Bradman and a handful of others who showed that they could make the transition from schoolboy obscurity to the big time with hardly a falter. On 12 December 1988, Tendulkar, batting down the order in the experienced Mumbai side, came in to face Gujarat's off-spinner Nisarg Patel at Mumbai's Wankhede Stadium. He defended the first two balls, cover drove the third for 4 and never looked back as he moved on to make a spectacular century in just 129 balls. The diminutive champion, whose pads seemed to slap his stomach as he ran, stroked 12 fours and became the youngest first-class centurion of the 20th Century. He ran off all the shots as though he had been playing at this level for years. From that performance on he was destined for a very early start to a Test career. That season the teenager collected another 6 scores over 50 without another century, scoring 583 runs at an average of 64.77. It was enough for selectors to consider sending him on tour to the West Indies early in 1989. Wisdom prevailed; the selectors had second thoughts about giving Tendulkar a baptism against the speed quartet of Marshall, Ambrose, Walsh and Patterson, who had recently formed the most lethal combination in modern cricket. Tendulkar thought he could cope but was not taken on the trip. As it turned out, only one batsman, Sanjay Manjrekar, demonstrated the will to withstand the West Indian pace.

A year later Tendulkar was selected to tour Pakistan. At Karachi in November 1989, aged 16 years and 201 days, he batted at number six, in his first Test, the fourth in the series. Despite a hideous attack of nerves—he said that 'butterflies were flying around in formation in my stomach'—he showed the cheek, confidence and courage of a person a decade older than him. Tendulkar The Daring put his hand up like a determined traffic cop to stop Wasim Akram in his tracks as he steamed in to bowl. Yet his mind was a blank. His feet remained static. Wasim Akram tore in at him and delivered four fearsome bouncers.

'It was very tough, too fierce,' Tendulkar told an Indian journalist years later. 'I didn't think I would ever play Test cricket again. At times I was beaten by pace. The ball went past my bat before I had finished my shot.'

Yet he did play some nice shots—a cover drive, a leg-glance, an on-drive—even if he couldn't remember them. A short time later Tendulkar was bowled for 15, but he had made his point. He had the mental strength to handle competition at this level.

His precocious hand movement probably swayed the tour selectors, who gave him another chance in the Fifth Test. After his harrowing introduction in the fourth, Tendulkar remarked that he never seemed to face pace like it again. He often wondered if he had run into a purple patch by Wasim or if his state of mind played tricks on his faculties. He decided that it was probably a little of each.

Rite of Passage

Tendulkar came to the wicket in the Fifth Test after an early collapse against the serious speed of Akram, Waqar Younis, Zakir Khan and Imran Khan. Back in the pavilion and already disposed of were Shastri, Srikkanth, Manjrekar and Azharuddin.

Tendulkar waddled in, his big pads dwarfing him. He wore a helmet without a grille because he felt uncomfortable peering through the steel bars. With the speedsters on top on a helpful wicket, the big Pakistani crowd bayed for blood. They got it. Not long into Tendulkar's innings Waqar bounced one hard off a good length, high enough to smash into the short teenager's nose. He dropped his bat, removed his helmet and attempted to stop the blood flow as the crowd roared their approval. Imran Khan went to check the damage. One or two Pakistanis sledged him to the effect: 'You're out of your league here, son.' Another suggested he should retire hurt. Urgent signals were made to the dressing room. The 12th man and a doctor rushed out. Head back, handkerchief to his face, Tendulkar waved a determined 'no' to a request by the doctor for him to leave the arena. He faced up again. Waqar tore in for the kill and did not waste a short ball on the youngster. Instead he speared in a good, swinging, full-pitch delivery. Tendulkar turned it into an excellent shot, square driving it for 4. The crowd fell silent, then revved up again as Waqar ran in faster for the next ball. He pitched it shorter outside the off stump. On tiptoe, Tendulkar struck the ball on the up through cover for another 4.

Was it the youth's rite of passage? Certainly he looked like a pro in command, not a quivering kid with a smashed nose. He went on for another 130 minutes compiling a solid, defensive 59 in an innings that would be remembered for its guts as much as its style. His stay staved off a Pakistan victory.

He had established that he had the gumption for this level of the sport, but he was still raw and sometimes could not control his aggression. On rare occasions it paid off, as in an exhibition match at Peshawar, Pakistan, in 1990 when he hit Abdul Qadir for 26 in one over—an effort that even earned the plaudits of the fine bowler himself. Yet his overuse of force, while thrilling the crowds, did nothing to advance his Test career. In his next 11 innings in Tests against Pakistan, New Zealand and England, he scored 8, 41, 35, 57, 0, 24, 88, 5, 10, 27 and 68, giving him an average of 33.61 and an aggregate of 437. He was still just 17 years old, but he had been playing Tests regularly for nine months and it was frustrating for him and his supporters, who expected bigger scores. After showing such promise against Pakistan, he was no match for New Zealand and the wily Richard Hadlee, who was arguably then the world's best bowler. He had a chance to make his first Test century at Napier when he was on 80 by the close of play on the first day. He visualised the next 20 over and over in his mind during the night, but in the first over of the morning he smashed 2 fours and was out at 88 going for a third.

Tendulkar failed twice (10 and 27) in the First Test in England, but in the Second Test at Old Trafford, he seemed to have taken on board a tip Gavaskar had given him—to play as late as possible. In the first innings Tendulkar revived India's flagging fortunes with 68. In the second, he hauled India away from defeat to a draw with an unbeaten 119 in a patient innings of more than five hours. His first Test century had taken him 14 innings. His average was up to 42.76. This grand effort was followed by further disappointments—21 in England and 11 against Sri Lanka in November 1990. It took a tour of Australia a year later in the 1991-92 southern season for Tendulkar to consolidate. He began poorly in the First Test in Brisbane, batting at number six behind a fine line-up of Shastri, Srikkanth, Manjrekar, Vengsarkar and captain Azharuddin, and made 16 and 7. At Melbourne at Christmas in 1991 he made 15 and 40. India lost both games and the squad's confidence was well down.

However, the tourists turned things around in Sydney early in 1992. In reply to Australia's 313, Shastri held the innings together until Tendulkar, now 18 years old, strode out with the score at 4 for 201. These two put on 196 in even time. The cricket world was forced to sit up and take notice of Tendulkar as he unleashed a range of aggressive strokes, backed by the control he had demonstrated at Old Trafford. Shane Warne, playing his first-ever Test, was on the other end of this assault and received a drubbing as Shastri went on to 206 before Warne had him caught in the deep. Tendulkar carried on to an unbeaten 148, and India was in a position to win. Only a rear-guard effort by Allan Border (53 not out) saved the home team from defeat. Tendulkar failed in the Fourth Test but came back in the Fifth on a hard Perth wicket to score a beautiful 114 off 161 balls. India lost again, making it a 4:0 series win for Australia. For India, Tendulkar's dazzling emergence was the one plus to come out of the tour.

The Fame Game

Tendulkar returned to India a hero. If he found fame difficult to cope with before, it was unbearable now. He couldn't go anywhere in his home city of Mumbai without being mobbed.

He had done just enough on the field to justify the fuss, with a middling series in South Africa in 1992-93. But at home in three Tests against England early in 1993 he didn't fail once and returned scores of 50, 9 not out, 165, 78 and 62. His career average was in the mid-40s. As he matured as a batsman and person, he was becoming more consistent and reliable. In five Tests from July 1993 to February 1994 against Sri Lanka he notched 28, 104 not out, 71, 142, 96 and 6. For the first time his average found some solidity at around 50, which, statistically, placed him in the top 17 players in cricket history. He stayed at the new ranking with scintillating performances at home—34, 85, 179, 54, 40 and 10—against the speed of the West Indies led by Walsh and Ambrose.

In the mid-1990s, Tendulkar had only a handful of sponsorship deals, including one with Action Shoes, for about US$10,000 a year. Mark Mascarenhas, American head of the communications company WorldTel, asked for and got the exclusive right to the Tendulkar name for five years. Within months, companies began lining up for sponsorship deals. His mother stopped him from advertising beer and cigarettes, which lost him US$800,000. It didn't matter. Footwear and soft-drink corporations, of which his parents approved, took their place. Later, a satellite TV group signed him for US$7.5 million over five years. Pepsi nabbed him for another big contract, which included the sweetener of an additional $25,000 for every century he scored for India, as did Visa, Philips, Colgate, a muesli company and a Madras rubber factory. Adidas India signed him to a sportswear deal worth more than US$4million over six years. His face appeared on billboards throughout India. You couldn't open a magazine or switch on a TV without seeing him. On top of this he had a good contract playing for India, worth more than US$200,000 annually. And he received 25 per cent of all prize money he earned in cricket tournaments, the rest going into the Indian team pool.

Tendulkar's financial future was assured early, but it came at a price. He now had superstar status in India and was said to be more famous than Mother Theresa. He was certainly the most popular entertainer in the country and more adored than film stars such as his own favourites, Amitabh Bacchan, Madhuri Dixit and Nana Patekar. Hundreds of millions of fans watched him perform all over the world via satellite TV.

He spoke of feeling free only when he was in the middle of a cricket field batting, bowling and fielding. There, he could be seen but not engaged by the fans. In the streets it was different. He stayed at home with his family and would not venture to the shops for fear of being engulfed by the crowds. A shy person, he vainly tried to hold on to some vestige of privacy. It was only possible inside the friendly compound in East Bandra where his parents lived. Kids from other apartments would often be seen playing cricket with him and many a youngster boasted he or she had bowled Tendulkar. Occasionally, late at night he would go for a drive in one of his cars, including a Maruti, a BMW and a custom-built Mercedes. It was the only time he could hope not to be recognised. He tried disguising himself as a street dweller by putting on raggy clothes, a false beard and a crumpled hat pulled down over his face. But he couldn't hide his walk, his voice, or his companions. People at a local cinema became suspicious when his beard slipped. A mob surrounded him. In the end, Sachin couldn't go to cinemas. It just wasn't worth the effort.

In 1995 he began seriously dating a young, attractive Anglo-Indian paediatrician, Anjali, the daughter of cosmetics magnate Anand Mehta and his English wife, Annabel. Sachin and Anjali had known each other since 1990.

'When I met my (future) wife she didn't have any clue about cricket,' Tendulkar said. 'Now she follows a little, but not much.'

They married early in 1996. Asia's Star TV wanted to televise the ceremony, saying it would rival the marriage of Charles and Diana in 1981. Tendulkar, just 22 years old on the big day, refused a large sum of money and barred all photographers until the reception the next day.

The couple took up residence in a luxury apartment above his parents' home in East Bandra, thus affording some measure of protection and a fraction more privacy. This added stability suited Tendulkar. He continued to perform well on the field.

Bradman on Tendulkar

In mid-1996, Tendulkar received the finest compliment of his life to that point from Don Bradman in an Australian TV interview with the Nine Network's Ray Martin.

Bradman ranked Brian Lara and Tendulkar as the best bats in the world, and found it difficult to judge which was better. He thought that Tendulkar had a very sound defence while Lara was marginally more aggressive and took more risks. By 2000, he held to the view that they were the best in world cricket, but that Tendulkar just pipped Lara as the world's number one.

He was first seriously impressed by Tendulkar when watching a one-day game in the World Cup on 27 February 1996. Australia won but not before a stunning 90 from Tendulkar that captured The Don's attention. He was most taken by Tendulkar's technique, compactness and shot production and asked his wife, Jessie, to have a look at the Indian as he felt that Tendulkar played like he had. Jessie agreed that they appeared similar. Bradman never missed a chance to see Tendulkar from then until the end of the 1999 three-match Test series in Australia.

The Times' cricket correspondent John Woodcock, who had seen both Bradman and Tendulkar in the flesh, commented:

The Bradman–Tendulkar analogy makes a fascinating subject.

Bradman was an inch or two taller but probably a pound or two lighter. Because of his oriental make-up, Tendulkar has the more exotic, chancier repertoire; owing to his cast of mind and strength of will, Bradman sold his wicket more dearly. Common to both is instinctive and lightning fast footwork, unquestionable genius, a wonderful capacity for placing the ball and a fine regard of the great game itself.

When Bradman's remarks were made public, Tendulkar was a few months over the age of 23. He'd scored 8 Test centuries from 55 innings, whereas at the same age Bradman also had 8 tonnes, but from only 21 starts. By then Bradman had hit 4 double centuries (including a 299 not out) and 1 triple century in Tests, whereas the Indian had yet to manage a double century. Tendulkar's average stood at 51.72. Bradman's at that point in his career was 94.45.

Tendulkar was in England when he heard Bradman's remarks and it seemed to boost him. In three Tests he recorded his best series yet—scoring 24, 122, 31, 177 and 74—428 runs at 85.60, lifting his career average to a healthy 54.92.

Captain

1996 was proving to be the biggest year of the 23-year-old's life. He had married, hit his best form so far as a batsman, and as a reward, in August was given the Indian captaincy. In the euphoria of his success, were Indian cricket officials getting carried away? Their thinking was straightforward: India was losing more than they were winning, so anything would be better. Azharuddin stepped down and India won a one-off Test against Australia by 7 wickets in Delhi in October. Tendulkar made 10 and 0, and could thank keeper-opener Mongia, who made 152, for the victory. He took his team to South Africa for the 1996-97 season and his slump continued with scores of 42, 7, 18, 2, 61, 36, 15, 4, 169, 9, 35 and 9, which brought his average down to 49.67. Tendulkar was having trouble juggling his form, the captaincy and all his off-field duties. Indian officials allowed him time to settle in against the West Indies in India, and his form improved with scores of 7, 15 not out, 88 (run out), 92, 4 and 83. He returned to top form in Sri Lanka in a five-Test series with 3 big hundreds in three matches—143, 139 and 148. In October 1997, in the middle of this purple patch, his daughter Sara was born. Tendulkar told Vinod Kambli that this gave him greater joy than any innings.

Under Tendulkar, India had drawn seven of its last eight Tests, and criticism mounted. His own batting was as brilliant, brave and risky as ever. Yet collectively, the Indian players appeared to be worried about losing, rather than striving for a win. The consequences in cricket-obsessed India were huge. In a one-day tournament against Pakistan, the West Indies and Sri Lanka following the Test series in December 1997, Tendulkar struggled. India lost a game in Sharjah and the team was pelted with bottles and stones as they left the field. Outside the team's hotel, fans rioted, hurling abuse and any projectiles they could get their hands on. It was a salutary lesson on the fickle nature of Indian spectators, who had been known to set fire to a stadium rather than see their team lose.

The officials' attitudes reflected those of the fans. They sacked half the side and axed Tendulkar as captain early in 1998. He had been skipper for just 18 months. Azharuddin took over again. Tendulkar, both upset and relieved, was able to concentrate on his batting. He did this with devastating effect against the Australians from February to March 1998 and India won the Test series 2:1 with attacking cricket.

Tendulkar kept up a terrific barrage in one-day games. At the end of 1998, his statistics read 202 innings, 20 not outs, an aggregate of 7,750 runs, and an average of 42.58. Michael Bevan of Australia, with an average of around 60, was ahead of him, as were England's Nick Knight on 47.32 and Lara on 46.91. Yet Bevan had just three centuries while Tendulkar had 21, at easily the best rate—one every 9.62 matches—of anyone in the game.

The Meeting

By mid-1998, after watching Tendulkar destroy Australia in Tests and one-day games in India, Bradman ranked him with Barry Richards, Arthur Morris and Garry Sobers. Not long after that series against Australia, Tendulkar received the invitation of a lifetime—to join Shane Warne in meeting Bradman at his Kensington Park home in Adelaide on his 90th birthday, 27 August 1998.

Both visitors looked nervous as they entered The Don's home in a quiet, tree-lined street, his refuge since 1935. Their friendly host, in an open-necked shirt and grey cardigan, put the two suited guests at ease as they were served tea by his housekeeper, Betty Joseph. Tendulkar was honoured to be told by Bradman that he was today's best batsman. They discussed Garry Sobers, whom Bradman had long regarded as the best cricketer of all time.

Bradman spoke about how his amateur status meant that he had to hold down a job to make ends meet while playing first-class cricket. Tendulkar and Warne have never experienced such a problem, but all three could agree that fame had its downsides. Bradman spoke a lot about modern cricket, and how the standard had gone up in every department, especially fielding. Bradman said he believed that players were under more pressure in modern cricket.

Tendulkar asked The Don how he prepared himself before a big match. Bradman replied that when he was in Adelaide he'd go to his job as a sharebroker for several hours before going to the ground. Sometimes he would even toss the coin still wearing his suit. After the game he would return to the office for several more hours. When he was playing games away from Adelaide, he would go for a long walk before and after the match.

Bradman told me after the meeting how impressed he was with Tendulkar, then 25 years old. He expected him to go on to even greater achievements.

'With a little luck,' the Don said, 'he'll have another decade at the top.'

Tendulkar has several ambitions beyond adding to his grand tally of international centuries. Among them is a fervent desire to win a World Cup for India, which he failed to do in England in May-June 1999. When his father died in the middle of that tournament, Tendulkar flew back to India for the funeral, then courageously resumed his place in the Indian team, knowing that his father would have wished it. Tendulkar will have two, perhaps three, more chances to win the Cup for his country. He also wants to become the first player to score a double century in a one-day international, which would break Saeed Anwar's record one-day score of 194. Tendulkar, at age 26, made his first Test double hundred (217) against New Zealand in late October 1999. It was his 71st Test and his 21st Test hundred.

In July 1999 one aim that Tendulkar was not in a hurry to achieve came his way. He was made captain of India again. Then, after a poor series loss to Australia away in 2000-2001, it was taken from him once more and given to Sourav Ganguly. A year later, he told the Internet site Cricinfo that he was open to leading India again.

By the end of the Test series against Australia in March-April 2001—in which India under Ganguly revenged their drubbing in Australia at the end of 1999 with a 2:1 series win—Tendulkar had scored 25 centuries in 131 Test innings, including two double hundreds, the other being against Zimbabwe. His average stood at 56.94. Tendulkar's mixed bag of spinners, mainly leggies, had snared 22 wickets at 38.09. In one-day internationals he had hit 28 hundreds from 261 innings and had averaged 42.58, with a top score of 186 not out. In 246 first-class innings he had accumulated 13,466 runs, including 43 centuries, with a highest score of 233 not out, and at an average of 61.20.

One record will elude Sachin Tendulkar: Don Bradman's Test average of 99.94. But just about everything else in Test and one-day cricket seems likely to fall his way.

CHAPTER 7

SIMPLY

THE BEST

GARFIELD ST AUBRUN
SOBERS

(West Indies)

28 July 1936—

'He is the best cricketer of all time.'

SIR DONALD BRADMAN

The time was 2.24 pm as Garry Sobers, on a pair, strode onto the MCG to bat for a World XI v Australia. It was the third day of the third game in the 1971-72 series. The 35-year-old skipper was said to be past his best and unlikely to ever again display the skills he'd shown for the West Indies in Australia in the 1960-61 series when he belted two magnificent centuries. So far he had struggled to find form in these matches with 20 not out, 15 not out, 0, 33 and another duck in the first innings, courtesy of the new Australian tearaway, Dennis Lillee, who displayed great speed, control and a very late swing. In the first innings the World XI had scrambled together a poor 184, in which Lillee had taken 5 for 48. Australia had replied with 285, giving them a lead of 101. Now, just after lunch on day three, 3 January 1972, the World XI was 3 for 146 with Zaheer Abbas at the wicket. They had a lead over Australia of just 45. Another quick breakthrough would give the game, and a 2:0 lead in the series, to Australia.

Sir Donald Bradman, who organised the World XI games after stopping the tour by South Africa in 1971-72, settled into his seat in the VIP box in the members' pavilion. As Sobers took block, Bradman said to Ian Johnson, Secretary of the Melbourne Cricket Club and his former Test team-mate: 'I hope Garry finds some form. He's due.'

Sobers got his eye in and then unleashed the power for which he had been known on every major ground in the world since he first played Test cricket in 1954. He hooked, drove, lofted on both sides of the wicket and threw in some of his unorthodox specials, such as cuts and drive–slashes off the front foot. He didn't spare anyone, including Bob Massie, Terry O'Keefe, Terry Jenner and Lillee, who had so far dominated the series.

Sobers delivered one shot that will stay forever with those fortunate spectators at the MCG. Lillee bowled a terrific in-dipper (away swinger to the left-hander) well up and nigh unplayable, except for someone with freakish skills. Sobers stepped as if he might go forward to drive, but then, with apparently plenty of time, made a backward movement and simultaneously smashed the ball like a bullet along the ground past Lillee for 4.

After 3 hours and 36 minutes of controlled mayhem, Sobers reached 139 not out by stumps, including 21 fours.

Bradman commented to Ian Johnson that he thought the innings to that point was 'perfection'. Sobers had not made an error, sustaining an unrelenting attack combined with a tight defence. The next day was a rest day and the West Indian relaxed with a round of golf. It allowed him to summon his energy for another assault on 5 January—if someone could stay at the wicket with him. Since Sobers had arrived at the crease, Abbas had gone for 86, Greig for 3, Engineer for 14 and Alam for 15. The next day, South Africa's Peter Pollock (54), coming in at number 9, provided support at one end as Sobers relaunched himself into his innings and reached 254 after lunch before Greg Chappell had him caught.

Sobers added 115 in 2 hours 46 minutes. In all, he batted for 6 hours and 16 minutes. He hit 35 fours and 2 successive sixes off O'Keefe. He had played at a furious pace all year round every year for nearly two decades, and his aging body was wracked with aches and pains.

'We (Bradman and Johnson) were totally engrossed in this

innings,' Johnson said. 'As it progressed we talked of the greatest knocks we'd ever seen. I mentioned a couple of his (Bradman's) own. Don recalled McCabe's 232 in 235 minutes at Trent Bridge in 1938 and Sobers' 132 in Brisbane in 1960.

'Bradman was smiling that little half-grin throughout (Sobers' 1972 innings). He loved it. When he (Sobers) was out, he (Bradman) said, with that, you know, typical certitude in his tone of voice—that always came from deep thought, long experience and a standard beyond the rest of us: "I don't think a better innings has ever been played in this country."'

Bradman made a public comment soon afterwards: 'I believe Garry Sobers' innings was probably the best ever seen in Australia. The people who saw Sobers have seen one of the historic events of cricket, they were privileged to have such experiences.'

There could be no finer tribute to a performance than this. Bradman had never been extravagant with praise, mainly because he judged things from his own phenomenal yardstick. He rated Sobers' effort better than any of his own great knocks in Australia, those of Macartney, McCabe, Ponsford, Harvey, Hutton and Hammond in Australia, and others by a long list of fine batsmen.

Bradman later said of Sobers:

> With his long grip of the bat, his high backlift and free swing, I think, by and large, Garry Sobers consistently hits the ball harder than anyone I can remember. This helps to make him such an exciting player to watch because the emphasis is on power and aggression rather than technique—the latter being the servant, not the master. The uncoiling of those long steely wrists, as he flicks the ball wide of mid-on, is a real joy to watch because it is unique and superbly controlled, whilst the full-blooded square cut is tremendous.

Bradman's appreciation of Sobers was established long before that blistering innings in early 1972. He had seen him perform over more than a decade. Sobers' all-round efforts with bat and ball caused Bradman to think as early as the 1960-61 series between Australia and the West Indies that he was the best all-round cricketer ever.

'Garry would be in my team for his batting alone,' Bradman said. 'If you consider that he could bowl left-hand fast-medium and spin with equal facility and great effect, he would also make any team as a bowler.'

Shaped by Tragedy

Garry's father, Shamont, was killed on 11 January 1942 when a German submarine torpedoed the *Lady Drake* as it was taking supplies to Barbados, his home island. The ship went down with all hands. Garry, fatherless at five years of age, matured faster than usual. With his father's death, his responsibilities in a household of six children increased. His upbringing was financially poor but rich in other important things, such as family and Christian values, good health, the abundance of fruit and fish on the island, and the opportunity to play sport. It was clear from the start that the young Garry was gifted at cricket, even when using his first bat, shaped from a wooden fence paling, and ball, crafted from tar and rags. Even as an 11-year-old, his bowling and batting left his adversaries and peers in awe. His capacities in the field stunned them. When he caught or gathered the ball it was as if he had an electronic extension to his long arms.

The young Sobers did have the beginnings of an extra finger on each hand. It is not known if this gave him an advantage, and the digits were later removed, but as former England Test player Trevor Bailey observed in his biography *Sir Gary*, it added to the mystique. Twelve-fingered spinners were certainly not common.

Sobers left school at 13 years of age. At this time he excelled at soccer, joining the Notre Dame Club as a goalkeeper—a position he would later hold for his country. (He would also represent Barbados at golf and table tennis, thus becoming perhaps the only sportsman to play for his country in four sports.)

Sobers' cricketing talent was first recognised by Garnett Ashby, the captain of the Barbados country districts team Kent. He persuaded Garry's protective mother to let her 13-year-old stay with him in the country on weekends to play cricket. The boy Sobers began by bowling accurate left-arm orthodox spinners, displaying a temperament that allowed him to slip easily into competition with men. By the third game, captain Ashby let Sobers set his own field. Sobers took 6 for 20 out of an opposition—the strong Sussex side—that made 52. By the sixth game Sobers ran through Sussex with 8 for 17 out of 39. The teenager perpetrated this kind of mayhem in the minor country league for nearly two seasons. And that was just with the ball.

Ashby had seen Sobers bat in school games and was aware of a raw brilliance here too. Yet the kid was apprehensive about facing the big rustic bowlers, until the skipper offered him the right moment to display his amazing skills with the willow. Kent, which had lost its specialist batsmen, had to make 38 to win in a match against a local side. Ashby gave Sobers the bat and sent him in. Sobers blocked the first couple of balls. The third delivery to him was short: a chest-high bouncer. Sobers swivelled and hooked hard. The ball was not quite middled, but it sailed over the fine-leg fence for six. He followed this stroke with a foal-like flurry of arms and legs in every shot. Despite the fact that all his limbs often seemed out of the correct orthodox position, the ball almost always went where it was meant to go, with force that could only have come from someone with exquisite timing. The game ended in four overs. The opposition had been chopped with the speed and brutality of a guillotine operator. Garry Sobers, all-rounder, was made. He never avoided the skipper's eye again when a batsman was required. He had a taste for the blood of opposition bowlers—it would not leave him for the next quarter of a century. Within a year, Sobers, now 15, was asked to join the Police XI, a member team of the Barbados Cricket Association, which chose the island's side for Caribbean games. Garry was still just 162.5 cm (5 ft 4 in) and in the Police XI matches was subject to much bouncing. In a match against Empire Cricket Club he was struck in the face by a former West Indian quick, Foffie Williams, and went down with a split lip and bloodied nose. He fronted the next week as if nothing had happened. In the eyes of the Barbados selectors his courage was an important asset in the Caribbean, where wickets ranged from unpredictable to awful. Anyone with a normal sense of self-preservation would be advised to play another sport.

Garry grew 20 cm (8 in) in a year. With his added height came performances with both bat and ball that could not be ignored by the island's selectors. He took 9 wickets in one game and made a quick-fire century in another. In 1952, he was selected as 12th man against the touring Indian team. The West Indian selectors had insisted that Barbados quick, Frank King, be rested. Thus Garry Sobers, just 16 years old, played in his debut first-class game. Showing the presence of mind of someone a decade older, he took 4 for 50 off 22 overs with 5 maidens in the first innings. In the second, he bowled a marathon 67 overs with 35 maidens, taking 3 for 92. His match figures against a near-Test side were 7 for 142 from 89 overs with 40 maidens.

In 1953, Sobers was entrenched in the Barbados team as a reliable left-arm spinner and hard-hitting middle-order bat. A year later, the 17-year-old batted at number five for Barbados and stroked an impressive 40 against the touring MCC. It may have helped his selection to play against the MCC in the 1954 series in the Fifth Test at Sabina Park, Jamaica, not as a batsman, but as a slow left-armer with all-rounder potential. The Windies won the toss and batted. The tall, lean and supple Sobers came in at number nine when the score was barely 100. He remained not out on 14 as his side scrambled to 139.

When England batted, he came on as the third change bowler delivering his orthodox spinners, which mostly left the bats of right-handers Len Hutton and Trevor Bailey, who opened the innings and were still together at 43. Bailey had never seen Sobers, but relished the change from Frank King's barrage of bumpers. Sobers dished up several innocuous balls on line that seemed to turn little. Then he threw one wide enough outside Bailey's off stump to tempt a cut. Bailey tried the shot, but was surprised to realise that it didn't turn at all. It was the teenager's arm-ball—a delivery that goes straight through. The result was a cramped shot that was caught behind. It was Sobers' first wicket in Tests. He was delighted to have picked up such a famous name on a score of 24. It was the first of 4 wickets (for 75 from 28.5 overs) as he finished off the tail in a tight, economical display. He made 26 in the second innings. The West Indies lost by 9 wickets.

Another year on, Sobers was selected for the Second Test of a series against Ian Johnson's Australians. He came in three places higher up the order at number six, and battled to 47 before being caught behind off Ray Lindwall. He hardly had a bowl (0 for 10 off three overs) as Australia climbed to 9 for 600 and he made 8 not out in the second innings of a drawn game. In the following Test at Georgetown—coming in after the famous three W's, Clyde Walcott, Everton Weekes and Frank Worrell—he only managed 12 and 11 with the bat, but took 3 for 20 off 16 overs with 10 maidens. Again, he was more than tidy, and also proud of his three victims—Keith Miller, Ron Archer and Ian Johnson.

His fourth Test, and the fourth of this series, at Bridgetown was the one that made the big names of the game sit up and take notice of his potential. The Windies were having trouble with their opening bats against the terrific pace of Lindwall and Miller. Captain, Denis Atkinson, felt they had nothing to lose by trying the youngster in the hot spot. To some, it was like throwing the Christians in with the lions. For Sobers, it was a challenge. He tamed the great Aussie speed men with an assault of 6 fours in his first 25.

Until then the Australians had viewed Sobers as just a back-up spinner for Alf Valentine. Suddenly he had to be seen as a young cricketer with serious and powerful all-round potential.

Ian Johnson relieved Lindwall and deceived Sobers with his flight and had him caught for 43. He was LBW to Archer for 11 in the second innings, but once again returned respectable figures with the ball—1 for 30 off 11.5 overs with 6 maidens—when everyone else took a belting as Australia amassed 668. In the second innings, he took 1 for 35 off 14 with 3 maidens.

He was dropped down to number seven in the Fifth Test at Sabina Park but went further in staking his claim as a genuine all-rounder, rather than bowling all-rounder, with 35 not out and 64 with the bat, and 1 for 90 with the ball from 38 overs with 12 maidens. This stint with the ball was against a powerful line-up that batted down to number nine (Benaud) and included three of Australia's all-time greats in Arthur Morris, Neil Harvey and Keith Miller. His chance to settle in to playing Tests could not have come against a more challenging line-up. He'd come through with a batting average of 38 and respectable bowling statistics.

Sobers toured New Zealand in 1956, and struggled on foreign soil. In four Tests he collected just 81 runs at 16.20, and was used as little more than a fill-in with the ball, taking 2 for 49 off 46 overs with 26 maidens. In his first tour of England in 1957 he was more promising with the bat, hitting 320 at 32. In England, his slow spinners were not a novelty. He sent down 134 overs including 24 maidens and took 5 for 355 at 71.00 runs per wicket.

Everton Weekes, who played as a professional in the Lancashire League, gave Sobers tips about English wickets that helped him score more than 1,600 runs for the season. Weekes also advised the just-turned-21-year-old to start saving some of the money he was earning. Sobers' fast living, centred on booze, gambling and women, did not impress the champion bat. Yet to the young, handsome star retirement from the game was 10, 15, maybe 20 years away. Why worry?

The Big One

In early 1958 when Pakistan toured the Caribbean, Sobers would have felt a sense of invincibility and never-ending youth. He was yet to score a century but it was hoped that he would against these relatively weak opponents who were playing away from their special conditions at home, which included wickets covered by matting.

The First Test was at Sabina Park. Pakistan batted first and notched a creditable 328. Sobers was again asked to open the batting after his moderate yet striking success there against the Australians three years earlier. The wicket was fast and true. Sobers played himself in, holding back some of his more audacious strokes. He opened up past 50 and reached his first Test hundred. He was elated, but instead of having a hoick, he took block again and put his head down. It paid off. Sobers was 226 not out at stumps on day two and in a strong second-wicket partnership with Conrad Hunte. The media and the public were confident that he could go on to break records.

Sobers always prided himself on being able to put the game

out of his mind and sleep well. For the first time in his career this strength deserted him. He didn't sleep until 4.00 am. But by the time he was at the wicket again, his mind was focused. He liked the reaction he had received after the previous day's play. Why not push on into uncharted territory?

He and Conrad Hunte batted on until they had put together 446. They had smashed records without even realising it. But they became conscious that they were approaching the best second-wicket stand in a Test: 451 by Bill Ponsford and Don Bradman against England in 1934. It made both of them tighten up. Hunte hit one to mid-off, and called for a suicide single. Sobers rejected it. Hunte turned back and was run out for 260.

Sobers, on 267, pushed on with Everton Weekes and reached the great Test milestone of 300. He knew of Bradman's 334, and the world record of 364 by Len Hutton. Only as a child had Sobers entertained travelling such territory, reserved for the gods of cricket. Yet now it was as if he could see the little man in the baggy green in the distance on the gold-paved road ahead, while on the horizon stood the Yorkshireman. Their mighty run-scoring performances were within reach. When Weekes was out for a superb 84, in which he outscored his well-set partner, Clyde Walcott came to the wicket and informed Sobers that the West Indies skipper, Gerry Alexander, was thinking of declaring. Sobers expressed his disappointment. Walcott said he would give him the strike.

Sobers seized the moment and pushed his score to 300. In his autobiography, *Cricket Crusader*, he recalled the tension and wondered why the ground didn't catch fire due to the human electricity. But nothing could upset him.

Sobers passed Bradman's 334, and a roar went up around the park. Then he drew level with Hutton's 364. Pakistan's Hanif Mohammed had been bowling right hand. He indicated he would deliver one with his left hand, a sure sign of surrender, and sportsmanship. Giving Garry Sobers the world record, he delivered the ball slowly. Sobers watched it on to his bat, pushed to the on and took off for run number 365 (not out)— and immortality. The 20,000-strong crowd rushed onto the arena and damaged the pitch. Play was abandoned for the day and the Windies (3 declared for 790) lost a chance to grab wickets from a fatigued Pakistan in the last hour of day three. But it didn't matter. Pakistan made 288 in its second innings and the Windies won by an innings and 174 runs.

Just to remind himself that his mighty performance was not a one-off, he scored 125 and 109 not out in the two innings of the next Test against Pakistan at Georgetown, and 3 other fifties in the series. From just eight innings in the series his Test aggregate was 824 and he averaged 137.33. Sobers was now considered a great *batting* all-rounder. His slow orthodox trundling was ineffective against the Pakistanis, who were used to far more fearsome turning deliveries at home. Sobers took 4 for 377 at 94.25 after his heaviest workload in a series to date.

Next up was a five-Test series in India in 1958. Sobers continued on his merry way, this time with the ball as well. He took 10 wickets on the more spinner-friendly Indian pitches for 292 at 29.20, and hit 557 (including 3 consecutive centuries) at 92.83 runs an innings with a top score of 198. Soon afterwards, without saying why, the Indians warned that he would not get a hundred in Pakistan when he toured there. He soon understood their pessimism. His sensibilities and sense of sportsmanship received a jolt when he was given three poor LBW judgments in his first three innings in Pakistan. They were so bad that Sobers felt victimised and cheated. The Pakistanis were getting back at him, he reasoned, for his walloping of them a year earlier. In the dressing room after the First Test in Karachi (and two poor decisions), Sobers packed his bags and declared he was going home. The team manager talked him out of it. In five innings he managed only 160 at an average of just 32, and he didn't take a wicket in 66 overs.

Sobers' Agony

In 1959, Sobers and his closest friend, the hard-hitting Jamaican batsman, Collie Smith were in England playing in the Lancashire League, in between series for the West Indies. One Saturday night they and a third West Indian, fast bowler Tom Dewdney, travelled by car up to London. Sobers was driving. Alongside him was Dewdney and in the back was Smith, catnapping. Sobers recalls rounding a corner, and 'the blinding blaze of headlights', then a crash. Smith was taken to hospital where he died soon afterwards.

Sobers returned to the West Indies after the 1959 season in England and sought solace in alcohol. He partied and had little sleep. He also stepped up his gambling. Once it had been for pleasure. Now it was serious.

Amazingly, none of this seemed to touch his cricket performances. England bore the brunt of his desire to play as if 'Collie was inside' him when it toured the West Indies in 1959-60. Sobers took command of England in the first game he played, for Barbados, when he hit 154. Fred Trueman, the best England speedster of the post-war era, tried bouncing him as he had successfully six years earlier in 1954. But Sobers was a raw teenager then. Now he was the best batsman in the world, and proceeded to destroy Trueman with ferocious hooking. In a practice match, he even turned on Wes Hall, who was also humiliated when trying to bounce him. These two express bowlers gave up the tactic against this opponent for all time.

Trueman said Sobers was the most devastating batsman— the best hooker and most powerful driver—he had ever encountered in Test cricket. Bradman endorsed this appraisal:

'Garry was by far the best player of short-pitched fast

bowlers I ever saw. He was absolutely murderous, miraculous. He mastered anyone who tried to bounce him.'

Sobers cracked 226 in the opening Test at Bridgetown in a near-record partnership of 399 with Worrell. This series restored Sobers' Test capacities after the debacle in Pakistan. He took 9 wickets for 355 (at 39.44) and notched 709 runs at 101.28, with a highest score of 226. At 24 years of age, Sobers had now plundered England, India and Pakistan with the bat. Of the major Test playing nations, only Australia and New Zealand were left to receive the force of his more mature bladesmanship (South Africa would only play against countries with white-skinned cricketers).

Series of the Century

It was Australia's turn next, in the 1960-61 series downunder. Sobers found Australians hospitable and he liked their relaxed lifestyle and sense of humour.

In Sydney in November 1960 the West Indies played a New South Wales team including half the Australian Test side. Sobers' form since arriving in Perth a few weeks earlier had been of concern. His inability to compose a good knock continued when Benaud bowled him with a wrong'un before his innings got going.

Bradman sensed that Sobers might be demoralised, so he went to the West Indies dressing room to console him, telling him about his own down moments. Bradman predicted Sobers would score at least two centuries during the series.

'Our pitches are generally good for shot-makers,' Bradman told him. 'You'll have plenty of chances.'

Bradman asked Sobers his opinion of the various wickets in Australia. Sobers said he liked the bouncy Perth wicket, which allowed him to play his shots. Bradman thought he would come to like the Sydney wicket best.

They chatted about past West Indian visits and Bradman told him that he was disappointed to have missed seeing Everton Weekes play in 1951-52. Bradman had taken time off from all cricket duties to help Lady Bradman look after their son John who was stricken by polio. (John recovered to later become an accomplished athlete.) Weekes, as it turned out, had an ordinary series.

The 1960-61 West Indies side, led by Frank Worrell, had a more dashing selection of players than any previous tour. Included in its number were Sobers, Worrell, Rohan Kanhai, Conrad Hunte, Seymour Nurse, Cammie Smith, Gerry Alexander, Wes Hall, Charlie Griffith, Lance Gibbs, Sonny Ramadhin and Alf Valentine. They were a formidable lot. Bradman decided to address the Australians, led by Richie Benaud, on the eve of the First Test at the Gabba, Brisbane in November 1960. It was an unprecedented act for the chairman of Australia's ruling cricket body, the Australian Cricket Board, yet he felt it was a necessary one. He gave the home side a gentle prod, first because they needed to bring themselves up a notch if they were to be competitive against Sobers and Co, and second, because of the dwindling attendances at Tests in Australia through the 1950s. Bradman knew a more attacking style of cricket would bring the spectators back. He was aware that Australians in general had more disposable income than before the war, which meant they had a wider choice of summer pleasure pursuits.

'They certainly weren't going to choose cricket if it were boring—not when they could drive into the country, or go sailing, boating or to the beach,' said Bradman.

Bradman reckoned the West Indies, especially with Sobers in its line-up, would stir passions for the game again. But not if the Australians didn't come to the party.

'I also did worry a little that our fellows might be outplayed if they didn't approach the series in a certain frame of mind,' said Bradman.

He told the players that the selectors would be predisposed towards individuals who played attractive, winning cricket—those who pulled in the crowds. Bradman was not overbearing or insistent. He simply stated what was in the best interests of the game. He didn't want another five dull Tests similar to those in Australia in 1958-59 against England.

Much had been made of the coming Test battle between Sobers and Australia's leg-spinner, Richie Benaud. The preliminary round in the tour game against New South Wales had gone to the Australian. It was accurately claimed by cricket journalists that Sobers couldn't pick Benaud's wrong'un. It could be his undoing in the Tests, they said.

Sobers set the tone for the series by slamming 132 in 123 minutes, not sparing Benaud or any of the Australian bowlers in an amazing onslaught. It ranked high on the list of 'Great Test Innings'.

Bradman was thrilled by Sobers' method and execution. It was this innings that made him think that the West Indian might be persuaded to play cricket in Australia professionally.

Bradman congratulated Sobers soon after the innings: 'Thank you very much, son, I knew you wouldn't let me down.'

He then added with that typically wry wit: 'It's a good thing you could not pick Richie (Benaud's wrong'un), or you would have murdered him!'

Sobers Turns to Seamers

The 1960-61 tour was where Sobers began to bring his seam bowling into the Test arena. His left-hand deliveries—mainly orthodox off-spinners and occasional wrist-spinners—had been useful, yet with Valentine, Ramadhin and young Lance Gibbs all pressing for selection, it was better for the team and

Sobers personally if he didn't compete with them but offered something different. The wickets would dictate the style he used, but all things being equal, on a normal wicket, Worrell would turn to him more and more to deliver speed and seamers.

Sobers had been bowling seamers in the Lancashire League where he was more likely to have success than with his finger-spinners. He had always been able to push through the faster delivery. Now he was doing it for its own sake and was developing into a real threat with his speed, seam and swerve.

Sobers had a perfect action. His body turned classically side-on just before delivery as he looked over the outside of his non-bowling (right) arm.

He landed on a braced right leg, and let go of the ball at the correct point of the arc of his follow-through, which was smooth. Sobers had terrific rhythm, which allowed him to deliver quicker off a shorter run than most recognised seamers. Speed, line and length featured, yet even at this early stage, he was toying with the subtleties of swing and seam. He liked switching styles, even in the middle of a spell.

'Garry always presented problems because he delivered a different line,' Bradman observed. 'Just when a batsman was used to, say, right-arm over the wicket, he would come on and disturb the equilibrium. He might also switch from speed to seam then spin, often presenting something different.'

This gave Worrell's 1960-61 team—and Bradman's 'dream team'—balance, variety and the surprise element.

Sobers was also a team workhorse. He was often asked to bowl up the hill when Wes Hall wanted to run down a slope. It was Sobers who would have to deliver into the wind when Charlie Griffith wanted it pushing at his back. This was not to say that Sobers wasn't quick. In that first revelation at Test level he was brisk. He was still youthful, yet not encumbered by the sort of injuries that often occur when a player delivers speed too young, or after ten years of wear and tear.

Sobers could 'slip himself' on occasions and send down balls as fast as a Hall bouncer or a Griffith yorker. Yet he relied on being able to bowl a good inswinger and one that moved away from the right-handed batsman off the pitch.

After his dashing innings in that First Test at Brisbane, Sobers opened the bowling with Hall. He made the break-through in dismissing Colin McDonald (57) in Australia's innings and later bowled the tenacious Ken Mackay (35), returning 2 for 115 off 32 overs. In his second innings, Alan Davidson, a fast-medium left-hander and now a model for Sobers to learn from, delivered a small lesson by way of a booming inswinger that bowled him for 14.

Australia needed 232 to win on the final day and began badly, losing 6 for 92. A fine partnership between Benaud (52) and Davidson (run out for 80) restored the home side's chances. But 3 late run outs brought about by brilliant Windies outfielding saw the game tied—the first in Test history.

Sobers had a lean time in the Second Test at Melbourne over the New Year into 1961. Benaud got him for 9 caught by Simpson in slip, and fellow leg-spinner Johnny Martin had him the same way for a duck in the second innings. Sobers was first change bowler and took an undistinguished 1 for 88 as the Windies went down by 7 wickets.

Bradman's dual prediction—that Sobers would like the Sydney wicket and score another century—came true in the Third Test. Sobers dominated the Windies' first innings with a power-laden 168 out of 339. He was more than useful in the field, bowling Norm O'Neill (71) when he looked like going on to a big hundred, and catching Harvey (9) in slips off Hall. He bowled little in the first innings, taking 1 for 14 off 5 overs with 2 maidens. In Australia's second innings he bowled Simpson (12) and caught Harvey (85) and O'Neill (70) off

Gibbs. His abilities and acrobatics in the slips, or anywhere, were enough to select him as a fielder alone. With Sobers in fine all-round form and Gibbs bowling his off-spinners well (8 for 112), the Windies levelled this enthralling series one-all.

In the Fourth Test, Sobers continued his duel with Benaud, who bowled him for 1 in the first innings. He was run out for 20 in the second. He opened the bowling again and was tighter on the good Adelaide wicket taking 3 for 64 off 24 overs with 3 maidens. O'Neill and Peter Burge were among his victims. In Australia's second knock, when Ken Mackay (64 not out) and Lindsay Kline (15 not out) hung on for 100 minutes in an unconquered last-wicket stand of 66, Sobers took 2 for 87 off 39 overs with 11 maidens.

This thrilling draw, characterised by Mackay taking the last ball in the chest from Hall rather than surrendering his wicket, set the stage for a sensational deciding Fifth Test in Melbourne. Sobers top-scored with 64 from 292 in the Windies first innings, and made 21 in the second. Notably, both times he was dismissed caught behind off Bob Simpson, another who could deliver effective leg-spin. Did he have a weakness against this type of bowling? Not according to Benaud, who said that even if Sobers did not pick a wrong'un, he still had time to alter his shot. He rarely missed the ball and refused to use his pads as a second line of defence.

Sobers, in a mighty marathon with the ball, took 5 for 120 off 44 overs with 7 maidens in Australia's first innings and kept his team in the match, while Gibbs backed him up by taking 4 for 74. Sobers' victims included both openers, Simpson (75) and McDonald (91) when they were set, Harvey (5) and Davidson (24).

After a huge tussle, Australia scraped in by 2 wickets in this game, and so won the series 2:1. But cricket was the winner, with record attendances at all games. Sobers' all-round skills would have given him the man-of-the-series award, if it had then been instituted. He scored 430 runs in 10 knocks at 43, and took 15 wickets for 588 at 39.20 runs per wicket.

During the series, Bradman approached Sobers about coming back to play the 1961-62 season with South Australian club team, Prospect, and the state team. Sobers jumped at the chance.

There were timing problems as the West Indian had commitments in England and at home, but the two men worked them through and Sobers arrived in South Australia in October 1961. The Australian cricket authorities had no funds then to employ professionals, but Bradman helped find sponsors for Sobers. He made guest appearances and gave endorsements for Victoria Car Services, a car accessories company. It was the first-ever job for Sobers, now 25 years old. Coca-Cola also employed him, offering an incentive clause of 10 shillings (about a dollar) a run and 5 pounds (10 dollars) a wicket.

The West Indian proved a winner for Prospect from 1961 to 1964 when he scored 868 runs at 41. He took 104 wickets at the exceptional rate of 13.5 runs per wicket. He went one better for South Australia, managing 1,000 runs and 50 wickets twice in the season. In 1961-62, South Australia, a weak state since Bradman's days, came close to winning the Sheffield Shield. Sobers scored a sensational 251 against New South Wales to end the season in February 1962.

He immediately embarked on a long plane trip to Trinidad, arriving on the morning of the first of a five-Test series against India. Despite jet lag and fatigue, Sobers took two stunning catches in slips. It seemed nothing could stop him. Sobers mowed down India with 23 wickets at 20.56 and hit 424 in 7 innings at 70.66 with 2 centuries, a 50 and a highest score of 153.

At the end of the series he flew to England for another professional season, his last at Radcliffe in the Lancashire League. From 1958 to 1962 he scored 5,728 runs at 65.35 and took

537 wickets at 11.29. Sobers arrived in Adelaide for the 1962-63 season after undergoing a knee operation. He was now fully acclimatised to Australian conditions. It showed, as he smashed 6 centuries and became the season's top wicket-taker. Not surprisingly, South Australia won the Shield. Sobers loved the experience as it meant less cricket at a more competitive standard than his seasons with Radcliffe.

Sobers felt that in Australia he was recognised financially for his skills as the world's best cricketer. But he and other West Indian big names such as Wes Hall were unhappy about the pittance the West Indian Cricket Board was prepared to pay them for another long tour of England. Sobers suggested he might not make the tour. It made headline news.

Sobers consulted Bradman about the problem, and Bradman agreed that he was underpaid.

'With your standing and ability,' Bradman told him, 'you should get more money in cricket than anybody.'

Sobers remarked that the situation was unfair. Bradman agreed, but then advised him to go to England on the board's terms.

'This is not the end,' Bradman added, 'but perhaps the beginning of something else for you.'

Sobers accepted this and toured England with the Windies.

Skipper in Training

Bradman's words reverberated in Sobers' mind during the 1963 summer as Frank Worrell groomed the disgruntled champion for the West Indian captaincy, consulting him about events in play. For the first time, as he turned 27 years of age, Sobers began thinking more consciously about his actions on and off the field, and was becoming more aware of his responsibilities. He was now one of the most experienced players in the team, and halfway through the 1963 tour found himself both 'one of the boys' and a leader. By the end of the season, Sobers had stepped up in the ranks, thanks to his own development and Worrell subtly drawing him out as a leader. He now also comprehended Bradman's advice, for he could look forward to captaining the West Indies, something that hadn't crossed his mind before. If he had not gone to England, he may never have had a chance to captain the West Indies.

Despite niggling knee injuries, Sobers had a fair series, hitting 322 runs from 8 innings at 40.25, with a top score of 102 in the Fourth Test at Leeds. His bowling was again out-standing as he took 20 for 571 at 28.55. His form continued into the Australian summer of 1963-64 when he scored 195, 138 and 124 for South Australia in Shield games and another 155 against the touring South Africans. A mighty season, in which for the second time he scored 1,000 runs and took 50 wickets, was capped off by two big performances. First, in the final Shield game against Victoria, he scored 124 and took 6 for 71—an effort that again gave South Australia the Sheffield Shield. Second, he hit 175 in 244 minutes in the Adelaide Club Grand Final in early 1964, which Prospect won.

Sobers had a 'light' year for the rest of 1964, playing for English club Norton and joining E W Swanton's XI Commonwealth Tour of Malaya. Early in 1965, he took over from the retired Frank Worrell as captain of the West Indies and prepared himself to take on the touring Australians under Bob Simpson. The series began at Sabina Park and Sobers, curtailed by a thigh muscle problem, had little impact on the game with bat or ball. Yet the Windies won by 179, thus getting his captaincy off to a satisfactory start.

He did better in the drawn Second Test in Trinidad where he was run out for 69 and trapped LBW by Simpson for 24. Australia (516) batted aggressively in its own innings with a dashing 143 run out by Bob Cowper. Sobers returned 3 for 75 and the game was drawn. In the Third Test at Georgetown he had a good game, being dismissed in the forties twice and taking 2 wickets in each Australian innings. The West Indies won by 212 runs.

The Fourth Test in Barbados was played on an excellent batting wicket as Australia compiled 6 for 650, with both Lawry and Simpson hitting double centuries. All bowlers returned figures they'd rather forget, including Sobers with 1 for 137. The Windies replied with 573, with Seymour Nurse making a double century. Sobers managed 55 and 34 not out in a game that ended in an exciting draw and gave the West Indies the series—the first time they'd ever beaten Australia. (In the final Test, again at Trinidad, Sobers had little influence on the game, which Australia won by 10 wickets.) Sobers was elated at the end of the Fourth Test. He had led his team to a victory that could allow him to claim they were the best in the world. It was his biggest thrill and moment in the game so far. *Wisden* gave him a profound endorsement as a thinker and leader by suggesting he was a 'worthy successor' to Sir Frank Worrell.

However, his figures for the series, 352 runs at 39.11 and 12 wickets at 40.83 each, suggested he might struggle to be a leader and perform at the top of his game. But this fear was allayed in the next two series against England and India, which were both won by the Windies. In the 1966 England series he returned his best all-round figures ever. In 8 innings, he made 722 at 103.14 with 3 centuries, 2 fifties and a highest score of 174. He also took 20 wickets at 27.25. At Lord's he figured in a 274 partnership with his young cousin, David Holford, when the Windies were in deep trouble. Sobers went on to 163 not out—which he said was his best-ever innings. England scraped through with a draw.

In 1966-67, against India in India he had just 5 innings and each time topped 50. Two not outs and a top score of 95 in the three-match series allowed him to mount an average of 114.00.

He was no less effective with the ball, taking 14 wickets at 25. This was Sobers' zenith as both a player and a skipper.

It all gave Sobers satisfaction, peace of mind and confidence. If possible, he became even more popular with women than before. It wasn't surprising that he fell in love with one of the most beautiful women in the world, Indian film star, Anju Mahendru, who was just 17 when they met in late 1966. They became engaged early in 1967. Anju planned to join Sobers in England when he returned there for the English summer. But she had a film to make in India. The relationship was dashed on the rocks of enforced separation, like many international affairs.

Sobers' leadership record early in 1967 stood at: 13 played, 7 won, 2 lost and 4 drawn. It was to be downhill from there, beginning with the next series in the West Indies against England in 1967-68. The first three Tests were drawn. At Kingston in the Second Test he struck 113 not out in the follow on to avert an innings defeat. Rather than play safe, he declared with less than 2 hours to play and put the pressure on England, which crumbled to be 8 for 68. In the Fourth Test, Sobers showed his gambling streak by declaring the Windies' second innings at 2 for 92, setting England 215 to make in 165 minutes to win. Sobers was attacked for the decision. His motive was simple: the series was deadlocked. He could have forced a fourth draw, a miserable option. Instead, he took a risk in striving for victory—and lost the game and the series.

Despite this minor debacle, he continued to flog England, whose bowlers had been cannon fodder to him now for several series. In 9 innings he made 545 at 90.83, hitting 2 centuries and 2 fifties, with a top score of 152. He took 13 wickets at 39.07.

In 1968 Sobers signed a £5,000 contract with Nottinghamshire for the England county season, making Sobers the highest-paid cricketer in the world. He had real impact, scoring more than 1,500 runs and taking 83 wickets. This helped lift the county from its long period at 15th—or bottom—of the championship table, to 4th. In one game against Glamorgan at Swansea he smashed 6 successive sixes from steady left-arm spinner Malcolm Nash—five pulls and hooks, and one straight drive—a first-class record. This assault was born out of necessity. Sobers needed quick runs in order to make a declaration.

His strong county season as leader and player was followed by a further five-Test series in Australia. Sobers, now 32 years old, had been playing all over the globe for 14 years, and he was beginning to consider life after cricket. He'd had a wonderful time as a single man. Women liked his looks, character, simplicity, warmth and directness. Now it was time for something responsible and long-term. He met an attractive Australian woman, Pru Kirby, in England and they became engaged early in 1969.

Meanwhile, the Windies began their 1968-69 series with a resounding win at Brisbane, thanks mainly to a second-innings century by Clive Lloyd and a great bowling performance by Sobers in Australia's second innings when he took 6 for 73. Sobers' form with the ball continued in the Melbourne Second Test when he took 4 for 97 in Australia's only innings. Batting at number 6, he made 67, top score in the Windies second innings. However, Australia's strong batting led by captain Bill Lawry (205) and Ian Chappell (165) gave the home side an easy innings win. The Australians kept up the pressure in the Third Test at Sydney early in 1969 and won by 10 wickets. Sobers made 49 and 36. The two teams fought out a close and exciting draw in the Fourth Test at Adelaide. Sobers had a fine double with the bat—110 and 52—but failed with the ball, taking 1 for 106 and 1 for 107. The draw gave Australia the series and restored it to its position as the number one team in the world. It was a worrying second successive loss for Sobers, who was skippering an aging side, which may have been one of the reasons they dropped 34 catches in the series. However his own all-round figures for the series were still respectable. He made 497 at 49.70 with 2 centuries and 2 fifties. His bowling load was heavy through the series and he kept attacking fields, often to the detriment of his analysis: 18 wickets at 40.72.

He went on an anti-climactic trip to New Zealand in early 1969—drawn one-all—and then a losing three-Test series in England. By now Sobers was jaded from the continual grind of cricket and the strain of leading a mediocre team. The bright spot in this otherwise unremarkable year was his marriage to Pru Kirby on 11 September.

Captain of the World

This loving union no doubt inspired him to greater perform-ances with a team much more to his liking when he captained a Rest of the World side against England after a South African tour was called off in 1970.

Sobers lifted, as a true champion will in illustrious company. In the First Test at Lord's in June he captained his team of international stars with skill and led from the front. He first destroyed England's batting with his best bowling in Test cricket, taking 6 for 21 with seam and swing in cloudy, humid conditions that suited him. He followed with a splendid, care-free 183. It was the third time he had made a century and taken 5 wickets in a Test innings. No other player had done it more than once. The change in the standard of players and the uniqueness of captaining a world-class side, which, on paper at least, was superior to any Test side, drew the best out of Sobers. It demonstrated that at 34 years of age, he had lost nothing in skill since his peak 7 years earlier.

The world side thrashed England in the First Test, but was shocked to lose the second at Nottingham. Perhaps complacency had set in. The obvious superiority of the world team was restored with a 5-wicket win in the Third Test at Edgbaston, when Sobers scored a blistering 80—the first 50 coming in an hour—in the first innings. He continued to be successful with the ball, taking 3 for 38 and 4 for 89 after a marathon 51.5 overs. He raced through 7,000 Test runs and took his 100th catch in this game.

In the Fourth Test at Leeds, he held his side together with a fine 114 in 270 minutes. This was slow for him, but the conditions and state of the game demanded caution rather than a cavalier approach. Sobers showed that he could be defensive when it was required to turn a game around. And it was a good thing too. England's players lifted to force a close game once more. The home team lost by only 2 wickets, giving Sobers' team a series win.

This would have been an excuse for any player at this level, and in this makeshift yet high-standard series, to take the foot of the accelerator for the final game. But Sobers would not accept any slackness in his talented foreign legion. In another tight match the West Indian superstar was forced to give his best to ensure victory. He took 1 for 18, and 3 for 81 off 42 overs, while exhibiting yet again his several gears as a batsman. In the first innings he slashed a powerful 79. In the second, he defended stoutly with 40 not out as his side struggled to win by just 4 wickets. The 4:1 series scoreline did not reflect the admirable fight put up by Ray Illingworth's strong England side.

Sobers walked away from the series with his reputation as a dynamic skipper restored after a few shaky series with the under-manned Windies. His figures were sensational. He topped the batting aggregates (588) and averages (73.50) for both sides, and took the most wickets of either team: 21 at 21.52.

Twilight, Star Still Bright

In keeping with his apolitical attitude to life, Sobers was surprised by the reaction in the Caribbean to his playing in a two-day, double-wicket competition in Rhodesia at the invitation of Ian Smith's white regime. He was criticised in the West Indies media and efforts began to displace him as captain. Politicians made much of his innocent visit to Rhodesia and he was forced to make a humble apology to the West Indies Cricket Board.

Yet, as ever, Sobers was able to rise above the turmoil and maintain the excellent form shown for the World XI in the Caribbean series against England in early 1971. He hit 597 at 74.62 with 3 centuries, 1 fifty and a highest score of 178 not out. He was also efficient with the ball, taking 11 wickets at 33.41. Unfortunately it was to no avail as the Windies went down by one game in the five-Test series.

In 1971-72 Sobers again profited from South Africa being stopped from touring, this time to Australia. Bradman hastily put together a Rest of the World team, led by Sobers, to play Australia.

In the first game at Brisbane in November 1971, Sobers and the Australian captain, Ian Chappell, tried to keep the rain-shortened game alive with sporting declarations but the contest ended in a tame draw with Australia on top. The second game in Perth saw Sobers struggling with both form and fitness as Dennis Lillee gunned down the much-vaunted World team, taking 8 for 59 and 4 for 63. Sobers fell to him for a duck in the first innings, in which the World could only manage 59. He made 33 in the second innings. In Australia's only knock, Sobers was serviceable, taking 2 for 69, claiming openers Bruce Francis and Keith Stackpole. Australia won easily by an innings and 11 runs, and Chappell and his young band of Aussie warriors felt they were a formidable unit as they

prepared for the coming Ashes series. They began the New Year
Test in Melbourne as they had left off in Perth, Lillee leading
the way with 5 for 48 as the World collapsed for 184. Sobers
fell to Lillee for another duck. Australia replied with 285 and
a handy lead of 101. They were held up by Sobers at the end
of the innings when he took 3 for 16 off 14.6 overs. Then at
the most critical moment of the series, he crashed that magnificent 254 that so transfixed a relieved Don Bradman. Had
Sobers not responded, the World team would have been
demolished a second time and most likely would not have
recovered in the series. The World team, and Sobers, struggled
in the Fourth Test at Sydney and just fell in for a draw after
Greg Chappell's graceful 197. This left the series at one-all
with the Fifth Test at Adelaide to play. Sobers failed with both
bat and ball, but the World team rallied to win well by 9
wickets, thanks mainly to Tony Greig with the ball (6 for 30 in
Australia's first innings) and Graeme Pollock with the bat (136
in the World's first innings).

Sobers' reputation as the world's greatest all-rounder
remained intact despite his reduced batting average of 48.71
with a 341 aggregate, and his mediocre bowling analysis of 9
wickets at 48.38. That great 254 maintained his image as a
champion and leader, but he was feeling the strain on body
and mind by the time New Zealand toured the Caribbean in
February 1972. Sobers, nearly 36 years old and slowing up,
managed to lift for one big innings of 142 in a 253 aggregate
and an average of 36.14. He fared reasonably with the ball,
taking 10 wickets at 33.20.

Sobers was by now the father of a baby son, Matthew, and
was going through a major transition in his life. After 39 Tests
as skipper, he lost the captaincy to Rohan Kanhai in 1972.
This—and his body—told him the end was coming. His knee
was never going to be 100 per cent right and a floating bone
in his shoulder had stopped him bowling his classy left-hand

spinners, and in particular the wrong'un (Chinaman), his best weapon in this form of bowling. Yet he still had his speed.

In the end it was a simple matter of a run-up that stopped his career, perhaps a year or two earlier than was necessary. The rules of early one-day competition in England dictated that he had to bowl his faster deliveries off a shorter run. This meant he had to change his rhythm. It put his knee under pressure and it buckled. Sobers missed a five-Test series against Australia early in 1973, which Australia won 3:0. The knee prevented his playing in the first three games—the first time he'd missed selection for a West Indian Test since he began in 1954. He felt right for the Fourth but the West Indies Board of Control did not select him. Sobers didn't play in the last two games and made his way to England to play county cricket for Nottingham in the midst of Australia's tour. The series was close. Sobers may well have meant victory for the Windies.

He didn't intend to play Tests again, but when the Windies toured England a few weeks later the board asked him to play after injuries to two opening batsmen. Sobers played in all three Tests under captain Rohan Kanhai and hit 306 at 76.20 with a highest score of 150 not out. Sobers was still the nemesis of the Old Country with the ball, too. He took 6 wickets at 28.16 runs each. Less than a year later, in early 1974, he played in another four Tests against England. He missed one through injury and fatigue, a sure sign that age was catching up on this mighty athlete, who was nearly 38 years old. He played his last Test in Trinidad. Batting down the list behind a talented line-up, he had just 5 innings in the series for a 100 aggregate with an average of just 20.00. Yet his bowling held up as ever, and he took 14 wickets at 30.07.

In 93 Tests he had 160 innings, in which he collected 8,032 runs at 57.78 with 26 centuries and 30 fifties. If you throw in his Rest of the World matches, his average rises to 58.63. He took 110 catches and captured 235 wickets at 34.03. In first-class cricket he scored 28,315 runs at an average of 54.87, including 86 centuries, and took 1,043 wickets. These figures, notched up over 20 years in the game at the highest level, represent the finest all-round performance in the history of the game.

Sobers now had more time for his family, which became even more important for him with the birth of his second son, Daniel, in 1974. Garry Sobers, the talented poor kid from Barbados, became Sir Garfield when Queen Elizabeth II dropped a sword on both shoulders and dubbed him a Knight of her realm in Barbados in February 1975. At the time there were only four other cricketing Knights: Sir Donald Bradman, Sir Len Hutton, the late Sir Frank Worrell and the late Sir Learie Constantine. His Knighthood was richly deserved and greatly appreciated, yet Sobers wondered how he could make a living. He was briefly connected as a consultant to the team around Kerry Packer during the World Series Cricket period. Since the early 1980s, his most regular employment has been with the Barbados Tourist Board as a consultant.

In a distinctive, articulate style, Sobers has produced several books on cricket, including *Cricket Advance* and *Garry Sobers, Cricket Crusader*, a history of cricket in the West Indies, and a novel, *Bonaventure and the Flashing Blade*. He wrote most of these during his halcyon days as a cricketer—writing was never to appeal as a permanent or stable profession later in life.

However, his home government of Barbados did not forget a favourite son. In 1994 it organised a fundraiser for him and raised about A$220,000 which was placed in a trust. In 1997, he was fortunate enough to win the Barbados state lottery, which brought him about A$500,000. Friends of Sobers joked that this was not really fair as it was only about half of what he had invested in horse racing.

Early in March 1999, the Barbados government declared Sobers, then 62, a national hero—he is the only sportsman out of 10 people to be given that title. He was officially recognised as a 'role model to thousands of youngsters from lower-income Barbadian families'.

He was also Don Bradman's first choice for his Dream Team.

CHAPTER 8

KEEPER
OF PREY

DONALD
TALLON

(Australia)

17 February 1916—7 September 1984

> *'Don Tallon was best described as like lightning with his stumpings.'*
>
> SIR DONALD BRADMAN

On the first morning of the Second Test at Sydney in the 1946-47 Ashes series, two of England's star batsmen, Len Hutton and Bill Edrich, had seen off Australia's speedsters and were set for a big partnership at lunch. During the break, keeper Don Tallon told his captain Don Bradman that he was itching to catch Hutton down the leg-side.

'He wants to play them,' Tallon told him. 'He just needs to nick one and I'll have him.'

'I'll bring Ian (Johnson, the off-spinner) on,' Bradman said.

Johnson opened the bowling after lunch. Don Tallon spoke briefly to Johnson mid-pitch.

'He (Hutton) likes to leg-glance,' Tallon said. 'Give him a couple (to glance).'

Johnson obliged, dropping a delivery just short of a length. Hutton moved back and glanced the ball in copybook manner. The batsman sensed it was 4 off the bat. He turned, expecting to see the ball skimming along the ground to the fence. Instead, Tallon flashed to leg and snaffled the ball in both gloves. The keeper held the ball aloft, roared an appeal and did a little jig towards square leg. Hutton, on 39, threw his head back in amazement and turned for the pavilion before the umpire's finger went up. It was a vital dismissal.

Keith Miller had removed Hutton, England's finest batsman along with Compton, twice in the First Test for 7 and 0. The Australians, particularly the old hands still playing— Bradman, Lindsay Hassett and Sid Barnes—had vivid memories of the last time they'd seen Hutton in a Test. It was the Fifth Test of the 1938 Ashes series at The Oval in England. Then, the opener scored 364 and broke Bradman's world record highest score of 334. It was the Australian skipper's intent to suffocate Hutton at the beginning of each innings and never let him dominate as he did in 1938. Part of his strategy was to mount the most menacing opening attack— Lindwall and Miller—Australia had fielded since Ted McDonald and Jack Gregory in the 1920s. An intricate part of Bradman's plan was a brilliant keeper who created opportunities for dismissals. Don Tallon was the man. The catch that sent back the England opener alone justified his selection.

England was now 2 for 88 as Denis Compton joined Edrich. Compton began confidently and was quickly on 5. Bradman brought Colin McCool on. The leg-spinner formed an outstanding partnership with Tallon. They worked instinctively together. McCool pitched one outside off stump. Compton slashed at the ball, misjudging the spin a fraction. The ball flew past Tallon, who was positioned a metre wide of the stumps, and crashed into Ian Johnson's chest at slip. The ball headed for the ground. Tallon spun around, dived backwards and just got his right glove under the ball. He rolled over and held his left hand up in appeal, as did an amazed Johnson. Compton waited for the umpire's decision, which confirmed the batsman's fears. The Australian keeper had just performed an acrobatic feat that would put any trapeze artist in the shade, taking one of the most brilliant catches in Test history. The effort was captured forever on film.

Only one of the game's greatest—if not the number one keeper ever—could have taken these two catches.

England was 3 for 97. Tallon put a further stamp on the

game by catching Hammond (1) smartly again off McCool to make England 4 for 99. It turned out to be a vital period in the game. Australia went on to win easily, with Tallon making 6 dismissals in 2 innings, and both Bradman and Barnes scoring 234.

This performance was the Test high point for Don Tallon, then 30 years old. It was only his second Test and he'd had a harder, longer road to the top than most.

The Boy From Bundaberg

Tallon was bred in the coastal Queensland sugar and rum town of Bundaberg, 400 km north of Brisbane and the birthplace of pioneer aviator Bert Hinkler. He learned the game playing on a backyard wicket with his three brothers and his father Les, a moulder at the Bundaberg foundry, and a good local slow bowler. At just seven years of age, young Don decided to be a wicket-keeper, and made his school team. He learnt to handle leg-spin delivered by his brother Bill, who later also played for Queensland.

'You are never out of the game (as a keeper),' the dry, laconic Tallon said during his Test career, 'and that suits me fine.'

His coach at North Bundaberg state school, teacher and former state keeper Tom O'Shea, saw Tallon's potential and made him captain of the school team at 11. At 13, he was chosen as captain of the Queensland schoolboys' team. A year later, the skinny little kid was playing A grade matches with men in Bundaberg's Hinkler Park. At 16, he progressed to the Queensland Country team that played at Toowoomba against Douglas Jardine's side during the 1932-33 bodyline tour.

In England's only innings, the lean youth, who had shot up to 180 cm (5 ft 10½ in), stumped opener Herbert Sutcliffe for 19 and let go just 5 byes in a total of 376. However, the rampaging Larwood, experimenting with bodyline, thwarted a possible showcase batting performance by delivering several throat balls before bowling the talented teenager for 2.

Tallon's finishing skills behind the stumps, whether taking spin or speed, impressed selectors. Yet he really caught everyone's attention in early 1933 when he kept during Country Week Carnivals, to Aboriginal player Eddie Gilbert, the speedster Bradman judged the fastest bowler he ever faced. Gilbert, a record-holding boomerang-thrower, had a short run-up and a suspect action. Chucker or not, he could deliver a cricket ball at around about 160 km per hour (100 miles per hour)—faster than Thomson, Larwood, Lillee, Wes Hall, Lindwall and Marshall. Tallon stood back further to him than anyone else in his career.

'Eddie let some rip that went clear over my head and one bounce to the fence,' he recalled.

At one point in a match, Tallon called to Gilbert:

'Slow up a fraction, Eddie, I can't see them.'

Yet he collected enough to ensure state selection later in the year, at the beginning of the 1933-34 season. He had his debut against Victoria. He let go just 6 byes in a score of 542. Tallon was only 17, and destined for very big things. But no-one could have guessed how long it would take him to fulfil that destiny. He was not chosen for the southern tour in his first year, but resumed his spot towards the end of the season and showed his prowess with the bat in his fourth game, against South Australia at Brisbane. He made 58 and 86 in two memorable knocks that included tussles against the world's finest leg-spinner, Clarrie Grimmett, who was then at his peak. A year later, at Christmas in 1934 he was again Queensland's keeper, taking over from Roy Levy behind the stumps. Tallon moved to Brisbane and took a job as a storeman for a car company, a position that kept him fit. In his late teens he began to take on the look and personality that seemed to represent, at least in England, the typical Aussie: tallish, tanned, lean and vociferous when he appealed. He was still forced to wait before he could push his way ahead of Eric Bensted, Levy's understudy.

Bradman at the Break

Tallon's biggest break came late in 1935 when Queensland played South Australia in Adelaide. It was one of Bradman's comeback matches after his 12-month lay-off since an operation in England for serious peritonitis. The Don, then a 27-year-old, made a brilliant return to his best, hitting his third successive double century against Queensland. Tallon kept throughout and marvelled at Bradman's precision, placement and skill. He hit 233 in just 191 minutes.

'You kept really well, nipper,' one of Tallon's brothers told him.

'Did I?' Tallon replied. 'I don't remember him letting anything through.'

Bradman hit almost every ball he faced that day, yet Tallon took two fine catches. One he would treasure forever was a nick from Bradman himself off Levy.

The young keeper's performance impressed Bradman.

'He let go 7 byes in our score of 642,' the Don recalled. 'It was a tireless, outstanding effort. I recall his great skill in taking balls down the leg-side to both pace and spin.'

What doubled the positive impression was Tallon's own talent with the bat in Queensland's second innings. He hit 88, including 10 fours.

'He had a clean-hitting, crisp style,' Bradman said. 'Don was attacking, positive and with a technique to rival most first-class batsmen at the time.'

This analysis would one day augur well for the Queenslander, but Tallon wondered when. He was from a 'minor' state in terms of Test selection, and apprehensive about making the big break into the highest level of the game. After all, he was still in his teens and there were some big names in front of him. Bill Oldfield had no immediate plans to retire and was entrenched as the country's number one keeper. Victorian Ben Barnett, who could bat a bit, had been the number two keeper on the tour of England in 1934. South Australia's Charles 'Chilla' Walker was another highly regarded player.

All Tallon could do was keep improving his technique behind the stumps and posting big scores. In many senses, he was an all-rounder more suited to the 1990s than the 1930s. He was a frequent and dramatic appealer. Many batsmen complained about the pressure he put on them. He played it hard but fair, in keeping with his country background and demeanour.

A few months after impressing Bradman with his mistake-free keeping and batting strike-power, he blazed a sensational 193 against Victoria. It was February 1936. He was still a week away from his 20th birthday and already established as easily the best batsman among the nation's top keepers. In 1935-36 he was Queensland's top batsman, scoring 503 for the season at an average of 55.88.

England toured for the 1936-37 Ashes series and once more Oldfield stood the wickets. Tallon toiled on for Queensland, dismissing three for the state against the MCC and taking 22 wickets for the season. He made the Test trial in 1936-37 in D G Bradman's team, but Oldfield—in V Y Richardson's side—kept wickets well enough to hold his Test place. Another season (1937-38) went by, and most astute observers bracketed Tallon at least with the other keepers, but none could match him with the bat.

Sorry Non-selection

When the selectors sat down to decide the team for the 1938 Ashes tour of England, Bradman opted for Tallon and his South Australian team-mate Walker, believing that Oldfield was past his best. The other two selectors—E A Dwyer from New South Wales and Bill Johnson from Victoria—outvoted him and opted for Barnett because of his experience in 1934, and Walker. The shock of Tallon's omission was overshadowed by the omission of leg-spinner Clarrie Grimmett. No official reason was given for the Queenslander not making the tour list. The unofficial version was that he was not used to keeping to the three spinners: Bill O'Reilly, Fleetwood-Smith and Frank Ward. Another reason was that Tallon preferred to stand back to medium-pacers. The truth was that it depended on the bowler. If it were Queensland's Geoff Cook, he stood back because Cook had a pronounced outswinger when delivering the new ball. There was no logic in missing catches from nicks to this kind of delivery while close up. When the ball was old, Tallon stood up to the wicket. He managed many stumpings off Cook, with his swift, clean style that saw him lifting the bails rather than crashing down the stumps.

Tallon was devastated not to tour England in 1938. He followed the form of Ben Barnett, who performed well, at times brilliantly, in the first three Tests (a fourth one was washed out). But in the Fifth, he missed stumping Hutton and Maurice Leyland off Fleetwood-Smith when both batsmen were on 40. Hutton went on to make another 324; Leyland, another 137. While Barnett was forgiven because of his previous performances, these incidents would not be forgotten, especially as England went on to 7 for 903 and a win that levelled the series.

Tallon brooded on his own misfortune during the Australian winter of 1938. He felt he had done enough and considered he was superior as both a keeper and batsman to the two chosen. Tallon was more talented, according to most expert observers, and less error-prone. And then there was his batting. He could take the number seven spot in the order, or even number six, and be confident he would do well.

Come September, when he turned up at the nets in Brisbane, he resolved to fight on.

Eviction Notices

A few months into the new season, Tallon was universally recognised as the nation's number one keeper. He reached a level of performance perhaps never attained by a stumpsman before or since. Records fell every time he turned out for Queensland, it seemed. He dismissed 34 batsmen in six first-class matches, the best-ever performance in an Australian season. On four occasions in 10 innings he removed at least six batsmen. At Sydney, Tallon caught 9 and stumped 3 New South Wales batsmen to equal Edward Pooley's first-class world record of 12 in a match for Surrey, which had stood for 70 years.

Tallon evicted seven Victorians in an innings to equal another world record for a first-class match. He caught and stumped fervently, sometimes furiously, and his appealing seemed a few decibels higher than before he missed selection to tour England. This runaway success gave him satisfaction as he out-kept and out-batted every rival in almost every game. Even in club matches, he played with a vengeance, perhaps against the national selectors, certainly to show his rivals, and proba-bly with a deep-felt distaste for all batsmen.

Queensland didn't have a regular spinner, and yet he still crashed through 100 wickets in 32 matches—the fastest return in Australian history. Also in 1938-39, he smashed a century before lunch—the first session was then just 90 minutes—

against New South Wales, becoming the only batsman to that date to achieve this in Brisbane.

Tallon couldn't wait for the Englishmen to turn up again in two seasons' time, 1940-41, when he would be just 24. It was a little later than he expected or deserved, yet his Test selection was coming—or so many told him. Unfortunately, war intervened, and first-class cricket was called off. It was another bitter blow. Tallon went into the Army in 1939, but was discharged with a stomach ulcer in 1942. Later, he had a major operation to remove part of his stomach. His chances of playing for his country ebbed with each year of the war. And he was getting older.

Better Late Than Never

He emerged again at the beginning of the Shield season of 1945-46. He was now approaching 30 years of age and pessimistic about his chances to play for his country. Then he looked around. Oldfield had long retired. Barnett, a captain in the Army, was a prisoner at Changi prison camp in Singapore for nearly four years. He courageously fought his way back to fitness and into the Victorian team, but he was nearly 40 and planned to retire at the end of the 1946-47 season. Charlie Walker joined the RAAF, became an air-gunner and was killed in a duel with German fighters over Soltau, Russia. No-one, especially Tallon, begrudged him his 1938 tour of England.

This left Tallon as the front-runner, but he was haunted by his lack of Test call-ups. He feared that a young buck would come through ahead of him. There were a few pressing for recognition, including New South Wales' Ron Saggers, South Australia's Gil Langley, Western Australia's Glyn Kessey, and Tallon's understudy in Queensland, Wally Grout. With this pressure, Tallon hit the Gabba running against New South Wales in November 1945 and snared 8 wickets—4 in each innings. Six were off McCool who had just transferred from New South Wales, which would prove a propitious move for both keeper and bowler. Three of the McCool dismissals were stumpings, indicating a special relationship had been born.

Tallon was more relieved than delighted to be picked to play his first Test against New Zealand at Wellington in March 1946. He managed a lightning stumping, a catch and a runout in New Zealand's 2 innings of 42 and 54, with Bill O'Reilly and Ernie Toshack running amok. He made just 5 in Australia's only innings of 8 for 199. The win unified the Australians under Bill Brown. Tallon drew praise from O'Reilly, who had rarely bowled with him as keeper. He bracketed him with Oldfield. It was a big endorsement, along with Bradman's reassessment of him. The Don felt selectors—including himself—underestimated him before the 1938-39 season when he emerged as the country's best keeper.

In 1946, Tallon married a Queenslander, Marjorie Beattie, which settled him off the field. His relationship with McCool allowed the keeper to display his versatility with the gloves, and to demonstrate that although it was seven years since his amazing 1938-39 season, he had lost little skill when taking pace or spin. He and McCool combined to dismiss six batsmen—4 stumpings and 2 catches—in their first game together in 1946-47. It was against the England team. Tallon took his tally of dismissals to 170 for Queensland in just 50 matches behind the stumps and gave selectors notice of his claims for further Test selection. His standard was so high in this match that a failed stumping of Edrich off Cook astonished commentators.

On the field, Tallon apologised to Cook, scuffed the earth vigorously with his foot and reproached himself with a few expletives. He was a perfectionist and blamed himself for any slips or failings, and never anyone else. His strong character had an unsettling effect on batsmen, who saw him as a predator in pads, playing to a standard in a galaxy all his own. His loud, demanding appeals also made him an alarming figure at the back of any batsman, especially those with insecurities. It wasn't helped by Tallon's laugh, which sounded like he was gargling with broken glass. Strangers didn't find him easy to approach. Batsmen found him impossible.

Even after his outstanding performance against the tourists, early in the 1946-47 season Tallon had sleepless nights as selection day approached. He was beside himself with nerves when an unscheduled radio news bulletin announced the team for the First Test against England. He was jubilant to hear his name, but the next morning awoke apprehensive.

Tallon did well behind the stumps in that game, taking 2 good catches, while making just 14. He remained worried and was relieved to be picked again for the Second Test at Sydney. His performance in Australia's big innings win—4 catches and 2 stumpings—and a fine knock of 30, lifted his spirits as never before. It was Tallon's finest hour, his joy only dampened by a dislocated finger.

Tallon felt he would now play the five Tests in the series. He didn't dare look further ahead than that. In the Third Test he kept proficiently without the spectacular opportunities of the previous game, and had another useful first innings of 35. In the second innings, he and Ray Lindwall forged a dashing eighth-wicket stand of 154 in 88 minutes. It was one of the best power-hitting partnerships in Test history. Lindwall reached 100. Tallon was caught and bowled by Doug Wright, for the second time in the series, for 92. His innings included some of the best driving both sides of the wicket and cutting for the entire series. Considering the array of stars on both sides, Tallon's innings set a standard he would find difficult to live up to.

He continued to keep with brilliance, especially in the second innings of the Fifth Test when he put paid to any doubts about his standing spinners by stumping Edrich, Ikin and

Bedser off McCool, and taking a catch off Lindwall. He broke all existing keeping records with 20 dismissals, and averaged 29 with the bat.

India toured Australia for the first time in 1947-48 and Tallon, now 31, was entrenched as the nation's senior keeper. He was expert at standing back to the pace of Lindwall and Miller, and quite the specialist in handling the wily spinning skills of Ian Johnson and McCool. Tallon's best was now nearly a decade behind him, yet his performances in Tests lifted in more exalted company, confirming the axiom that the better the bowler, the better the keeper, and vice versa.

The Indian skipper, Amarnarth, who had played international cricket for 15 years, said after the 1947-48 tour that Tallon was the 'greatest keeper' he had seen. It was a big statement considering the Indian had witnessed such fine players as Englishmen George Duckworth and Les Ames. But a long list of Test players supported the Indian. England's Godfrey Evans, himself no slouch behind the stumps, said he was the best and most nimble keeper ever. Arthur Morris had no doubts. Alan Davidson called him the 'Bradman of keepers' because he was so far ahead of his rivals.

Cold, Coiled and Courageous

Tallon was in Bradman's mighty squad to tour England in 1948 with the solid and capable Ron Saggers from New South Wales as his understudy. He was happy on the lazy boat trip to England, enjoying the warm to hot weather. But the Queenslander was warned about things to come. When the boat docked at Tilbury, Tallon experienced the cold that sometimes lingers after a particularly bleak English winter. It stunned him. His first concern was his fingers. He normally wet his inner gloves, but this wasn't going to be possible. Arriving at Worcester for the first game of the tour, the team found it was bitterly cold and wet. Even when the sun peeped through, many of the 15,000 spectators remained rugged up.

'Bit different from home, hey Don?' McCool said to Tallon.

'Yeah,' he responded, 'from Bundaberg to iceberg.'

Some of the bowlers would be wayward in their aim as it took their fingers time to warm up. The keeper was pitied as he dived for a full toss from McCool down leg, then an over later when he dropped to his knees to intercept a wide. Yet McCool made amends with a well-flighted leg-break that drifted past a batsman drawn forward. Tallon flicked off the bails with such alacrity that when you watch film of the action at normal speed you wonder if he actually had the ball. As if to dispel any doubts, he held it aloft and yelled a throaty appeal.

At The Oval a few weeks later on a grey and misty morning, Lindwall built up some real speed. He bounced one hard, which flew over the batsman's shoulder. Tallon lost it and put his glove to his face for protection. The ball crashed into his right middle finger and bruised it.

'I didn't pick it up either,' slipper Ian Johnson said. 'It flew out of the mist.'

'Not bloody missed by me!' Tallon said through clenched teeth, shaking his hand.

It would have been an easier season for Tallon if Bradman had used the spinners more. But he was relying on the fierce pace of Lindwall and Miller to smash through the English batting.

'With a new ball available every 55 overs (in the Tests),' Bradman said, 'Don was forced to stand back more than normal, and probably more than he would have liked. It didn't allow him to display his stumping skills as much.'

Thus not all English supporters witnessed his eye-blink fast and precise stumpings. Yet they did become familiar with his lean, sun-dried look. To the English Tallon was the mythical outback, craggy-faced stockman who could ride a bucking brumby. Spectators couldn't hear his comments on the field, but they could sense them from his body language. There was a rhythm in his preparation for each ball that second-rate mimics and enthusiastic kids began copying across England.

Film of the 1948 tour in the Cinesound archives shows Tallon at his peak. He was relaxed between deliveries but as the bowler reached his mark he would go down like a coiled white spring waiting for whatever would be delivered—wide, wayward, wicked or wonderful.

Each ball could be different, especially with a genius like Lindwall delivering a yorker, a bumper, a slower ball, an inswinger, an outswinger, one short of a length. The stumps-guardsman had to adjust himself to each unknown as he uncoiled. He could move to leg, or the off, high or low. Then his movements were quick and crab-like, with short steps. Perhaps he would dash for the stumps. Then it would be hamstrings at full stretch to reach a quick return from a fieldsman. He stood nearer the stumps than was fashionable then for both pace and spin. He squatted lower than most to wait for the delivery and uncoiled himself further and with greater speed than any keeper before or since.

And it wasn't all reaction with Tallon. Often he had a sixth sense of what was coming, and had no need to consult with the bowler. Tallon would read batsmen just as well, if not better. He would know in advance when a paceman sniffed fear. That would mean a ball aimed around the throat or heart. And Tallon would be ready for a flying ball, nick or high slash. He would slip into position ready for the batsman's false shot, indiscretion or miscue.

Tallon, the indefatigable, was the nerve centre in the field, around which was built Australia's exceptional, rounded attack.

Fame and Fate

In the First Test of 1948 at Trent Bridge, Tallon was instrumental in breaking through England's early second-innings batting with fine catches to dismiss Washbrook (1) and Edrich (13) off Miller and Johnson respectively. During Compton's long, magnificent 184, Tallon kept his cool and humour, waiting for the main chance. At one point when Compton was jogging a second run, Tallon smacked his gloves, crouched over the stumps and cried, 'Get it in!' to a phantom fielder. It caused the tired batsman to scamper. Compton was puffing and smiling at Tallon's cheek.

Later Tallon snaffled his English counterpart, Godfrey Evans (50), off Johnston, when he was holding up Australia's progress. Australia won by 8 wickets and the Invincibles marched on to Lord's for the Second Test.

Australia batted first and managed 350 thanks to Morris (105), and some attacking and stylish batting by Tallon (53). He figured in useful tail-wriggling stands with Lindwall (15), Johnston (29) and Toshack (20 not out). Tallon had saved his best form for the right moment. It was too much for England, mainly thanks to the brilliance of Lindwall (5 wickets in the first innings, 8 for the match) and Toshack (5 wickets in the second innings). During the game, Tallon was often seen diving down the leg-side for spectacular saves and stops. His acrobatics saved about 40 runs and he did not let one bye go through in the first innings of 215.

In the second innings, English opener Cyril Washbrook, on 37, and looking set, received a full toss from Ernie Toshack. Washbrook was surprised. He went to drive, caught an inside edge and the ball flew towards Tallon's boots. He managed to snaffle the catch.

'I don't know how he (Tallon) got his gloves under it,' Bradman marvelled. 'It was a miraculous effort since it virtually ended up a yorker by the time it reached Don's feet. Keepers are not expected to perform miracles.'

Tallon paid the price for skill and determination by diving for one from Lindwall down leg-side that was destined for the fence. He damaged his left little finger and had to be x-rayed during the game. It wasn't broken but badly bruised. The pain didn't stop him stooping low behind the stumps as the throws came in from fielders. He applauded—gloves above his head—accurate throws from Hassett. But such was his mood that when Bradman whipped in a return at his feet, he made a rebuking movement with his hands which said, 'Get the ball over the bails'. The Lord's crowd watched in surprise, but there was no confrontation. Bradman waved a 'sorry' and trotted back to his position at mid-on grinning in mild embarrassment. The skipper knew that he had transgressed and that his keeper was struggling.

Australia and the injured Tallon had a lean time in the Third Test at Old Trafford, which they struggled to draw. Yet Tallon still managed a freakish catch off Lindwall to dismiss opener George Emmett for a duck in England's second innings.

'It was one of the grandest low and wide right-hand catches ever in Test cricket,' Bradman commented.

There could have been a magic moment for Tallon if he'd had the benefit of modern video cameras and appeals to third umpires. Ian Johnson drifted a beautiful arm-ball past Compton, then just 35 in the first innings, and Compton's foot slid out of the crease. Tallon whipped off a bail. Umpire Frank Chester, Bradman's favourite of all time, firmly shook his head and said 'Not out!'

Tallon, and fielders at square leg and point, were in no doubt that this time the brilliant Chester was wrong. The score sheet would show forever that Compton went on to a dashing 145 not out.

After the game, the keeper's little finger was up like a balloon. He injured it again in a game against Middlesex and was ruled out of the Fourth Test at Leeds.

He looked on from over the fence at the famous Leeds Test (won by Australia) with mild anxiety as his understudy Saggers performed up to Tallon's own standards for the tour, taking three catches but scoring just 5 runs. Tallon's experience and record with the gloves and his superior batting meant there was no question about his return for the Fifth Test at The Oval. He maintained his keeping average with three catches and performed well with the bat, notching up a useful 31. His batting, while not up to his top standard of the 1930s, was still consistent. No opposition could count Australia out unless its number nine was back in the pavilion, a situation that demoralised England's fielders when they saw the scoreboard registering Barnes, Morris, Bradman, Hassett, Miller, Harvey, Loxton or Johnson, Lindwall and then Tallon. The opposition knew that by technique, style, temperament and courage, this number nine could bat as high as number six in any Test team, at least in the immediate post-war period.

Tallon kept his standards up with bat and gloves right through the tour. Bradman would not allow anyone to relax during any of the games. He was determined—even obsessed—about not losing any of the 34 fixtures. Keith Miller thought he should have relaxed in the festival games, but not The Don. Tallon and everyone else were expected to do their best to achieve victory in each match, right through to a game against Scotland at Aberdeen. Only when that game was as good as won did the captain smile when Tallon fooled around behind the stumps. Tallon was even allowed to remove gloves and pads and bowl the leg-spinners that secured him plenty of wickets in club games after his retirement from big cricket.

During the 1948 tour, Tallon made 43 dismissals—29 catches and 14 stumpings—compared with Saggers, also with

43, who took 23 catches and made 20 stumpings. The discrepancy in the manner of dismissal reflected that Saggers played more non-Test matches and stood to more spinning, since Bradman was preserving his pacemen for the big matches. In the final analysis, form being roughly equal, Tallon would always pip Saggers for a place because of his batting capacity.

Yet the Queenslander would never rest easy. He was just two years into his Test career and still feeling pressure on his spot in the team. He refused to take much comfort from *Wisden* making him one of the five best cricketers of 1948. It even noted that his hands were like those of a violinist. Bradman remarked that Tallon's hands were unmarked and that all his 'fine, longer fingers were intact' as if he had never played the game.

'I don't know any other keeper at any level who played as long as Don who didn't have gnarled knuckles and bent fingers,' Bradman observed,.

In *Farewell to Cricket*, The Don rated Tallon a better wicket-keeper than any of his predecessors. Though he ranked Bert Oldfield as a more graceful keeper, he still thought Tallon was an attractive performer for a man of his height. Bradman had never seen a faster stumper, whether to spinners or standing up to medium-pacers. He thought him 'abnormally' safe, but noted that there were odd days when his performance slackened. He told me he believed that Tallon's off performances may well have been due to medical problems, particularly his troublesome and agonising ulcers.

Bradman judged him best at keeping to fast bowling but said that once he got used to McCool's round-arm leg-breaks, he demonstrated lightning responses to catches and stumpings. Bradman chose Tallon for his keeping first, while noting that only England's Les Ames, who scored 2,434 runs at 40.56 in 47 Tests, was a sounder bat. Yet he still ranked Tallon as the most brilliant stroke-player of all keepers.

The Fading Star

Tallon played in Bradman's Testimonial in front of 53,000 spectators at the MCG in December 1948. The Don thrashed a stylish 123—his last first-class hundred—and was nearly upstaged by Tallon and Lindwall, who also stroked powerful centuries. Tallon's performance was a timely reminder in front of a big audience that despite his unspectacular run of scores, he was more than just a capable bat. He could mix it with the best when luck and opportunity came his way. This was followed by another century in a one-off unofficial Test against New Zealand the next year. His keeping record now, plus his standing as the best bat among contemporary glovemen worldwide, meant he was first choice to tour South Africa in 1949-50, but he withdrew because of illness caused by stomach ulcers. His place was taken by Saggers, with Langley as his deputy. Saggers took 21 wickets in five Tests, including 7 (4 stumpings and 3 catches) in the Second Test at Cape Town.

Tallon's travels abroad and interstate took a toll on his marriage, and he and Marjorie divorced in 1950. Ever the pessimist, he felt his cricket-playing days were numbered but Saggers made no impact with the bat in South Africa. Selectors were now bracketing Saggers with Tallon, but the Queenslander would still get the nod, for services rendered, and his batting. He was chosen for the First Test at Brisbane against England in December 1950. Tallon knew he was on trial again. He took just one catch, but kept neatly in a winning team, which the selectors were reluctant to change.

At only 34, he was becoming increasingly deaf, and this earned him the cruel nickname 'Deafy' during the series. In one game, Hassett told his team, which was batting, he would soon signal for them to appeal against the light. A wicket fell, Tallon was in. Hassett left him with the instruction to 'Go for the light.' Tallon misheard and thought he directed him 'Go for a lash.'

He had a bash, got himself out and had some explaining to do to the skipper when back in the pavilion.

Tallon had a poor series with the bat, yet demonstrated that he still could deliver with a fine 77 in a 150-run stand with Hassett in the Third Test at Sydney. This effort came just in time as there were rumblings about him being replaced after the first two Tests. It was a case of: forget about the critics, join the skipper in a match-winning stand. It was enough to retain his spot until the end of the series. Yet the next season, 1951-52, he was replaced by Langley for five Tests against the Windies in Australia. Tallon's lingering stomach illness, age, deafness and a tendency to fumble late in his career kept him out of contention for the 1952-53 two-all series in Australia against South Africa. Tallon's decline corresponded with Australia's fall from number one spot in world cricket.

The selectors gave him one last hurrah on the Ashes tour of England in 1953. He was chosen ahead of Langley for the First Test at Old Trafford and took two good catches. Yet that fumbling problem was his undoing. He made a duck and 15, not enough to save him this time. Skipper Hassett and his deputy Arthur Morris made the hard decision and dropped him. Langley took over and did better. Tallon continued to perform ordinarily in the county games, despite making every effort to lift. On the boat trip home, he knew that his Test career, at age 37, was over. He was not unhappy. After his misfortune early with non-selection, war and illness, Tallon counted himself lucky to have been the country's top keeper for seven years. He could also lay claim to the number one spot from 1937 to 1939, giving him nearly a decade as the best. The end of his cricket career saw the beginning of his second marriage in 1954 to a Bundaberg woman, Lynda Kirchner. They had two daughters, Catherine and Jane. Tallon's main work after cricket was in a corner store in Bundaberg that he ran with his brother Mat.

Tallon played 21 Tests. He kept in 41 innings and made 58 dismissals, taking 50 catches and 8 stumpings. His rate was about 1.5 wickets an innings, which is not exceptional. Rod Marsh, Ian Healy and Langley are nearer two. Despite his ability with the bat, Tallon's Test figures were also not outstanding. He batted 26 times (with 3 not outs), and scored 394 at 17.13 with 3 fifties. Plenty of keepers, including Gilchrist, Knott, Dujon, Healy and Marsh had superior averages over more Tests.

Yet Tallon's record is one where figures do not tell the complete story. He snared big Test wickets at key moments with freakish efforts. He hit 9 first-class centuries and each one was delivered with class and style.

'Don's brilliance inspired and often flattered the figures of bowlers,' Bradman observed. 'His batting could be outstanding. He drove strongly, and liked to score quickly. His fleet-footed style was also attractive to watch.'

His rivals with the bat were Ames, Alan Knott, Healy and Marsh. Bradman placed Tallon ahead of the lot in terms of his keeping skills, and at his peak with the blade before World War II, as the most skilled bat of all keepers he had seen. On this basis, Don Tallon was in the number six spot in Bradman's best-ever world team. More accurately, he was the first batsman in a long tail.

CHAPTER 9

ATOMIC RAY

RAYMOND RUSSELL
LINDWALL

(Australia)

3 October 1921—23 June 1996

*'He was technically the best
fast bowler I ever saw.'*

RICHIE BENAUD

Harold Larwood turned at the top of his mark. The big Sydney crowd on day two of the First Test of the 1932-33 Ashes series hushed. He pushed off without a rush, building pace with each smooth stride as he approached the wicket. Then he made that characteristic side-on turn of the body without changing his perfect rhythm or interrupting his momentum. He made his sleek slide of the inside of his right boot, followed by the transference of weight to his left leg. Finally he looked over his left shoulder at the target—either the stumps or some point on the batsman's head or chest—a split second before the revolution of his right hand, beginning somewhere round his left buttock and ending near his left knee.

This 173 cm (5 ft 9 in) dynamo from the coal-mining area of Nottingham propelled the ball at such a pace that Australia's batsmen were in disarray. The only one able to handle him that day was Stan McCabe, who dashed from 120 not out overnight to 187 not out. He played the finest innings in that infamous bodyline series, where the aim of Larwood and his partners, Voce and Bowes, was to intimidate batsmen with well-directed bumpers and a stacked leg-side field, close-in.

On Sydney's Hill, a fair-haired 11-year-old looked on in awe and saw his destiny. His name was Raymond Russell

Lindwall. He wanted to emulate this lethal machine that threatened the limbs—even the lives—of batsmen. And after young Lindwall had done damage with the ball his desire was to bat like Bradman and McCabe, smashing the ball all around the park.

That evening young Ray returned with his older brother Jack to suburban Hurstville and played cricket on the road using a garbage tin. Ray insisted on bowling, attempting for the first time to copy Larwood's action, which he would later perfect. Ray was athletic and Larwood's performance was still fresh in his mind. Two days later at school at nearby St Mary's he repeated the mimicry and was thrilled that every now and again he was able to sling the ball with pleasing speed, causing his little mates some trepidation. He enjoyed seeing the whites of their eyes. It was a crude beginning that took on some refinement a year later when this grandson of Swedish and Irish immigrants began secondary school at Kogarah Marist Brothers. The headmaster, Brother Aidan, could play the game well and was an enthusiastic coach. He and his fellow teachers were always on the lookout for potential champions who could bring the school prestige in sport. They put time into instruction, and it paid off with boys like Ray. He was bright enough to achieve academically if he applied himself. Yet his heart was not in scholarship but in fields of play. Brother Aidan taught him every shot in the Bradman coaching manual, without curtailing his natural aggression.

'Hit it hard at every opportunity,' was the order.

Like most boys, Ray wanted to impress with speed. Brother Aidan encouraged this, but taught him the importance of accuracy and variation. At 13, Ray was leading the under-15 team at Kogarah and opening the batting and bowling. At 14, he played in two different Saturday competitions—in the morning with schoolboys and in the afternoon with adults in the local B-grade competition with Carlton Waratahs. Once he

Windies Wallop. Garry Sobers never missed a chance to exert dominance over a bowler by lofting him out of the ground. He holds the record for 6 sixes in a first-class over.

Losing with Grace. Garry Sobers fills the glass of Australian captain Bill Lawry with champagne after losing the Second Test at the MCG in the 1968-69 series, Australia versus the West Indies. Lawry scored 205. Sobers still had a good match, scoring 67 and taking 4 for 97 in Australia's only innings.

Two 20th Century Masters of the Game. (The future) Sir Garfield Sobers and Sir Donald Bradman enjoy a chat. Bradman was instrumental in getting Sobers to play for South Australia in the 1960s. He regarded Sobers as the greatest cricketer of all time.

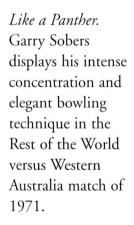

Like a Panther. Garry Sobers displays his intense concentration and elegant bowling technique in the Rest of the World versus Western Australia match of 1971.

Like Lightning. Don Tallon has removed a bail neatly. The batsman can't believe the speed of the keeper's action, but he's out, like scores of Tallon victims before him.

Up and Right. Don Tallon displays his batting style in 1946-47. In the Second Ashes Test at Sydney that season he and Ray Lindwall forged a dashing eighth-wicket stand of 154 in just 88 minutes. Tallon made his highest Test score, 92, while Lindwall made 100.

Rhythm and Power. Lindwall copied his delivery from England's Harold Larwood. Most good judges said Lindwall had the best fast bowler's delivery of all.

Concentration Plus. Don Tallon was all concentration and determination behind the stumps.

Partners, Real and Mythical. Lindwall (left) with his great opening fast-bowler partner, Keith Miller, and Dennis Lillee on the right, in 1987 at the Australian Sport Hall of Fame.

Applause for a Champion. Ray Lindwall walks from the MCG with the then world Test record of 218 wickets. He is applauded by his team-mates and England batsmen Colin Cowdrey and Peter Richardson. Lindwall went on to take 228 wickets at 23.03 runs a wicket.

Coming at You. Dennis Lillee was a
fearsome sight for batsmen, especially
before he broke his back in 1973.

The Speed Demons' Union. Dennis Lillee chats to England's Harold Larwood— the main purveyor of Bodyline in the infamous 1932-33 Ashes—during the Centenary Test in Melbourne of 1977.

Above: An Appealing Sight for Australian Fans. Dennis Lillee is airborne in his appeal to umpire Tony Crafter.

Left: Australia's Three Musketeers. Rod Marsh (355 victims as a keeper), Greg Chappell (the first Australian to score 7,000 runs in Tests) and Dennis Lillee during their last Test for Australia—versus Pakistan at Sydney in January 1984. They all retired after this game.

scored 219 and 110 not out in two different games—329 in a day.

Lindwall's physique had filled out by the time he was 15 in 1936, his final year at Kogarah. He excelled in his sporting pursuits, which now included athletics and swimming (and later, golf). Ray's mother, Catherine, had died of pneumonia when he was seven. Lindwall's father, Arthur, had a steady job at the Water and Sewerage Board, but he couldn't afford to support the five children beyond school-leaving age. Ray was inclined to stay on, aware that a better education would help him progress in life. He showed he could apply himself intellectually when it was necessary by winning a half-scholarship to Marist Brothers Darlinghurst for 1937 and 1938. He continued his accelerated development in cricket and rugby and neglected his studies enough to fail his Leaving Certificate in his final year of school.

O'Reilly's Rule

He concentrated more on his batting in his high school years and built a reputation as a dashing stroke-player. In early October 1938, in his last few months at school, he and 30 other promising players were invited to practise at the SCG with the state team. Jack Fingleton, just off the boat from England after the 1938 Ashes tour, turned up for a net. The New South Wales coach, George Lowe, asked for volunteers to bowl to him and Lindwall was first to put his hand up. By now he had a bumper and a yorker. He let a short one go at Fingleton, who swayed into it with ease. The next few deliveries swung away from the Test opener. He missed one and nicked another. Lindwall delivered a better bouncer. Fingleton shaped to hit but at the last moment had to duck. Then the young streak bowled a yorker that slid under Fingleton's bat and bowled him. The batsman shook his head and grinned at Lowe. Lindwall gave him another short ball, followed by another yorker that crashed into his stumps again. In the space of 15 minutes, Lindwall bowled him four times and broke through his defences with several other deliveries. According to John Ringwood in his book *Ray Lindwall, Cricket Legend*, Lowe stepped over to Fingleton as he left the nets looking unsettled and asked what he thought of Lindwall. Fingleton told him not to take any notice of what had just happened.

'I'm just off the boat,' Fingleton said, 'I'm not seeing the ball.'

The remark hurt the 16-year-old Lindwall. It taught him to hate all batsmen, no matter how exalted. He wished right then that he could bowl to Fingleton in a club match. He seemed a long way from that, starting the season with St George's Thirds, but by Christmas he was in the Firsts alongside Arthur Morris, and early in 1939 under captain Bill O'Reilly. The lanky Irishman had planned to rest his troublesome knees and shins for the rest of the season but changed his mind and played. He had a big impact on Lindwall and was a kind of father figure. The man judged by Bradman to be the world's best bowler watched his new young charge and then dictated his career course. Before his first club game against Waverley, the young Lindwall regarded himself as a swing, into-the-wind bowler. O'Reilly, who felt fast men were superfluous and good for three or four overs with the new ball, directed him to lengthen his run-up and bowl as fast as he could.

Jack Fingleton was opening the batting for Waverley. Fresh in Lindwall's mind was the put-down in the nets three months earlier. Fingleton also hadn't forgotten his humiliation by a junior. He stayed up the other end and let his partner take most of Lindwall's three overs, which was all O'Reilly allowed before he brought himself on. Lindwall removed the other opener. O'Reilly took 5 wickets and later Lindwall took another 2 wickets, giving him 3 for 71 off 13 overs. He was nervous. It translated on field as looseness. There was no word of encouragement from O'Reilly. Lindwall was not happy with his own form, but could have done with some verbal support.

He wanted to bat more than bowl. The skipper, heedless of any of his teenage charges' ambitions, had decided that St George needed bowlers. It had plenty of quality batsmen. The youth was at number eight in the batting order for the game and didn't get a hit. In the next match, Lindwall's third in the Firsts, he was listed at number nine. It upset him. He saw himself as a number four. He wanted to complain to O'Reilly but knew it would be useless. He would just have to show the skipper, *if* he got a chance. He did, and made 51 in 86 minutes, nearly saving St George. This was followed the next week by 48 not out. It was the only way to make a point.

The young Lindwall never missed practice and once earned the wrath of O'Reilly for belting the ball out of the nets.

'He made me bowl all the next practice session,' Lindwall recalled. 'And I didn't get a hit.'

O'Reilly was against coaching. He relied purely on natural ability. It meant that Lindwall would not be helped or encouraged to develop his batting. He had to grow primarily as a bowler. Arthur Morris, who wanted to bowl his left-arm spinners, had to bat. It was Bill O'Reilly's topsy-turvy world, but by good judgment, dumb luck or circumstance, it worked well for the careers of both. Morris would never have played Test cricket as a bowler. Lindwall may have made it as a batsman, but he was up against a strong array of champions in Australia. However, as a speed bowler he had little competition. The dominance of spin by O'Reilly, Grimmett, Fleetwood-Smith, Ward and others in the 1930s had thinned the ranks of capable pacemen.

By the end of the 1938-39 season, Lindwall was not a

stand-out at anything in the eyes of critics. Charlie Macartney had a look at St George and could only see O'Reilly. The former star batsman lamented the lack of talent and substance in batting and bowling. This was a fraction premature, given that there were several teenagers at the club. But it hardly mattered to Lindwall, who was back at school in 1939 trying for his Leaving Certificate again. He played third-grade rugby league and impressed with his tenacity and goal-kicking.

Ray's father died in July, and the five already close-knit siblings pulled together even more. The elder three, Eileen, Jack and Thelma, supported Ray and Margaret at school.

During the 1939-40 summer Lindwall was buoyed by gaining his Leaving Certificate. This gave him the option of going to university, but he couldn't see how he could combine tertiary study with playing sport, while chipping in his share for the family. Instead he took an office job with Commercial Steel and Forge Company, which made aeroplane parts and bomb fuses.

Batting at number six for St George, he made 282 at 25.6 and finished fourth in the averages. His bowling was steady without being penetrating through 115 overs. He took 15 wickets at 34.93. These figures, and all others at the club that year, were overshadowed by O'Reilly's. He took 86 wickets at 7.4. However, Lindwall was only 18 years old, and O'Reilly, at 34, had 15 years' experience in top cricket. St George won the premiership and Lindwall did well with a solid 49 not out in support of Morris' 85 in a winning score of 271.

Lindwall played first-grade rugby league in the winter of 1940 and began the 1940-41 cricket season with confidence, but misgivings. The war had begun, and the club ranks were becoming depleted as players joined the armed services. Lindwall struggled with the bat in first-grade cricket but made a big leap with his bowling, taking 34 wickets at 16.45 runs per wicket, which was twice as good as in the previous season.

He was selected to play for New South Wales alongside heroes McCabe and O'Reilly against Queensland in Brisbane in October 1941, just after his 20th birthday. Like many a debut, it was ordinary. His nerves showed. He was wayward and took 0 for 81 off 15 overs. He was bowled for 1, batting at number 10.

A few weeks later, on 7 December 1941, the Japanese bombed Pearl Harbor. The war that had been confined to Europe and Asia had now spread to the Pacific. Australia prepared for conflict. The Shield cricket competition was abandoned, but Sydney grade games continued. While Lindwall helped St George win its third successive premiership, taking 27 wickets at 22.2 and scoring 405 runs at 27, Malaya fell to the advancing Japanese and Darwin was bombed. He played first-grade rugby league through 1942 with distinction, his goal-kicking continuing to be a feature.

He tried to enlist in the Air Force but was rejected because the employees of the company he worked for were exempt from military service. Lindwall gave up his job and joined the Army. By May 1943, in the Anti-aircraft and Fortress Signals unit, he was on his way by ship to New Guinea as the Japanese reached the Kokoda Trail, close to Port Moresby.

Lindwall and his unit were bombed while ashore, and he was fortunate not to be killed. He served until 1945 and suffered from bouts of the tropical diseases dengue fever and malaria. He returned to Australia and despite lack of strength—he was just 73 kg (11 st 6 lb) and looked thin for his 178 cm (5 ft 10 in)—he was picked for New South Wales.

Ray of Hope

He began steadily against Queensland and South Australia, then, in a game against Victoria, cricket opponents, fans and officials saw Lindwall's real force for the first time. In 38°C

(100°F) heat and a day after a mild malaria attack, he turned on a burst of four overs in Victoria's second innings, the like of which had not been seen since Larwood in 1932-33. It brought him 3 wickets.

He bowled with accuracy and speed but, on advice from O'Reilly, resorted to a bumper against a player who seemed uncomfortable against a ball rising into the chest. It was not bodyline, which had been outlawed, but its impact was similar. O'Reilly's encouragement caused Lindwall to add the short-lifter to his armoury. Yet he still relied on knocking down the stumps, or snicks from his outswinger to the stacked slips field.

On 31 January 1945 he played in the Shield game against Queensland at the SCG and bowled even faster than in Melbourne. He introduced the short ball again and immediately had Don Tallon in trouble, crashing one into his shoulder before bowling him. The resultant bruising prevented Tallon from keeping when New South Wales batted. Lindwall now turned on his best batting in a remarkable innings of 134 not out in 180 minutes, which featured superb driving and cutting.

In this game, Lindwall, 24 years of age, announced himself as a stunning all-rounder—someone who could open an innings with speed and take a capable attack apart with the bat. He was now recognised as an enormous talent. The mature young man knew he had arrived in big cricket. He played for New South Wales against the famous Australian Services side that had played in England in the 1945 Victory Tests. Lindwall starred with three wickets in each innings and served notice to the world of his menace with brutal, quick lift off the easy-paced Sydney wicket. He was outshone only by Keith Miller's dashing 105 not out. Lindsay Hassett was impressed with Lindwall and thought he was the best fast-bowling prospect he had seen in a decade.

Lindwall took 33 wickets for New South Wales and this was enough to be selected for the one-off Test against New Zealand at Wellington in March 1946. Lindwall bowled economically and well, taking 1 for 13 and 1 for 16 in a match dominated by O'Reilly, who took 8 wickets for the game, which was won easily by Australia.

Eight months later, in November 1946, Lindwall was selected for the First Test of the 1946-47 Ashes series against England. His boyhood friend, Arthur Morris, was also chosen and they flew to Brisbane together. Lindwall met Australian captain Bradman for the first time. He'd watched Bradman play for St George from 1928 to 1934, and then in Tests. The Don had been Lindwall's batting model. He was in awe of his boyhood hero.

'He put me at ease straight away and treated me as an equal,' he recalled, 'but I still thought of him as "the boss".'

'No-one could have treated me better than Bradman,' Lindwall wrote in his autobiography, *Flying Stumps*, 'and after playing under him in nearly 20 Test matches, I still say the same about him. Bradman was always ready with a word of encouragement. He consulted me over all my field placings, suggested alterations but never insisted, and allowed me to bowl my own way.'

Lindwall was thrilled to play under Bradman at the Gabba. The skipper was under pressure too. If he failed it might signal an end to his career, just as Lindwall's was beginning.

'He never showed any tension,' Lindwall said. 'He was always calmly but firmly in control. His presence was inspiring for all the team.'

Lindwall had a long, nervous wait over two days as Australia compiled a huge score. Bradman made 187 after a 276-run partnership with Lindsay Hassett (128). Lindwall came in to bat at 7 for 599, with the opposition flagging and wondering if there would be a declaration. He was apprehensive but free to play his strokes, which allowed him to settle down quickly. Lindwall batted impressively, making 31 as the team finished on 645.

Australia won easily, but Lindwall developed chicken pox during the game and was forced to miss the Second Test at Sydney. He was chosen for the Third Test in Melbourne and it was one he would not forget. For one thing, 343,675 people— a world record for a cricket match to that point—watched the game, and paid a record £44,063. For another, Lindwall snared his first Ashes wicket, Len Hutton, caught by McCool for 2. It couldn't have been a more satisfying trophy. Later he trapped Edrich LBW for 89, giving him 2 for 64 on a batsman's paradise, and in the second innings 1 for 59 (Hammond, bowled for 26). When Australia batted, Lindwall was bowled by Bedser for 9. In his second hit—his fourth innings in Tests—he struck top form with the bat and figured in a partnership of 154 with Don Tallon (92) that lasted just 87 minutes. They both played a wide range of strokes, with cuts and drives featuring. Lindwall was 80 when he lost Tallon. Then Dooland went for 1, leaving Lindwall on 81 not out with just a bunny, Ernie Toshack, to come. Toshack put his head down and defended. Lindwall managed an even 100 before Bedser had him caught. The innings had lasted 113 minutes and 88 balls, then the second-fastest in Australian history behind Jack Gregory—67 balls against South Africa in 1921-22. (Since then, Adam Gilchrist did it in 84 balls versus India in 2001.)

Lindwall had made his mark with both bat and ball in just his second full Test match. He continued to have impact in the next Test, taking 3 wickets in four balls to wipe out the England tail. He took 4 for 52 in the first innings and 2 for 60 in the second, while scoring a useful, tail-wriggling 20 in his only hit.

Australia was ahead 2:0 in the series with one to play when

the teams reassembled in Sydney for the Fifth Test. Lindwall was in good shape, taking 10 for 73 in a state game against South Australia before the Test. He emulated this form on a good Sydney batting wicket by ripping through England to take 7 for 63 off 22 overs with 3 maidens. He generated enough genuine pace to knock the bat from Compton's hand.

This matched Keith Miller's devastating 7 for 60 when he bowled medium-pace and off-breaks on a sticky wicket in the First Test in Brisbane. These two efforts were among the best in history for Australia. (No Australian paceman had taken 8 wickets in an innings till that point.) The home team went on to a 3:0 series win, with Lindwall the leading wicket-taker at 18 at 20.38. He scored 160 runs at 32.00.

En Route to Invincibility

Lindwall repeated his 7-wicket feat against India in the Fourth Test of the 1947-48 season at Adelaide. He had another consistent series with the ball where he was again the top wicket-taker with 18 at 16.88. He also made 70 runs at an average of 14.

His future was threatened by two things, first, an injured leg tendon and second, his foot drag on delivery, which was beginning to concern the press and umpires in the lead-up to the 1948 Ashes tour of England. Bradman stepped in to help on both counts, introducing him to his Melbourne masseur, Ern Saunders, who had the leg right in two weeks, and stating publicly that he thought Lindwall's delivery was fair.

The drag problem was not over though, and Bradman spoke to Lindwall on the boat trip to England about the strategy he should follow through the Ashes tour. Bradman thought he should keep his right, dragging foot even further behind the crease than usual to avoid being no-balled. He advised Lindwall not to bowl at full speed until he had been scrutinised and passed by the Test umpires.

Bradman recalled how on the Ashes tour of England in 1938 Ernie McCormick was no-balled 35 times in the first game at Worcester and it destroyed his confidence for the tour.

'Even if you don't take a wicket beforehand your place in the Test team is assured,' Bradman told Lindwall. 'Concentrate on passing the umpires. Taking wickets must be a secondary consideration for the time being.'

When the team docked at Tilbury a reporter asked Bradman about 'the problem with Lindwall's bowling action'.

'What problem?' Bradman replied. 'There is no problem. Lindwall has been passed by umpires under the rules all his career.'

This put the issue back in the MCC's court. It chose two experienced umpires, Fred Root and Dai Davies, to stand the first game at Worcester so that they could adjudicate on his bowling. The Australian strategy worked. Lindwall was not no-balled then or for the rest of the tour.

Lindwall built to top speed in the game against Nottingham and took 6 wickets—3 with yorkers. In the next contest against Surrey he took 11 for 59—5 of them clean-bowled by yorkers.

In the First Test at Nottingham, Lindwall took 1 for 30 before straining a groin muscle. He couldn't field but he batted without a runner and limped his way to 42 and a century partnership with Hassett who made 137, second-top score to Bradman's 138. This lifted Australia's first innings score to 8 for 575 declared. It was enough to eventually win by 8 wickets despite a fine 184 by Denis Compton.

Bradman gave Lindwall a tough examination on the morning of the first day of the Lord's Test. The captain was worried that his top bowler couldn't recover from a groin problem so quickly. Lindwall was adamant he was fine.

When he saw that he had not convinced Bradman, he said,

'Look, Don, I'm absolutely sure I'll be all right. Leave me out on form if you want to—but not on fitness.'

'Keep your hair on,' Bradman said. 'You've talked me into it. We'll take the gamble.'

Australia batted first, giving Lindwall more time to recover. He scored 15 of 350 (Morris 105). When England batted, Bradman wished him luck and handed him the new ball to deliver to Hutton. The speedster measured his 16 paces, ran up to bowl at three-quarter pace and felt pain in his groin again. Lindwall stole a glance at Bradman. Had the skipper noticed his short step in the follow-through? It didn't seem so, though The Don didn't miss a trick on the field. The damage wasn't too bad, although the pain was severe as Lindwall delivered. In his fourth over he caused Cyril Washbrook to edge one to Tallon. Soon after, he clean-bowled Bill Edrich and Tom Dollery in three balls. England was 4 for 46 and Australia was in command. Lindwall went on to take 5 for 70 and England made 215. Australia's second innings brought 7 for 460 declared. All batsmen got runs, including Lindwall, who was stumped by Evans off Laker for 25.

England was dismissed for 186 in the second innings and beaten by 409 runs. Lindwall took 3 for 61 (giving him 8 for 131 for his debut match at Lord's while carrying a groin injury), and Toshack 5 for 40.

Five years later, while walking back to the pavilion from net practice on the eve of the 1953 Ashes Lord's Test, Lindwall chatted with Bradman, who was in a very good mood. Bradman let Lindwall know he knew that he had injured his groin in the Test of 1948. Lindwall asked him why he hadn't said anything at the time.

'I noticed that you were trying so hard to hide it from me and I reckoned you might bowl better if you thought I didn't know about it. I wasn't far wrong was I?' Bradman replied.

Stinging Ray

Lindwall's short-pitch bowling at Lord's in 1948 caused Hutton problems and was said to be the reason Hutton was dropped from the Third Test at Manchester. The Australian camp rejoiced. All the bowlers thought he was the best bat in England, with Denis Compton not far behind. Compton showed why in the Third Test by scoring a fine 145 not out in England's first innings of 350. Lindwall at one point felled him with a short ball that didn't get up as much as expected. When Lindwall batted in Australia's innings, Bill Edrich bowled him five successive bumpers and hit him once on the hand. Part of the crowd applauded. Lindwall battled on to 23 and helped Australia avoid the follow on as they struggled to 221. He thought that if he bowled short to Edrich in England's second innings, it would be viewed as retaliation. Lindwall dismissed George Emmett for a duck when Tallon took a fine diving catch. Bradman walked over to Lindwall and for the only occasion in Lindwall's career influenced his bowling by asking him not to bowl any short-pitched deliveries at the next man in, Bill Edrich. Bradman said that if Lindwall delivered bouncers, the crowd would react and the English media would make headlines out of it. Bradman, shrewd as ever, knew that the bouncer was a legitimate and highly effective weapon in the Test series, if used judiciously.

Lindwall had another good game, taking 4 for 99 and 1 for 37, and scoring 23. Australia forced a draw, although England was on top for most of the game.

The night before the only fixture preceding the Fourth Test, the match against Middlesex at Lord's, Lindwall went to a London nightclub and drank too much. The next day, Bradman overheard some of the players talking about the convivial evening. Lindwall didn't feel like bowling, but had to. He wasn't going to complain to Bradman after the 'boss' had told everyone at the start of the tour that they could do what they wished in their free time so long as they were fully fit to play when chosen. In other words, party if you will, but don't turn up hungover on the morning of any game. Lindwall struggled in his opening spell on a hot July day and looked forward to it ending after four overs. But Bradman tossed the ball to him for another over, then another. After eight overs, Bradman let him have a break.

'Have a good night last night, Ray?' the skipper asked him, with that little half-grin.

Lindwall was 100 per cent fit when the Fourth Test began on 22 July. England hit 496 thanks to Hutton (81), Washbrook (143), Edrich (111) and Bedser (79). Lindwall took 2 for 79 and Sam Loxton took 3 for 53.

In Australia's innings, Miller (58), Harvey (112), Loxton (93) and Lindwall (77) brought Australia's tally to 458, just 38 short. Lindwall and Loxton joined in some big hitting. England replied with 8 for 365, leaving Australia to make 404 to win. They lost three wickets securing the magnificent win, Morris scoring 182 and Bradman 173 not out.

The Australians celebrated the next day with a private £100 dinner paid for by Bradman and team manager Keith Johnson.

There was still one Test to play at The Oval. England captain Norman Yardley won the toss and batted on a pitch affected by rain. Lindwall dismissed Compton brilliantly caught by Morris for 4 before lunch. After the break he took 5 wickets for 8 and ended with 6 for 20 from 16.1 overs. He clean-bowled four victims with yorkers. The last victim was Hutton (30), who had stayed right through the innings, defying the extraordinary bowling. The batsman leg-glanced. Tallon dived full stretch for the catch, which Lindwall branded the best he'd ever seen.

'Ray's spell (after lunch) that day was the most devastating and one of the fastest I ever saw in Test cricket,' Bradman said.

England scored just 52. Australia replied with 389, a tally that featured 196 by Morris and a second-ball duck by Bradman in his last Test innings. England managed just 188 in its second dig, with Lindwall taking 3 for 50 (giving him 9 for 70 for the match), and Bill Johnston 4 for 40. This gave the series to Australia 4:0. Lindwall took 27 wickets at 19.62. He made 191 runs at 31.83. For the entire tour, he took 86 wickets at 15.68, including one 10-wicket haul. He took 5 wickets in an innings six times. He scored 405 runs at 24.17.

In Bradman's testimonial game at the MCG, beginning 4 December 1948, Lindwall was the star of the first day, smashing 104 in 86 minutes for Hassett's XI. Bradman scored 123 and received about £10,000.

Into the Post-Bradman Era

Lindwall had an ordinary tour of South Africa in 1949-50, taking 12 wickets at 20.66 and scoring just 41 at 13.66. A groin injury, fibrositis and a stomach disorder reduced his effectiveness in four Tests and he was dropped for the Fifth. He fought hard to make it back into the XI for the First Test at the Gabba in the 1950-51 Ashes series against Freddie Brown's visiting MCC team. Lindwall batted solidly, making the second-top score of 41 in support of Harvey (74) in Australia's mediocre 228. Rain made the wicket sticky and Lindwall wasn't needed as Johnston and Miller bowled effective medium-pace, reducing England to 7 for 68, when Brown declared. Australia fared worse, reaching 7 for 32 before declaring also. The Australian lead was 192. It was enough under the conditions, especially after Lindwall yorked opener Reg Simpson first ball. He took 2 for 21. Jack Iverson's spinners mopped up the tail and Australia won by 70 runs.

Lindwall continued to improve his fitness and form by the Second Test in which he dismissed 5 victims, including Brown and Godfrey Evans in successive overs with the second new ball of England's second innings. It was a vital breakthrough as England had just 179 runs to make for victory. They fell 28 short. Lindwall played second fiddle to his good friend and bowling partner Keith Miller in the Third Test. Miller made 135 not out and took 4 for 37. Jack Iverson took 6 for 27 in England's second innings. Lindwall, however, still made an impact in his customary fiery spells, clean-bowling Brown and Bedser and breaking Bailey's thumb. The combination of terrific pace, accuracy, swing and well-directed bouncers always menaced the opposition. Australia won by an innings and 13 runs, giving it an unassailable lead in the Ashes. It was the fifth successive series win by Australia since the war. Lindwall had been a major part of his team's winning way, and Australia rightly claimed to be the best cricket combination in the world.

In the Fourth Test at Adelaide in the 1950-51 series Lindwall took 3 for 51 in England's first innings and made a watchful 31 with the bat in Australia's second innings as they headed for a win by 274. In the Fifth Test in Melbourne in February 1951, Lindwall (3 for 77) and Miller (4 for 76) crashed through England's middle order in their best combined display of the series, but it wasn't enough, the tourists winning by 8 wickets.

Lindwall took 15 wickets at 22.93 and made 124 runs at 15.50.

Off the field, his future was taking shape. He married a Queensland woman, Peggy Robinson, in May 1951 and switched from a job working in Stan McCabe's sports store to being a salesman for a wine and spirits company.

The West Indies arrived for the 1951-52 season after beating England 2:1. The squad included the famous batting trio, the three W's: Frank Worrell, Everton Weekes and Clyde Walcott. The side also featured the spin twins, Alf

Valentine and Sonny Ramadhin.

Lindwall, now 30 years old, had taken 9 wickets in a Shield game against Queensland and was in good form with bat and ball for the First Test at the Gabba in November 1951. In his first spell he was too quick for the Windies batsmen who had never faced someone as fast and as accurate. Yet it was Miller who caused a stir by bowling dead-eye straight medium-pace bouncers at a couple of troublesome tail-enders. Lindwall took 4 for 60 in the Windies' first innings. He top-scored with 61 as Australia struggled to a lead of 10 runs. They were set 236 to win, and thanks to a sixth-wicket stand of 54 between Lindwall (29) and Graeme Hole (45 not out), Australia scraped in by 3 wickets.

More bumpers were bowled in the Second Test in Sydney. *Wisden* complained later about the 'relentless bumper tactics'. But the West Indians, although unsettled, didn't complain. John Goddard, the skipper, thought the bouncer legitimate and that his men should counter-attack.

They reached 362, with Lindwall taking 4 for 66. He was run out for 48 in Australia's reply of 517 (Hassett 137 and Miller 129). In the Windies' second dig, Lindwall struck Jeff Stollmeyer in the head with one that he ducked into. It reminded many of the bodyline season two decades earlier, yet there were differences. Lindwall didn't bowl 'leg-theory' but used two men in close on the leg-side and one in the deep, not seven—even eight—as Larwood and Co did. Larwood's field would often have just one fielder forward of square, and with the bowler and keeper always moving to leg for each delivery there were always effectively 10 fielders on the leg-side. Lindwall's short ball was delivered over middle or off stump every time. The bodyline trio of Larwood, Voce and Bowes aimed outside or on leg stump, lifting into the ribcage. Nevertheless, Lindwall's short ball was brutal. It skidded at the batsman's throat. Opposition teams facing Lindwall and Miller became conscious that the Australians were setting a trend.

Australia won the Test by 7 wickets and moved on to Adelaide at Christmas. A sticky wicket offered Lindwall little and he had an ineffective match as the Windies fought back to win by 6 wickets. The teams reassembled for the Fourth Test in Melbourne over the New Year. Lindwall had another unspectacular game, although his 29 in the second innings helped Australia towards the target of 260 for victory. The unlikely heroes for Australia were Doug Ring (32 not out) and Johnston (7 not out), who figured in a thrilling last-wicket stand of 38, giving Australia victory by 1 wicket.

The highlight of the Fifth Test in Sydney was a battle of wits between Lindwall and Weekes. The Windies began the final day on 2 for 112, needing 416 to win, a possibility given their strong batting line-up. Lindwall and Miller began the first session with a bigger dose of bouncers than normal. In Lindwall's sixth over of the morning he bounced Weekes, an accomplished hooker. The batsman hesitated and missed in a late attempt.

Stollmeyer, the team vice captain who was batting at the other end, ordered Weekes not to play the hook shot. Lindwall heard the instruction. It would be difficult to imagine any bowler in Lindwall's league—Larwood, Marshall, Lillee, Ambrose or Trueman, for instance—not doing what Lindwall did next. Weekes shaped to hook again but ducked the short one. Stollmeyer took a few steps towards Weekes and again advised Weekes to ignore the hook. Miller in slips intervened with a provocative remark suggesting Stollmeyer had no right to instruct Weekes how to bat. This confused the batsman even more. Lindwall's third successive bouncer sailed close and Weekes shaped but declined the shot again. In the press area, O'Reilly and ABC radio commentator Alan McGilvray were upset by the tactics. They later said they would have been angered even if they had been privy to the by-play at the wicket. Lindwall delivered his fourth bumper in a row. Weekes shaped up, went halfway through with a shot and was caught behind. Lindwall won the mind battle and the game for Australia, taking 5 for 52 off 21 overs with 4 maidens, but also gained opprobrium for his actions.

Regardless, Australia won 4:1, their sixth successive series win since the war. Lindwall played a big all-round part, securing 21 wickets at 23.04 and making 211 runs at 26.37.

Surprising Springboks

Lindwall joined Nelson in the Lancashire League for the 1952 season for £600 and bonuses, which did not include boat fares for him and Peggy. He performed well, taking 96 wickets at 8.37, and learned to bowl the inswinger on advice from an English umpire who refused him LBW decisions with the outswinger. On Lindwall's return to Australia with Peggy and their four-month-old son, Raymond Robert, the press discussed whether he was as good as he had been before turning 'pro' for a season. He was 31.

Lindwall answered them with the ball a few weeks later, and just for good measure, his bat as well. He made 70 out of 148 on a 'sticky dog' in Adelaide in what Keith Miller said was the best innings he'd ever seen under such conditions. Observers noted his new lethal inswinger, and the continued force of his yorker. After his season in England, it was better than before, if that were possible.

His all-round versatility was evident in the First Test at the Gabba against Jack Cheetham's South Africans who were in Australia for the 1952-53 season. Lindwall made a more than useful 38 not out in Australia's second innings and took 5 for 60 in South Africa's second innings of 277 chasing 337 to win. He made the difference, and Australia won by 96 runs.

Miller returned to the side for the Melbourne Test over

Christmas 1952 but the old combination, which took 12 wickets, was not enough to prevent the tourists from winning by 82 runs, thanks to Russell Endean who made 162 not out, and Hugh Tayfield, who took 6 for 84. It was a shock for the Australians and South Africa's first win in 42 years.

The tourists moved on to Sydney early in January 1953 and faced the wrath of Lindwall and Miller on their home turf, with a big crowd in support. Miller (3 for 48) bowled a few bouncers, which put the opposing batsmen on the defensive, while Lindwall (4 for 40) used that inswinger, and his always effective outswinger. Australia replied to South Africa's 173 with 443 (Harvey 190), then Lindwall (4 for 72) and Miller again caused enough havoc to hold the South Africans to 232, giving Australia victory by an innings and 38 runs.

Lindwall and Miller demonstrated their importance in the next two Tests. At Adelaide in the Fourth Test, they both broke down and were unable to bowl. Australia scored 530 (Colin McDonald 154, Hassett 163) and 3 declared for 233 (Harvey 116), as against South Africa's 387 and 6 for 177. The game was drawn with Australia 199 ahead. At Melbourne in the Fifth Test, they were unfit to play and Australia lost by 6 wickets despite scoring 520 (Harvey 205) in the first innings.

The absence of Lindwall and Miller's powerful opening attack enabled South Africa to draw the series 2:2. It drove home the fact that Australia had to replace these great bowlers eventually. Richie Benaud was coming on as an all-rounder who bowled leg-spin, but he was some years from maturity. Otherwise there wasn't much on the horizon, apart from another raw all-rounder from New South Wales, left-armer Alan Davidson.

Top of the Tree in '53

Lindwall was fit again for the Ashes tour of England in 1953 and he reached his zenith, producing a sustained, sensational season of brilliant, powerful and intelligent fast bowling. By the time the two teams lined up for the First Test at Trent Bridge, he had cut a swathe through England's finest batsmen, from old hands like Hutton and Compton, to new stars such as Peter May and Tom Graveney. Against Yorkshire it was important for the speedster to gain an advantage over Hutton. He bowled him in the first over with an unplayable inswinging yorker. At The Oval against the county champions, Surrey, it was vital that Lindwall attempt to work over the best post-war prospect in England, Peter May. This has been a tradition with all teams since the inception of Tests. If you could gain the upper hand over a potential champion early, then that potential might never be fulfilled, or might at least be delayed. Lindwall's first-ever over to May contained six unplayable deliveries—three inswingers and three outswingers—which left the new boy bewildered and uncertain about his claims to success at the game's highest level. Lindwall said it was his best over ever in any form of cricket, even though he didn't officially take a wicket. Unofficially, the shaken and stirred May was his. Ron Archer bowled him in the next over. The future England champion's time would come but not this summer in England, not against the world's best fast bowler.

Lindwall's stunning form continued into the rain-affected Test that was ready-made for Alec Bedser, who took 7 for 55 in Australia's struggle up to 249. Lindwall's response was blistering pace and swing which led to 5 for 57 and a collapse by England, who could only manage 144. Bedser did more record-breaking damage in the second innings with 7 for 44, and Australia made just 123. England chased but the rain and time beat them as they reached 1 for 120—128 short with 9 wickets in hand. By the last hour the honours went to the home team.

At Lord's in the Second Test, Australia batted first and

notched 346 (Hassett 104, Alan Davidson 76). England was 1 for 177 at stumps on the second day, with Hutton and Graveney—in just his Second Test—in command. Though they never worried much about lengthy preparation Lindwall and Miller discussed tactics that night and decided that the next morning they would attempt to bowl Graveney (78) under his high backlift, which was a feature of his fine stroke-making. Lindwall succeeded and yorked the young star. Hutton went on to 145 and England 372, highlighting the ineffectiveness at that time of Australia's bowlers after Lindwall and Miller.

Australia rallied in the second innings to make 368, with Lindwall (50) backing up Miller (109) and Morris (89). Lindwall's 50 in 48 minutes was the fastest ever recorded from scratch in Ashes Tests. He hit 2 sixes and 5 fours.

England (7 for 282) hung on for a grim draw on a dead Manchester pitch, Australia this time on top. So far, there had been three games for three draws.

Hassett won the toss for the fourth time in the series and sent England into bat on a slow wicket at Headlingley. Lindwall's second ball was a fast, inswinging yorker to Hutton, which took out his middle and leg stump. For the big Yorkshire crowd it could have been a video replay of the earlier game against the county as they watched their champion trudge back to the pavilion with nought against his name. Only Graveney (55) held up Lindwall's onslaught as he took 5 for 54 off 35 overs. Australia replied with 266. England's Bailey delayed Australia's advance with 38 in 260 minutes in the second innings as the home team reached 275. Lindwall took 3 for 104, giving him 8 for 158 for the match from 89 overs. Miller took 6 for 102 for the match, again showing how dependent the tourists were on this duo. Australia was set just 177 to win, and were well on the way when captain Hutton and his key bowlers, in this case Bedser and Bailey, introduced 'leg-theory' balls that swung away down leg-side and were difficult to score off. It slowed Australia just enough (4 for 147) to force a draw. The visitors fell 30 short. Bailey's negative cricket with both bat and ball had saved England, although it diminished the game as a spectacle.

Now four Tests had been played for four draws.

The teams met at The Oval for the decider, perhaps. Australia only managed 275 in its first innings. Lindwall crashed a face-saving, quick 62 to be top scorer. New England paceman Fred Trueman, who worshipped Lindwall and even asked him for tips earlier in the season, impressed with 4 for 86. Lindwall took 4 for 70 in England's first innings. But the Surrey spin-twins Jim Laker and Tony Lock on their home wicket took 9 wickets between them and ran through Australia (162) in the second innings. England had no trouble picking off the 132 to win by 8 wickets, giving them the Ashes 1:0— their first such victory since the bodyline series in Australia 20 years before.

It certainly was not Lindwall's fault. He took 26 wickets at just 18.84. He also scored 159 at 17.66, with two timely, high-class attacking knocks. His entire season amounted to 85 wickets at 16.40 (compared to his 1948 statistics of 86 wickets at 15.69.) At 32 years of age, he had lost nothing in pace, but had gained in guile, range and the effectiveness of his deliveries to maintain his position as the world's best fast bowler.

State of Change

The Lindwalls moved to Brisbane in late 1953 and Ray took a job with the bus company Cobb and Co. He continued playing for New South Wales and had an ordinary season by his high standards, taking 22 wickets at 30.14. More worrying was his batting, which fell away. He scored just 14 runs in 6 innings. Was Lindwall past it? the press asked. He began 1954-

55 playing for Queensland and took over the captaincy a year later. His new life in the sun refreshed him and his wife Peggy was happy to be living in Brisbane.

In the First Test of the Ashes series, he had a good all-round game. His batting was back in tune and he notched 64 not out for Australia's score of 8 for 601 (Morris 153, Harvey 162) after Hutton sent the home side in. Lindwall removed Hutton for 4 and took 3 for 27 as England fell for 190. In its second innings he took 2 for 50 as England reached 257, giving Australia a resounding win by an innings and 154 runs.

Lindwall had a drink with England speedster Frank Tyson after the game. Tyson asked him his thoughts on how to bowl a bumper more effectively. Lindwall said he would show him next time they met. That was in Sydney at the pre-Christmas Second Test. Lindwall (2 for 47) contributed to England's third successive mediocre batting display. He'd bowled Tyson for a duck in the first innings and when he came in at 5 for 222 in the second innings after Australia made 228, Lindwall gave him a trademark lethal bouncer. It hit the deck just short of a good length and skidded towards the batsman's throat. Tyson turned his head and was hit on the back of the skull. He was taken to hospital and x-rayed. When found not to have a fracture he resumed batting and was soon bowled by Lindwall.

'Thanks so much for showing me the bouncer,' Tyson said to him later.

Peter May, coming of age in Ashes contests, made 104 before Lindwall (3 for 69) bowled him with the second new ball. England ended with 296. Australia had just 223 to make. Tyson turned on the speed for which he was highly reputed, and with Statham ripped through Australia (184, Harvey 92 not out) and gave England victory by 38 runs.

In the Third Test at the MCG, which began on New Year's Day 1955, Lindwall removed May for a duck, but looked lacklustre as Miller and Archer dismissed England (191).

Lindwall had hepatitis and a leg muscle strain, both of which contributed to his below-par effort. Australia replied with 231, and in a game hauntingly similar for the Australians to the previous Test, England rattled on 279 in its second innings, with May reaching 91. Lindwall took 0 for 52, while Bill Johnston returned 5 for 85. Tyson then took 7 for 27 in a burst of pace that rivalled all the great speed efforts in Tests past. It reduced Australia to 111, a number that pleased the more superstitious English. The tourists won by 128 runs, giving them a 2:1 lead with two matches to play.

Lindwall pulled a muscle in a state game and missed the Fourth Test at Adelaide, which England won by 5 wickets. He was back for the Fifth at Sydney and again removed Hutton early. It was the wicket that gave the Australian most satisfaction, for he still regarded the captain as England's best batsman. However, Tom Graveney played a magnificent innings of 111 (not so pleasing to the English) and England built its biggest score for the series. Evans became Lindwall's 99th wicket, and in the push towards a declaration, Bailey (72) threw his wicket away to give him his 100th victim in Ashes Tests.

The game was drawn. Lindwall ended the series with 14 wickets at 27.21 and made 106 runs at 26.25. The critics, headed by Bill O'Reilly, called for new blood. O'Reilly even called for new selectors, claiming Australia was at its worst in four decades. His former star pupil was high on his list of those who should be chopped.

Lindwall had no thoughts of bowing out as he packed his bags for a tour of the Caribbean under Ian Johnson. He was determined to have a good time after his recent illness. He and Miller renewed friendships with Weekes, Worrell and Walcott in convivial card games at night and sporting rivalry by day. However, Lindwall's full recovery from hepatitis was dependent on good rest and a strict diet. He was not quite the revelling mate Miller knew from past tours.

A steady diet of wickets would always help his morale. After Australia compiled 9 for 515 (Harvey 133, Miller 147) in the first innings of the First Test at Sabina Park, Jamaica, Lindwall (4 for 61, and 2 for 63) led the way in confining the West Indies to 259 and 275. Australia won by 9 wickets. The team flew on to Queen's Park, Trinidad and this time there was more resistance from the star Windies line-up, with Walcott making 126 (after 108 in the First Test) and Weekes 139 in a tally of 382. Lindwall took 6 for 95 from 24.5 overs and 3 maidens in a sustained, quality performance that culminated in a spell of 4 for 16. His haul included Garry Sobers (47) in his first-ever Test innings.

Australia responded with 9 for 600 declared (Colin McDonald, Morris and Harvey scoring centuries), of which the in-form Lindwall contributed 37 not out. He broke down with an Achilles tendon problem in the West Indies' second innings as the game fizzled to a draw.

In the Third Test at Bourda, Georgetown in what was then British Guyana, Lindwall (1 for 44), Miller and Archer were upstaged by the ever-improving leg-spin of Richie Benaud (4 for 15) as the West Indies was all out for 182. Australia managed 257 and the West Indies was in trouble against Australia's balanced attack, making just 207 (Lindwall 1 for 54). Australia mopped up the 133 needed, losing just 2 wickets and winning the game by 8 wickets.

The tourists benefited from winning the toss and batting first in the Fourth Test at Bridgetown, Barbados. In front of a packed crowd under a boiling sun, the Australians, led by Miller (137) and Archer (98), blazed their way to 6 for 439 before Lindwall arrived at the wicket. He thrashed 50 in 69 minutes and was on 80 not out at stumps. The next morning he went on to 118, his second Test century, hitting 2 sixes and 16 fours. His two attacking hundreds were eight years apart and this one meant more to him than the first. It was exhilarating stuff for the crowd, and for Lindwall. At the age of 33, and performing well with bat and ball, he felt that he could go on for a long time yet. His tough rugby league days had taught him how to carry and hide injuries, and he felt he could overcome all obstacles.

A tough time in the field as the West Indies rattled up 510 didn't change his attitude. One spell with the second new ball by Lindwall and Miller was decidedly quick. There was still petrol in both tanks when they needed it.

The game was drawn. The teams clashed for the final Test at Sabina Park. Round one went to the home side when the West Indies batted and made 357 (Walcott 157). It was Miller's turn to take a bag (6 for 107), but as ever Lindwall (2 for 64) backed him up. Australia then lifted for a big finish as McDonald (127), Harvey (204), Miller (109), Archer (128) and Benaud (121) forced the score up to 8 for 758 declared.

The West Indies reached 319 in its second innings, losing the match by an innings and 82 runs. Australia won the series 3:0. Lindwall and Miller took 40 of the 85 opposition wickets to fall. The team broke out the champagne as news came through that Peggy had given birth to their second child, Carolyn Gail.

Lindwall's figures of 20 wickets at 31.85 were up to his usual level considering the fine opposition (Clyde Walcott scored 827, including five centuries, a Test series record) and that most wickets favoured batsmen. His 187 runs were made at the highest Test average of his career—37.40—thus emphasising his importance as an all-rounder.

No Sign of Decline

Lindwall didn't experience any serious decline in the domestic 1955-56 season as he took 30 first-class wickets at 28.97, and made 383 runs at 32.55. It was enough for him to tour England in 1956 with Ian Johnson's squad, which lost the Ashes series 2:1. He was dogged by wet weather, spinners' wickets and his old groin injury, which caused him to miss nearly two complete Tests. His return of 7 wickets at 34 had many writing him off. But Lindwall didn't think he was in decline or over the hill. To him, these criticisms were from journalists who didn't know or appreciate him.

On the way home, the squad competed in the first-ever Test against Pakistan at Karachi in October 1956. They played on matting, which did nothing for Lindwall and the other fast men. Australia lost by 9 wickets. Next stop a week later was Madras, India, for the start of a three-Test series.

Lindwall toiled in the cauldron of Corporation Stadium on day one and gave way to Benaud, who took 7 for 72 as India was toppled for 161. Lindwall was stricken with a severe stomach complaint and spent most of the next two days in his hotel bed as his team-mates pulled together to reach 319. He went to the ground, pottered around for 8 runs and went back to bed. He returned on the fourth morning feeling terrible, but was determined to play. And play he did, crashing through the Indians. In three sensational spells he took 7 for 43. Lindwall claimed he also had sunstroke.

'I wanted a beer after that effort on a good batting wicket,' he said, 'but didn't have the stomach or head for it.'

With Ian Johnson and Miller ill, Lindwall captained Australia for the only time in a Test, at Mumbai. He injured his knee, and along with Davidson (who had a stomach complaint) and Crawford (who had pulled a muscle), left the Australian attack struggling. But Lindwall led the 'crocks' (injured) well and managed to curtail the Indians to 251. Australia rallied for a big effort with the bat and reached 7 for 523 declared (Rutherford 161, Harvey 140), Lindwall hammering 48 not out. The game petered out to a tame draw.

Johnson returned as skipper for the Third Test at Calcutta. Benaud was brilliant, taking 11 wickets. India collapsed for 136 in both innings, as opposed to Australia's not much more impressive 177 and 9 for 189 declared. The weary tourists got home by 94 runs. Lindwall was well pleased as he made second-top score (28) in the second innings and took 3 for 32 from 25.2 overs with 12 maidens in India's first innings. Thus his Indian series yielded 12 wickets at 16.58 which was more like his figures at his best. He made 92 runs at 30.66, demonstrating his consistency with the willow once more.

In the 1956-57 domestic season Lindwall took 27 wickets at 23.74 and made 243 runs at 27. His great partner Miller retired before he was pushed. Lindwall, on the other hand, had no reason to be other than confident of his continuing Test selection. After all, at his second-last outing for Australia hadn't he been the player most responsible—by a long way— for winning a Test in conditions that were against him?

Unfortunately, neither form nor sentiment was on the Australian selectors' minds when they announced the squad that would tour South Africa in 1957-58. Lindwall's name was not on the list. He heard about his omission on the radio while working in the outback. He was stunned, hurt and bewildered. It didn't seem possible. The pacemen chosen—Ian Meckiff, Davidson and Ron Gaunt—were not in his class.

Lindwall returned to Brisbane and sought an explanation. The only reason for his omission that made sense was that the selectors had adopted a youth policy. Ian Craig, the new skipper, was to be furnished with young men with potential. For the first time, Lindwall felt the weight of his 36 years and the winds of change. It was a tough period. He had moved from job to job, knowing that he was a cricketer first and foremost in life, even if he wasn't a professional. Now he had to start thinking about life after cricket. But not quite yet. While the potential stars were away beating South Africa,

Lindwall was performing as well as ever, taking 26 wickets at 25.77 and making 274 runs at 34.25.

Comeback

Lindwall argued that his performances in the last two series against England in 1954-55 and 1956 had not been an indication of his true form because he was suffering the after-effects of hepatitis. During the winter of 1958, as he approached his 37th birthday, Lindwall set himself a tough fitness program. He ran 5 km a night through the streets near his home. He topped and tailed the run with vigorous stomach and back exercises. If it were raining, Lindwall rode a stationary bicycle in his garage. Neighbours could hear him pedalling and grunting as he did standing jumps, sit-ups, press-ups, and ran on the spot. He would be a lather of sweat at the end of up to two hours' training six nights a week. He was determined to make the national team at least once more. He had 212 Test wickets, just four less than Clarrie Grimmett's Australian record. Lindwall needed just five to become the record-holder—something to go out with, if he had to go. He felt he could do it in one more appearance. Nothing would divert him from his mission to be reselected. Not even the £6000 offered to him by an English paper to cover the 1958-59 Ashes series as a journalist.

His rigorous training regime paid off and he took wickets in early Shield games. Then the MCC team arrived in Brisbane for the warm-up game before the First Test. Lindwall's bowling was sensational as he dismissed Watson, Milton, Cowdrey, Bailey and Laker cheaply, ending with 5 for 57 from 15.4 overs. He was on his way to wreaking equal devastation in the second innings, dismissing both openers again for 7 runs each. Rain finished the game early and robbed him of a 10-wicket match that would have forced the selectors to take notice.

Seven for 73 for the game was proof enough of his sustained ability, but there was a problem. Not one selector was there to see his fluidity and form. He was not chosen for the First Test. The success of the home team's bowlers in a poor spectacle ensured Lindwall was kept out. Ian Meckiff, despite having a suspect action, and Davidson were performing too well.

Lindwall toiled on and continued to take Shield wickets and make runs, despite hearing a rumour that the national selectors, including Bradman, had written him off.

Bradman said the rumour wasn't true.

'I think you'll find Jack Fingleton behind that one,' he said. 'At that stage of the season the form was with those selected. But to say any of us would have written off Ray is wrong.'

Meckiff and Davidson devastated England in the Second Test at Melbourne, making Lindwall's return even more remote. Yet in the Third Test Meckiff was injured and was not certain to play in the next Test. Would this leave the way open for at least one other fast bowler? Lindwall showed his mettle by lifting for the state game against South Australia in Adelaide a week before the Fourth Test.

Did Bradman say anything to him before the game?

'We spoke, of course,' Bradman recalled, 'and I wished him luck. He was aware there could be replacements. He knew that Dudley Seddon (another national selector) would be watching as well.'

Bradman remembered that the elements were against the speedster.

'We had a heat wave,' he said. 'The temperatures were up around 42 and 43 degrees—not ideal for pacemen. And the wicket was as good as ever.'

South Australia batted on the first day and Lindwall bowled 29 eight-ball overs, taking 3 for 47. The next morning he delivered another 12 overs, taking 4 for 45, giving him 7 for 92 for the innings, perhaps his best displays ever in a state game. He walked off the ground to a standing ovation from the members, including Bradman.

'He bowled superbly,' Bradman said. 'Control, accuracy, swing, change of pace, the yorker—everything was there.'

Bradman was unaware of the severe nature of the hepatitis Lindwall was recovering from and his recurring groin injury. The bowler had kept them quiet, fearing it might put him out of contention for selection. The Don spoke to him after the game and asked him how he made his comeback, referring to his lack of form in the recent Ashes contests.

'I didn't make a comeback,' Lindwall replied. 'I've never stopped playing.'

'How come you're fitter now than you were in England in 1956?' Bradman persisted. He suspected Lindwall had carried his injuries with courage. The bowler circumvented the question, not wanting to complain or dwell on his injury problems.

Lindwall felt from Bradman's enthusiasm for his Adelaide effort that he would have a chance for the Fourth Test, and was overjoyed to be named in the 12-man squad for the Adelaide Test when Bob Simpson was dropped. But Meckiff and Gordon Rorke, the express bowler for New South Wales, were also in the squad. In the end, Meckiff was unfit to play and both Lindwall and Rorke were in. Lindwall's inclusion met with excitement from the media and cricket fans. There had been few more popular players at Test level. But beyond the superficial reaction, the feeling was that Lindwall had earned his place. Lindwall didn't want to characterise his selection for the Test side as a comeback, but it was probably the most remarkable return to top cricket for a fast bowler in his age bracket in history.

May shocked Benaud by sending Australia in at Adelaide— a major blunder on the good batting wicket. The home team reached 476 (McDonald 170), with Lindwall coming in at number 10 and scoring 19 before Trueman bowled him. Benaud did him the honour of letting him open the bowling ahead of Rorke, another suspected chucker, who—whatever he was delivering—was the fastest on either side.

The other opening bowler, Davidson, lamented the fact that Lindwall would have to bowl into the wind. Even though Davidson was the beneficiary of the breeze at his back, he felt badly about it.

'He was my hero,' Davidson said. 'He was the greatest. It seemed silly to me to be given the choice over him.'

Lindwall, however, was not miffed. He was thrilled to be back and to have a chance to crack Grimmett's record. He soon removed Peter Richardson (4) LBW, and Benaud (5 for 91) did most of the rest. Lindwall ended with 1 for 66 from 15 overs. In England's second innings, again he was first to break through, this time removing the other opener, Bailey (6), caught by keeper Grout. He went one better and bowled Cowdrey (8) before he got a start. Australia won the game by 10 wickets, giving it a 3:0 lead so far. Lindwall's figures were 2 for 70, which left him 1 wicket short of that record. The press now wondered if he would maintain his place for the final Test in Melbourne, where a fit Meckiff was sure to make his return.

The selectors kept the faith after Lindwall's serviceable effort in Adelaide and dropped a batsman, Les Favell, to make way for Meckiff. It gave the team an unwieldy look, with four pacemen. Benaud surprised this time and sent England in.

Davidson opened the bowling with a maiden to Richardson and then settled in slips to await his hero bowling to Bailey. Benaud, indulging in gamesmanship, sat close enough at silly mid-off to touch the batsman. Lindwall bowled a short ball that didn't threaten Bailey as it rose. He flashed at it and Davidson took a smart catch. It was the third successive occasion Lindwall made the first breakthrough, and very early in England's innings. Lindwall had now drawn level with

Grimmett at 216 wickets. He showed his prowess in the field by taking two fine low slips catches. Lindwall gave his three quicker partners a lesson in the basics of fast bowling—direction and accuracy. Although he bowled steadily and with menace at times, he couldn't snare another wicket in his 14 overs, taking 1 for 36, with England dismissed for 205. Australia made 351 (McDonald 133).

There was an electric atmosphere when Lindwall ran in to bowl late in the afternoon of the fourth day in front of 28,000 Melbourne fans willing him to take the record. In his first over, he bowled two outswingers to Bailey and then a stunning inswinger on a perfect length, to which the batsman could play neither forward nor back. Bailey was bowled for a duck, giving Lindwall the Australian wicket-taking record. No-one suggested that Bailey threw away his wicket to give Lindwall this one. The crowd erupted. Lindwall ran down the wicket, hands above his head like a boxer, and was embraced by his teammates.

He now looked something like the Lindwall of previous Ashes triumphs as he steamed in with that rhythmic run. May was lucky to survive an outswinger that he nicked through slips for 4. In his next over he had May (4) caught by Harvey at slip. England went to stumps at 2 for 22, with Lindwall's figures reading 2 for 8. He was given a standing ovation as he left the ground, his sweater draped over one shoulder. England's batsmen, Cowdrey and Richardson, stood aside and applauded. He went on the next day to take another wicket, giving him 3 for 37. Australia won by 9 wickets.

He took 40 wickets for the 1958-59 first-class season at 20.55 and, at 38 years of age, went on tour to Pakistan and India with a 15-man squad under Benaud at the end of 1959. Illness plagued him but he still managed 2 innings, claiming 3 wickets apiece. This lifted his final wicket tally to 228 wickets (at 23.03), just 8 short of Alec Bedser's then all-time Test record. In his last Test innings he scored 10, taking his run tally to 1,502 at 21.15. This made him the first player ever to score 1,500 and take 200 wickets in Tests.

Lindwall arrived home in February 1960 and announced his retirement from all forms of cricket, effective at the end of the 1959-60 season. Robbed of several years of the game due to the war, Lindwall had still managed to play 15 years at the top.

After 1965, he and Peggy ran a successful florist shop in Brisbane. He also put something back into the game by coaching. In the late 1960s a young, hirsute bowler from Western Australia sought his help in the nets, and Lindwall was later proud to take a little credit for his development. His name was Dennis Lillee, The Don's choice to open the bowling with Lindwall in his World XI.

CHAPTER 10

THE BATSMAN'S MENACE

DENNIS KEITH
LILLEE

(Australia)

18 July 1949—

> *'Dennis' comeback is one of the most inspirational stories in Australian sporting history.'*
>
> SIR DONALD BRADMAN

D ennis Lillee felt terrible. He had the flu on the morning of the second day of the Second Test, Australia v Rest of the World, in December 1971. He didn't want to leave his bed. He had played in four internationals and Tests against New Zealand (in an Australian Second XI), England and the Rest but had yet to cement a place in the Australian side. Early in the year he had started promisingly, taking 5 for 84 against England the first time he bowled. But wickets had come in ones and twos since then. Lillee couldn't afford to drop out now, even if there was a risk that the Rest batsmen might belt him. He would be bowling on a typical WACA wicket: fast, bouncy and true. Australia had rattled on 349 the day before, with Walters crunching 123.

Lillee let his skipper, Ian Chappell, know he was ill. Chappell told him to bowl a few overs to see how he felt. The speedster, urged on by a partisan Perth crowd, ran in to bowl to Sunil Gavaskar. The delivery was nearly a wide and had keeper Marsh diving to take it. Lillee stopped halfway down the wicket. He raised his eyebrow. The wicket had 'sweated' a bit under the covers over night. Did it have more zip than the day before, or was that ball a fluke? Intrigued, and forgetting his condition for a second, Lillee tore in and delivered another ball just short of a length. It kicked and grazed Gavaskar's shirtfront on the way through. The batsman let the next ball slide through, but the fourth delivery soared at Gavaskar's chest. He fended it off. It touched his glove and was snaffled by Marsh, who threw the ball high in his gleeful manner. The team rushed to embrace the bowler. For a moment, the excitement and the adrenalin supplanted the discomfort of the flu. In his third over he caught and bowled Farokh Engineer (13). By the end of the fourth, his figures were 2 for 29. Loose deliveries between the unplayable kickers had been belted for 7 an over. In the meantime, the Rest lost Rohan Kanhai (10), caught off Graham McKenzie, and Zaheer Abbas (14), run out.

Lillee again told Chappell he was feeling unwell, but Chappell knew his man and recognised that the unusual wicket was very much in the bowler's favour. He asked Lillee to bowl another over. Lillee did as requested and sent down his fifth over, a maiden. He rolled in for the sixth over and dismissed Clive Lloyd (14), caught behind, Tony Greig (5), caught in slips, and the prize wicket of Garry Sobers, caught behind for a duck. Lillee's figures were now 5 for 29. He sweated and his head ached, but he went another over, in which he had Richard Hutton (0) and Intikhab Alam (1) caught, boosting his figures to 7 for 29. Chappell had Doug Walters bowling his swingers from the other end. He was expensive, yet it mattered little. At the beginning of Lillee's eighth over, the score was 9 for 59. He had R S Cunis (0) caught in slips with his first ball. His figures had changed from 2 for 29 off 4 overs, to 8 for 29 off 7.1 overs. He took 6 wickets for no runs in his last 13 deliveries, in one of the most destructive spells of fast bowling ever seen. The complete innings of 14.1 overs took 90 minutes—it wasn't even lunch.

The bowler trudged off the field, head down and not smiling much, with his team-mates behind him applauding. It was the toughest 90 minutes he'd experienced in cricket, but there was no time to rest and savour the moment. Chappell enforced the follow on and Lillee had to bowl a couple more overs before lunch. He had Engineer (4) caught in the second of the two overs he delivered, giving him 9 wickets for the morning. That was it. He went home to bed. (The next day he recovered just enough to take another 3 wickets, giving him 12 for 92 for the game.)

Lillee was thrilled but kept things in perspective—he thought the wicket was the fastest he'd ever bowled on, the crowd gave him a lift, and there were some great catches by Marsh, Stackpole, McKenzie and Sheahan. Nevertheless, his confidence was high for the first time at Test level. After an uncertain rise to international cricket he now felt comfortable.

Hall of Fame

Lillee's early inspiration was the West Indies' express bowler Wes Hall. At the age of 11, Lillee jumped the fence at the WACA Members' Stand to talk to him. Hall was friendly and answered all Lillee's questions, showing interest in the wide-eyed youngster. Not only did Hall put fear in the hearts of opposition batsmen, with his size and flaying, aggressive run-up, but his selflessness also inspired their admiration. Hall was a big man in every sense, but not so big that he couldn't reach down to youngsters. His warmth and humility touched Lillee, who wanted to be like big Wes, just as Lindwall before him had wanted to be like Harold Larwood. In cricket, inspiration traverses national boundaries.

Lillee's truck-driver father, Keith, was another inspiration. He encouraged his sons, Dennis and younger brother Trevor, to play all sports, with an emphasis on Aussie rules and swimming rather than cricket. Dennis' lean, broad-shouldered physique looked more like that of a swimmer, yet it was at cricket that he shone. At first, the lanky teenager was more of a batsman, but by the time he had played four seasons in grade cricket in Perth, it was his capacity to bowl fast, with not much science or subtlety, that caused state selectors to take notice. In 1968-69 Lillee took 41 wickets at 15.61. The next year when Western Australia's two leading fast bowlers went to India with the national side, Lillee came into contention for state selection in October 1969. The day that the selectors were due to announce the state team at 5.00 pm, Lillee was playing in a grade game at Fletcher Park. Keith Lillee would sound the car horn at the game if his son was selected.

And at 5.00 pm the car horn sounded, followed by many others around the small ground. Lillee, at 20 years of age, was on his way with a cacophonous fanfare. His first state game was against Queensland at the Gabba on a flat wicket. He was enthusiastic more than nervous, and he sprayed the ball like an out-of-control water-sprinkler. He returned 2 for 60 and picked up another wicket in the second innings. Pushed along by hard taskmaster, Western Australian captain Tony Lock, Lillee bowled his fastest. His season's figures were 32 wickets at 22.03 runs a wicket, at the excellent strike rate of a wicket every six overs.

Off the field, his life took an important turn: he married Helen, his girlfriend of three years. He may have been young at 21, but he felt the responsibility would be good for him. Marriage matured and settled Lillee, and it showed on the field.

At the beginning of the next season—1970-71—observers in Perth touted him as a Test prospect, but he had to play second fiddle to McKenzie and bowl into the wind. This affected the tyro's wicket-taking ability and he took only 6 wickets in four matches on a tour of the eastern states. On 21 November he faced Barry Richards (playing for South Australia) en route to 356 runs in little over a day. The South

African belted everyone and was severe on Lillee, who ended up with 0 for 117. The speedster was dropped for the next game against the touring MCC side, but put back in when McKenzie was unfit to play. Lillee only succeeded in knocking Boycott's cap off in the first innings, but in the second he dismissed the big-name England opener and Colin Cowdrey cheaply.

Bradman, in his last season as a national selector, took note when Lillee snared 6 wickets in the next state game against Queensland in Perth. Lillee toiled on and kept taking wickets for Western Australia throughout the summer. His reward came in the Sixth Test of the season when he was picked for the national side.

In the series so far, England's John Snow had troubled Australia's batsmen with speed and bouncers and some journalists perceived Lillee's selection as an attempt to counter England with short deliveries. They predicted a bumper war. The impressionable young Lillee was confused. Should he become a macho man and take on Snow, bouncer for bouncer? The Australian had the fire to try, but not the experience. He felt pressured by the media to intimidate the England batsmen, until he spoke with Bradman at a function in Adelaide before the game.

The Chairman of Selectors knew all about the fineries and crudities of the bouncer, and its effects. Bowlers tried for 20 years to bounce him out with very little success. He knew that Lillee would be in two minds about what to do.

'He was very quick but raw,' Bradman recalled, 'and I knew he would have been reading the press reports. Bowling bouncers should have been the last thing on his mind, especially in his first Test.'

Bradman told Lillee that he had been picked to bowl his normal way, not to engage in a skirmish over short-pitched deliveries. If he adopted his usual style, he would succeed,

Bradman told him.

Lillee walked away from the chat twice as tall. Bradman was always sparing in his words, mainly because he felt that it was not his place to interfere. But when he did say something, he went to the heart of any issue. Lillee was honoured that Bradman had taken a genuine interest in him and realised intuitively that the bumper problem would be on his mind.

Lillee wrote in his first autobiography, *Back to the Mark*, that Bradman's advice not to get into a bumper war was invaluable. He was too inexperienced. If he had tried to match Snow it might have set back his progress.

Lillee needed all the bolstering he could get. England won the toss and lost only Boycott (run out 58) on the way to 276. Lillee came on into the wind again with the second new ball and had John Edrich caught in slips by Stackpole for 130. The tyro had toiled all day for his first-ever Test wicket. He finished his initial day in the international arena with 1 for 41 off 14 overs, but had not been penetrating. Lillee, a perfectionist long before he reached the big time, was not satisfied.

The next morning, Australian skipper Bill Lawry threw him the ball to deliver with the wind, the way most speedsters preferred. It paid dividends. The ball started to swing away from the right-handers and Lillee, swept along with the breeze, found rhythm. He removed nightwatchman Alan Knott (7). Later in the day he bowled England skipper Ray Illingworth with a sensational delivery that swung in the air and dipped in after hitting the pitch. Lillee added John Snow and Bob Willis to his bag and finished with the very satisfying figures of 5 for 84 off 28.3 overs.

That night, with a free day in front of them, Lillee got nicely inebriated with Rod Marsh and, with emotions running, cursed the fact that he had talked his number one supporter, his father, out of driving the 3000 km from Perth to see him play. Beforehand, Lillee was not sure the trip would have been worth it; now he regretted Keith not being there. He vowed to perform as well in the future in his father's presence.

Although Lillee played his part in the next Test (1 for 32 and 2 for 43) he had to wait until Perth nearly a year later before doing better, taking 8 for 59 in the first innings of the Second Test in the series against the Rest of the World. He followed this up in Melbourne in the first innings of the Third Test with 5 for 48, sending back a substantial haul: H M Ackerman (0), Gavaskar (38), Pollock (8), Sobers (0) and Engineer (5). Lillee and the confident Australians were brought back to earth in the second innings when Sobers smashed 254 to win the game for the Rest. Yet still Lillee took 3 (Ackerman, Abbas and Engineer) for 133 off 30 overs, giving him the good figures of 8 for 181 for the game.

Backbreaker

Lillee took just 1 wicket in the Fourth Test against the Rest at Sydney early in 1972. During the Rest's second innings, Ian Chappell urged him to bowl faster, saying that if he wanted someone to bowl spinners he'd put on Terry Jenner. Lillee responded by tearing in at Gavaskar. The paceman felt severe pain at the base of his spine after he had delivered the ball and was put out of action for a few weeks. His four games against one of the best line-ups world cricket could provide saw him take 24 wickets at 20.09. His back injury had to be carefully managed, and before the First Test of the 1972 Ashes series at Old Trafford he underwent manipulation of his spine under anaesthetic. In the second innings he took 6 for 66, although England won by 89 runs.

In the Second Test at Lord's, Bob Massie took 16 wickets in one of the finest-ever exhibitions of swing bowling. Lillee took the other 4 and Australia won by 8 wickets. The Third Test at Trent Bridge was drawn and Lillee again performed well, taking 6 wickets for 75 off 54 overs, demonstrating his pace and economy. The Fourth Test wicket at Headingley was devoid of grass and blatantly prepared for spinners, especially England's star, Derek Underwood, who took 8 and won the game for the home side. The disgruntled Australians moved on to The Oval where Lillee took his second 10-wicket haul in Tests (if the games against the Rest of the World are counted), taking 5 for 84 and 5 for 123. He did the most to secure a 5-wicket victory for the tourists. This squared the series at 2:2, and while the Ashes stayed in England, The Oval game was a turning point for the fortunes of the Australians under Chappell.

Lillee topped the bowling averages with 31 wickets at 17.67, then a record for an Australian in England. Suddenly Lillee found himself in excellent company, including Lindwall, Miller, McKenzie and Benaud.

The downside was that he was overworked, delivering 29 more overs for the tour than the next bowler, Ashley Mallett. And there was no respite. No sooner was he off the plane in Perth than he was preparing for the home summer of Shield games and Tests against Pakistan. In the space of six weeks he bowled 207.2 overs, 38 maidens, and took 44 wickets for 778 runs. It was by far the biggest bowling effort and success rate in the country, but it was taking its toll. Lillee could feel himself slipping as the Tests began. Nevertheless, he took 4 for 49 and 1 for 53 in the First Test against Pakistan at Adelaide over Christmas 1972, which Australia won by an innings and 114 runs. By the Second Test at Melbourne over the New Year into 1973, he was hoping the team would bat first so he could rest. His performance was flat. He took just 3 for 149 as Australia won by 92 runs.

In the Third Test at Sydney Lillee's back troubled him. He took 5 for 102 but his spine was very sore. The selectors were not perturbed, but Bradman, now retired as a selector, suggested he take a complete rest for the month or so before touring the West Indies. Lillee took Bradman's advice and felt fine on arrival in the West Indies and in the lead-up games before the First Test. But in a game against the Leeward Islands at Antigua, he collapsed.

'I think my back is broken,' he told Chappell. In fact, Lillee had not one break in his spine, but three. After the series, which Australia won 2:0, he sought treatment with a Perth orthopaedic surgeon, who encased him in a plaster cast from buttocks to chest. He was relieved to shed the cast several weeks later, but still had to wear a back brace for some time and was nowhere near fit enough to resume bowling. He still had to earn an income for his family though. Lillee, like many top cricketers, struggled with finding suitable employment and making ends meet. Cricket was a year-round occupation, but the remuneration was poor. Lillee had worked in a bank, then in his own contract cleaning business for 13 hours a day, but sold it so that he could recover from his back problem. Lillee got a job in a car company, which was flexible in letting him have time off.

Perth made Lillee captain–coach for the 1973-74 season and as he couldn't bowl, he went back to batting, scoring 654 runs from 18 innings at 43.6. Lillee, always a fitness fanatic, did twice as much exercise as prescribed to strengthen his back. He also worked on his fielding and took his captaincy seriously.

The 1973-74 season wore on and Lillee could not resist the temptation to bowl. He did this without pace and concentrated on line and length, never his forté in his early days of hellfire pace. Into the New Year he bowled more and more in short spells and built to a lively pace by the end of the season. It did his morale good to take wickets, 48 of them at 15.8, which was a fine return even in grade cricket.

At this time Lillee out of necessity reinvented himself as a bowler of quality. He used a shorter run, changed his action to reduce back stress, and worked on variations in pace and the inswinger, which had never been his strength. Lillee learned to bowl to his less attacking field, and improved to a huge degree in the technical side of the art. Thus, having a back problem at such an early stage of his career (he was only 23) was the making of D K Lillee, Master Bowler.

Comeback

Lillee's rehabilitation took just 21 months, but he had missed 11 Tests against the Windies and New Zealand between February 1973 and November 1974. Despite feeling apprehensive, and having a run-in with the Cricket Board over medical bills, he walked straight back into the side to play against England in the Ashes tour in Australia in 1974-75.

Lillee began cautiously, knowing that if he let rip at full speed it might be the end of his career. Fortunately, his new opening partner, Jeff Thomson, was doing all the 'ripping' for him with his sling action, which propelled the ball faster than anyone since Frank Tyson. This took some of the pressure off Lillee, who now bowled steadily, with patches of controlled speed. England bowled short to Lillee and Thomson when they were batting in the First Test at Brisbane. This began a bumper war that carried through the series, won 4:1 by the Australians. England won in the Sixth Test at Melbourne when Thomson couldn't play after injuring his shoulder in a tennis match on the rest day of the Fifth Test at Adelaide, and Lillee couldn't bowl more than six overs because of a bruised foot. The Lillee n' Thomson combination dominated the rest of the series, Thomson taking 32 wickets and Lillee 25 wickets at 23.84. He was relieved and thrilled to get through the season without any back problems.

In early 1975 Lillee joined the Australian team on a tour of

Canada before the first-ever international one-day World Cup in England. Australia reached the final against the West Indies, lost narrowly and then embarked on a four-Test Ashes battle. They won the First Test at Edgbaston, when England skipper Mike Denness put Australia in. The tourists batted evenly and reached 359. Lillee then took 5 for 15 from 15 overs with 8 maidens on a rain-affected pitch, and England was dismissed for 101. In the next innings, Thomson snared 5 for 35 and the home side reached just 173, giving Australia a win by an innings and 85 runs.

Lillee took 4 for 84 in England's first innings of the Second Test at Lord's, which was drawn. The Third at Headingley was abandoned when a political protestor ruined the pitch the night before the last day, when the game was evenly poised. The Fourth Test was also drawn, with Lillee taking 4 for 91, giving Australia the series 1:0 and the retention of the Ashes. Lillee ended with 21 wickets at 21.90, a good return given the strength of England's team, which was unlucky to lose a tight series. Lillee left that series with a leg-cutter in his armoury, taught to him by John Snow.

Lillee's back held up again, and while the injury would remain manageable, he would never be rid of the nagging fear that his glorious career could be cut short by the hauntingly familiar pain. Even more on his mind at 26, with a wife and two small boys, was survival. After giving up his job for cricket he was unemployed and only picking up occasional promotional and advertising work. It seemed unfair for someone bringing enormous credit to his country as a top sportsman.

He battled on into the 1975-76 season in Australia with new challenges from a strong West Indies side. Lillee had studied them in the Caribbean when he had to sit out the series, and during the 1975 World Cup. He saw Alvin Kallicharran and Clive Lloyd as the tourists' danger batsmen, while Andy Roberts, Michael Holding and Lance Gibbs would cause trouble for Australia with the ball.

Lillee was consistent in the First Test at the Gabba, taking 3 for 84 and 3 for 72, ably supported by speedster Gary Gilmour, who took another 6 wickets. By scoring a century in each innings, Greg Chappell did most to win the game for Australia by 8 wickets. The West Indies fought back in Perth (Fredericks 169 and Lloyd 149), amassing 585 and winning by an innings and 87 runs. Four Australian bowlers, including Lillee (3 for 123 from 20 overs), conceded a hundred runs. During the game, scientists from a Western Australian university clocked Thomson bowling at just under 100 miles per hour (161 km per hour), Roberts at 93.6 miles per hour (151 km per hour), Holding at 92 miles per hour (148 km per hour) and Lillee at 86.4 miles per hour (139 km per hour). This reflected Thomson's hostility, but not the science in Lillee's improved technique.

In the Third Test at Melbourne Lillee and Thomson at last hit their stride together in the series. They demolished the opposition in the first innings for 224, Thomson taking 5 for 62 and Lillee 4 for 56. In the second innings, the West Indies did better, making 312 (Lloyd 102), but not enough to avoid going down by 8 wickets. Lillee's form was consistently fine and he took 3 for 70.

Lillee missed the Fourth Test due to a minor form of pleurisy, yet Australia still won well by 7 wickets, mainly thanks again to the brilliance of Thomson (6 for 50 in the Windies' second innings) and Greg Chappell, who scored 182 out of Australia's first innings of 405. Lillee returned to take 2 wickets in each innings of the Fifth Test as Australia rolled on to another big win, this time by 190 runs. He reached top form in the final Test, snaring his best bag for the series with 5 for 63, and then 3 for 112 in the Windies' second innings. This effort had most influence on the game, which Australia won by 165 runs, giving it a 5:1 series win. Lillee took 27 wickets at 26.36 for the series, while Thomson captured 29 wickets.

In the mid-1970s Australia sat on top of the unofficial world table, thanks in large measure to their capacity to blast out such a strong West Indian batting line-up, which included Fredericks, Viv Richards, Rowe, Kallicharran and Lloyd. Lillee and Thomson, ably supported by Gilmour and Max Walker, were able to set low scores for Australia's batsmen, led by the Chappells and Ian Redpath, to chase. Another factor supporting Australia's dominance in the mid-1970s and its fast bowlers' success was the skill of Rod Marsh behind the stumps.

The Peak

Lillee's career peaked in 1976-77 when in six Tests he took 47 wickets at 21.62. He secured 21 against Pakistan in three Tests, 15 in two against New Zealand and 11 in the Centenary Test against England. Lillee thrice took 10 or more wickets in a game. In all Tests and first-class games for the season combined he sent down 477.4 overs and snared 93 wickets at an average of 18.92 a wicket. It was no coincidence that with Lillee in this devastating form Australia maintained its winning edge despite Ian Chappell standing down for his brother Greg, and other personnel changes. Western Australia also won the Sheffield Shield and the Gillette (one-day) Cup, a feat never before achieved by the one state.

Even when Thomson hurt his shoulder in an on-field collision that ruled him out for the rest of the summer, Lillee ploughed on, taking all before him. His aggression came to the fore and his image as a longhaired larrikin was set. He was not above 'colliding' with batsmen as they went for a run. When an umpire warned him in the Melbourne Test against Pakistan early in 1977 for an excess of bouncers, he churlishly made as if to deliver underarm, and then feigned a delivery with a balloon. This was followed by some rude exchanges with men in the members' pavilion. The confident, popular Lillee thrived on the new image of Australian cricketers in the 1970s. In the 1960s, teams led by Benaud, Simpson and Lawry played it hard but fair, with less of a need for snarling or histrionics. Ian Chappell changed the demeanour of the national side on the field in the 1970s, using more aggressive tactics to gain the edge. This new style was in keeping with an era of anti-establishment, nationalistic fervour in Australia that made a virtue out of the ocker image as portrayed by Barry Humphries in the Bazza McKenzie films. Lillee exemplified the change in the mythology of the Aussie sporting hero and national character when he was presented to the Queen at the MCG during the March 1977 Centenary Test to mark a hundred years of Tests between England and Australia. He asked for Her Majesty's autograph—and later received it on a photograph capturing the cheeky but harmless incident.

The Australian crowds loved Lillee. He was the warrior, the country's jousting knight. What's more, Lillee smiled a lot and enjoyed himself on and off the field. He loved performing at the MCG where the huge crowds gave voice with the chant 'Lill-ee ... Lill-ee ... Lill-ee'. With that simplest of mantras ringing out around the vast stadium, he always lifted his rating.

Lillee's performance went up a notch in the Centenary Test, despite his body screaming for a rest after a hectic, strenuous non-stop season. Big crowds—250,000 for the five days—turned out for the match, which lived up to expectations. Lillee routed England in their first innings, taking 6 for 26 off 13.3 overs of fire and mayhem. In their second, he took 5 for 139 and kept Australia in the game (as did his good mate Rod Marsh, who scored 110 not out) when Derek Randall (174) threatened to steal the contest for his country. It was Lillee who trapped the dangerous keeper/batsman Alan Knott (42) LBW to end the struggle. Australia won by 45 runs, the same margin as in the first game at the MCG in March 1877.

Lillee bowled 34.4 overs in that last innings. But there was a price for being Australia's match-winner and gaining everlasting fame. His vertebrae nearly gave way again. Lillee was ordered to rest, and missed the entire tour of England in 1977.

Packer Man for a Penny

Lillee was the first person to suggest the idea of a breakaway cricket competition, which grew into Kerry Packer's World Series Cricket. Lillee was frustrated at being underpaid, and enjoyed being involved in clandestine moves against the Australian Cricket Board. The board had not made the changes needed to meet the modern demands of the game and represented establishment values to which Lillee had never aligned himself. As one of the two best cricketers in Australia at the time (the other being Greg Chappell), Lillee had tangible power, and was just the person to thumb his nose at the board's intransigence and assist Packer.

With a three-year contract in his pocket, Lillee took on the challenge of making the World Series Cricket games attractive to the public. He needed to look no further than the opposition teams: a World XI and one from the West Indies. They included a galaxy of great batsmen such as Gordon Greenidge, Barry Richards, Viv Richards, Clive Lloyd, Asif Iqbal, Tony Greig, Imran Khan, Roy Fredericks, Eddie Barlow, Zaheer Abbas and Clive Rice. Lillee recruited talent from within Australia's ranks, including the retired Ian Chappell, his brother Greg, who was the current Australian captain, Doug Walters and others.

In the first so-called Supertests in 1977-78, Lillee took on the biggest workload of any bowler, sending down 152.4 overs in five matches and taking 21 wickets at 36.43. His best effort was 5 for 82. In the one-day competition, he took just 3 wickets at 33.33. These figures were not Lillee's best, but conditions, easy-paced batting wickets, and the weight of the competition were unfavourable.

Packer's gamble of risking millions on the project looked in jeopardy after the first season when it took some time to capture the public's imagination, but in the second, 1978-79, World Series Cricket took off. Early in 1979 about 50,000 people jammed into the SCG for a day–night game, and thousands more were turned away. Packer secured agreements with politicians and unions. Better grounds and pitches were used. With ratings lifting on his Nine Network, he was able to charge more for advertising.

Improved conditions lifted Lillee's ratings as he again bowled more overs than any other competitor in the Supertests while taking the most wickets, 23 at 16.60. In the one-day series he took 23 more wickets, this time at just 12.56.

The success of World Series Cricket forced the board to the negotiating table, and a compromise with Packer. The board gave Packer the rights to broadcast the game in Australia— which was Packer's original aim—in return for him abandoning the World Series Cricket experiment. Lillee had something in the bank for the first time, and the board had agreed to improved pay and conditions for players, although it was a long way from giving him or any other star cricketer a sense of security.

As You Were

Lillee was back in the unified national team for the 1979-80 season and three Tests each against England and the West Indies. Australia won all three Tests against England with Lillee dominant, taking 23 wickets at 16.87. His leg-cutter was now a serious weapon and the England bats struggled whenever he bowled. He had refined his skills against the world's best batsmen in two seasons and he was too much for England, despite stars such as Randall, Geoff Boycott, David Gower, Graham Gooch and Ian Botham. Lillee took 6 wickets in each of the first two games, then 11 in the Third, including his best return for the summer of 6 for 60.

The story was different against the West Indies line-up which featured a powerful batting order: Greenidge, Haynes, Viv Richards, Kallicharran, Lance Rowe and Lloyd. Yet Lillee's return of 12 wickets at 30.41 was respectable, and he managed 5 for 78.

In the first game, Lillee used an aluminium bat that he and a business partner were trying to market. The West Indies players laughed it off, but when he tried it again against England, their captain, Mike Brearley, complained and Lillee was ordered by the umpires not to use it. No-one could ever accuse him of missing a marketing opportunity.

The Australian summer was followed by another three-Test series in Pakistan. Lillee suffered in these games from slow, flat wickets. His counterpart in Pakistan's team, Imran Khan, also complained about them after the series. Lillee went wicketless in the first two games and took 3 in the last. He ended the tour with 3 for 303. He left Pakistan vowing never to come back, annoyed about the doctoring of wickets to suit the local spinners. Until the late 1990s Pakistan was never a happy hunting ground for visiting teams.

Lillee found the second Centenary Test—to mark the first Test ever in England—more enjoyable. It was staged in late August and early September 1980 at Lord's. The original match had been played at The Oval and the result was a 5-wicket win to England (Grace hitting 152 for England and Murdoch 153 not out for Australia). In 1980, weather played havoc with the game. Lillee was shocked to see the umpires—Dickie Bird and David Constant—jostled by angry Lord's members, who felt the game should be under way despite the conditions.

Lillee took 4 for 43 in England's first innings of 205. Australia's Kim Hughes made 117 and 84 not out in an outstanding double, but with weather interruptions and Geoff Boycott in form (62 and 128 not out), it wasn't enough to press home a win.

Lillee returned to his normal wicket haul for six Tests in the 1980-81 Australian summer against New Zealand and then India. He took 16 wickets at 15.31 against the Kiwis, with 6 for 53 in one innings in Brisbane and 5 for 63 in another in Perth. Australia won 2:0. India provided tougher resistance. Lillee took 21 wickets at 21.52 and the series was 1:1. He took 4-wicket hauls on four occasions and maintained a consistency throughout the summer that was a credit to his maturity and his dedication to fitness.

One Last Tilt

Lillee, approaching 32, arrived in England in April 1981 for one last tilt at the old enemy on their home soil. It didn't begin well, as he picked up a pneumonia virus that put him in hospital. The virus left him feeling exhausted after his early county games. His spirits lifted when he was made an MBE, and this seemed to carry him into the First Test at Trent Bridge in which he took 3 for 34 and a match-winning 5 for 46. Australia won by 4 wickets.

Before the Second Test Lillee had an angry argument with the MCC secretary, Jack Bailey, at Lord's when he and Allan Border were nearly prevented from getting in some unscheduled practice. Lillee and the ultra-conservatism of cricket headquarters were never likely to be easy bedfellows. He had not forgiven the Lord's members for their treatment of his mate, Dickie Bird, during the Centenary Test a year earlier.

The Lord's Test began magnificently for Geoff Lawson, who took 7 for 81 in the first innings, while Lillee went wicketless. He did better in England's second innings, taking 3 for 82, including the prize wickets of Boycott and Gower. The game ended in a tame draw.

Lillee, ever the headline-maker, put a £10 bet on England to win the Third Test at Headingley on the fourth day when the odds were 500 to 1 against it. The home team's score was 7 for 135, leaving them 191 runs behind, with Australia able to bat again if they needed to. Rod Marsh put £5 on at the same odds. The two Australians collected £5,000 and £2,500 pounds respectively, thanks to Ian Botham scoring 149 not out in his best-ever knock for England, and Bob Willis (8 for 43) rolling Australia for just 111 in its second innings, leaving the tourists 18 runs in arrears.

Morale on the tour had not been high, with Lillee and Marsh not always seeing eye-to-eye with skipper Kim Hughes, but it reached rock-bottom after this shock loss. The cavalier punting didn't help, although Lillee and Marsh at least shouted the rest of the team a drink or two out of their windfalls.

Even with Lillee and Alderman doing damage in the next Test at Edgbaston, Australia again failed to reach a small target (150) in the last innings, being sent back for just 121, mainly thanks this time to Botham (5 for 11). Somehow the tourists had thrown away two Tests, which would have given Australia the series 3:1. Instead, they went down 1:3. It was the fault of neither Lillee nor Terry Alderman. Lillee had held fine form as he paced himself through a long summer of six Tests. He took 39 at 22.30, only to be pipped by Terry Alderman, who took 42 wickets and created a record for an Australian in an Ashes series. Lillee's best effort was 7 for 89 in the first innings of the last Test at The Oval, which was drawn.

Lillee had an extra incentive for the 1981-82 season in Australia with three Tests each against Pakistan and the West

Indies. He was closing in on Lance Gibbs' record of 309 Test wickets. He began well in the First Test at the WACA, taking 5 for 18 in Pakistan's first innings of just 62. In its second, Javed Miandad pushed his bat hard into an unsuspecting Lillee's ribcage as he went for a run off the bowler, who had turned at the end of his follow-through. Lillee pursued Miandad and pushed his foot at the Pakistani's pad. It was no more than a tap, but the media in Australia and elsewhere turned it into a kick. In England it became one of the biggest news items featuring Australia for years, the other most recent being the story about a dingo running off with a baby at Uluru.

Lillee was depicted as the Australian larrikin-turned-yobbo. But when this incident passed into history, Lillee was a champion fast-bowler en route to a world record. Australia won the Test by 286 runs and he achieved sweet revenge in the Second Test at the Gabba by dismissing Miandad twice for low scores as he took 5 for 81 and 4 for 51. This effort and a fine double hundred by Greg Chappell sealed the tourists' fate in another win for Australia, this time by 10 wickets.

Lillee was out of sorts in the dead rubber in Melbourne, and Pakistan picked up a win. Eleven days later he turned up at the MCG for the First Test against the West Indies. He was sitting on 305 wickets and needed only 5—his average per Test—to take the world record. Australia won the toss, batted, and was quickly 4 for 26. Only a brilliant century by Kim Hughes saved the side from humiliation by the tourists' great bowling attack of Holding, Roberts, Joel Garner and Colin Croft. The Australian innings ended late in the day at just 198, giving the West Indies 30 minutes until stumps. The huge MCG crowd, feeling cheated of some fine Aussie batting, gave voice as never before to their hero, D K Lillee.

He bowled from the outer end with the fans chanting: 'Lill-ee … Lill-ee … Lill-ee'. His first over was unremarkable.

Then Alderman at the other end took a wicket. Lillee tore in, the crowd finding more voice. He had Haynes caught for 1, and the West Indies was 2 for 5. Moments later he had night-watchman Croft LBW for a duck. The scoreboard read 3 for 6. In marched the 'master-blaster', Viv Richards, unperturbed by the situation. The Melbourne outer was now ecstatic. Lillee stopped, turned at the top of his mark and charged in. The ball was outside off stump, but very quick. Richards stabbed forward. The ball beat him for pace, caught the inside edge and cannoned into his stumps. The roof of the outer stand was lifted by the mighty roar that greeted this triumph, perhaps the most inspiring moment in the bowler's entire sporting career. The West Indies was 4 for 10 at stumps. Lillee was one wicket short of equalling Gibbs' record.

The next day, he removed Dujon after lunch. At 2.55 pm, with the last ball of his 19th over, he had Gomes caught by Greg Chappell at slip to take his wicket tally to 310, a new world record. The 44,894 fans stood to salute their champion in one of the greatest moments in Australian sport.

Lillee's wife Helen and their sons, Adam, 7, and Dean, 5, were watching from the Members' Stand as he confirmed his ranking as king bowler of all time. Lillee paid tribute to his wife and to her father for instilling a passion for fitness into him and his parents for encouraging but not pushing him. He also acknowledged Rod Marsh, who had taken 83 catches off his bowling, and who often signalled his ideas about how to dismiss a batsman.

'Dennis had tremendous energy and courage, which coupled with his great skills made him the most formidable bowler produced by Australia since Ray Lindwall,' Bradman noted. 'Dennis' comeback is one of the most inspirational stories in Australian sporting history.'

Lillee finished the innings with 7 for 83, his best figures ever in a Test innings, and in the second innings he took another 3 for 44, giving Australia victory by 58 runs. He took another 6 wickets in the next Test in Sydney, which was drawn. He injured his groin in the Third Test at Adelaide, and the West Indies won by 5 wickets. In the six Tests he took 31 wickets at 20.93, thus maintaining an amazing consistency throughout another long season, which included Shield games.

Lillee was not enthusiastic about the three-Test tour of New Zealand that followed. He was hampered by the groin injury, which caused a disc in his spine to be thrown out of place. This was capped off by a knee injury, which needed two operations. Lillee's injuries kept him out of big cricket for six months. He only managed one Test against England at the WACA in 1982-83, but he was fit for a one-off Test in Sri Lanka in April 1983—the first between the two countries, which Australia won by an innings and 38 runs. Lillee struck early in the first innings, taking 2 wickets, and again in the second when he put back an opener early on.

It was hard for the aging lion to accept that he was losing his pace and effectiveness. Lillee felt the chilling edge of the axe in the England summer of 1983 when he was dropped for the first time in his career during the World Cup one-day competition. He decided there and then he would work hard to get fit for one last glorious summer in 1983-84 in a five-Test series against Pakistan.

In September 1983, Western Australian captain Kim Hughes told him he would be needed only as a change bowler in state games. It was the final needle for Lillee. He was determined to play alongside Greg Chappell and Rod Marsh, who, it was thought, would probably also retire at the end of the Pakistan Tests. Lillee overcame niggling pain in back, knee and groin, and the howls of critics, to return to the Test arena with 20 wickets at 31.50. This included one marathon of more than 50 overs in which he took 6 for 171. In the last Test at Sydney, his favourite ground, he took 4 for 65 and 4 for 88.

Marsh took five catches in the Pakistani second innings, which brought his number of dismissals to 355 (coincidentally, the same number as Lillee). Greg Chappell, in his last-ever Test innings, made a splendid 182 and became the highest run-getter in Australian cricket. These Three Musketeers of the Australian game, who had been associated with each other for 12 years, bowed out together with panache in a game won by Australia, who took the series 2:0.

Lillee, at 34, ended his 70-Test career with 355 wickets at 23.92. He took 10 wickets in a Test on seven occasions, and 5 wickets in an innings 23 times. He enjoyed every wonderful, painful moment of a turbulent career.

After cricket, Lillee was seen for a time as the cheerful workman in a TV ad for Carpet Call. More permanent, and fitting, has been his contribution to the game as a fine coach of pace bowlers in Australia and other countries such as India. Every so often, a player is spotted with a long-striding smooth run similar to the master paceman. Chances are he has been given a tip or two by Dennis Keith Lillee.

CHAPTER 11

THE LION

OF SURREY

ALEC VICTOR
BEDSER

9

(England)

4 July 1918—

*'No batsman played him with
anything like approaching relish,
and, for once, the adjective
"great" carried no exaggeration.'*

WISDEN.

A packed crowd and many millions more watching on BBC TV were keyed up for the first day of the 1953 Ashes series. It was the first time since 1926 that Australia had faced England without Bradman in its line-up. English supporters were optimistic their team had a strong chance to win the Ashes for the first time since the bodyline series of 1932-33.

Two decades were a long time to wait to sniff success. Despite the dull early June conditions and the promise of rain at Trent Bridge, Nottingham, an electric atmosphere greeted Australia's opening batsmen Graeme Hole and Arthur Morris as they walked out to bat.

In the crowded press box were Sir Jack Hobbs, Bill Bowes, Douglas Jardine, Bradman, Sid Barnes, Bill O'Reilly and Jack Fingleton. They were just as excited as the crowd.

Alec Bedser, England's brilliant, big aging medium-fast bowler was pleased that Bradman and Barnes, combatants of his from the last Ashes series in England in 1948, were there to see him perform. He had built a strong friendship with The Don, and naturally wanted to impress.

Bedser had been let off practice the day before by Hutton because he had bowled 24 overs (taking 2 for 80) for Surrey the day before that. The press suggested that the 34-year-old, 190 cm (6 ft 3 in) bowler was unfit, but he was 100 per cent right and ready.

The crowd hushed as Bedser ran in to bowl the first ball to Hole. He cannily delivered an innocuous over below top pace, feeling that the batsman might be unsure of the wicket and lulled by the way the ball came through. He knew that Hole was vulnerable to a well-directed inswinger. The first over was a maiden. In the second, Trevor Bailey conceded two runs to Morris at the other end.

Bedser ran in to begin his second over with one aim in mind. He would bowl the quickest inswinger he could manage. The key was to put it on the spot in line with off stump. The ball landed perfectly. Hole played too late. His middle stump was removed. The crowd roared. What a start for England!

Tight bowling kept Australia to 1 for 54. Morris was watchful, especially of Bedser's fast off-break to the left-hander (the leg-cutter to the right-hander), while Hassett gave a masterly display of batting with 'soft hands'—slackening the wrists and relaxing the grip on the bat as the ball hit it.

It drizzled during lunch, making the ball difficult to grip and the outfield slower. The Australians took the score past 100 without further loss and there was a dulling sense of 'as you were' for the fans. Those damned Aussies were pulling the game around and ruining their fervent hopes for a change of fortune.

At tea, rain held up play for 20 minutes. The rested Bedser looked forward to the new ball, which was due in the last session. He thought he could make it skid faster, but the wet outfield would remove the shine. The moisture on the pitch would soon disappear. The decision had to be made quickly. It was up to the captain. Hutton thought about it and took the gamble, calling for the new ball.

Bedser bowled Morris three inswingers then his fast off-break, which caught Morris on the crease and plumb in front. The classy Australian's finest international adversary had snared him once more.

Another top-line left-hander, Neil Harvey, replaced Morris. Bedser knew it was best to attack him first rather than let such a batting dominator take the initiative. Like Bradman, his predecessor at number three for Australia, Harvey always tried to get off the mark as soon as possible. A psychological tactic for both these great bats, it often set a tone for an innings. Bedser brought in another short leg and put Denis Compton at short fine leg. With deliberation, the bowler hurled down a ball intended for movement away off the pitch down leg-side. Harvey picked the line and tried to force it to the square-leg fence. If the ball had come straight on it would have reached its intended destination. Instead, it was flicked fine and fast to Compton. The fielder bobbled the ball and caught it in his arm. It was a superb grab, considering the pace at which it flew.

'Don't frighten me by juggling such easy catches,' Bedser scolded. Compton was about to respond in no uncertain terms when he saw that the bowler was joking. Australia was 3 for 128. Bedser had all three wickets to fall. At stumps the tourists had reached 3 for 157 off 92 overs of quality medium-fast, accurate swing bowling. Bedser sent down 25 overs, 12 maidens, and conceded just 26 runs for his 3 wickets. Day one of the 1953 Ashes had been a classic battle between fine bowlers and batsmen. Honours were even. Hassett was still in occupation.

It rained through the night, and the uncovered wicket and outfield were wet in the morning. Bedser didn't like the conditions as the ball would become wet and tough to grasp; it would lose its hardness; the stitches would soften; and it would come through slower and wouldn't swing. Bedser's only choice was to bowl dead straight and wait until the outfield dried out.

Hassett and Miller added 80 in an overall partnership of 109 that took the score to 237. Then Johnny Wardle tempted Miller (55) into a big hit, only to see Bailey take a fine catch on the run. After lunch the new ball was due. Bedser, anticipating a dry outfield but still a heavy atmosphere that would bring back his prodigious swing, did some stretches and exercises during the break: deep knee bends, sit-ups and side bends. He wanted to be loose and ready to tear in from the first ball of the second session. Bailey removed the young Richie Benaud and Ray Lindwall, both brilliantly caught by Godfrey Evans behind the stumps. Bedser did the rest, clean-bowling Hassett (115), Davidson, Tallon and Jack Hill, to give him 7 for 55 off 38.3 overs with 16 maidens. This was one of the best bags in Test history. Only Hill in this haul was not capable of turning a Test match with brilliant or vigorous batting. Australia was dismissed for 249.

No sooner had Bedser put his feet up in the dressing room than his Australian counterpart, Lindwall, sent back three England batsmen for just 17 runs. It meant that Bedser could not relax. Not only that, he had been struck on the foot by a Lindwall yorker just before being trapped LBW by him. Well into day three, Saturday, England was all out for a miserable 144.

Demonstrating that he was made of sterner stuff than most, Bedser did not take his boots off back in the dressing room, but instead kept walking around to avoid his instep becoming swollen and sore. This courageous ploy worked. Bedser went out and responded as perhaps only someone with his enormous strength could.

He found that the ball wasn't swinging as much without the heavy cloud cover, so he decided to attack on the batsman-friendly wicket by setting a most attacking close-in field. This positive approach worked. Bedser removed Hole (5) with an identical inswinger to the one he received in the first innings. Hassett came in. The bowler asked his captain for a shorter than short leg and a close gully. Bedser then held the ball across the seam and dug it into the pitch as hard as his big frame could manage. The ball reared up, surprising Hassett (5), who popped an easy catch to Hutton close in. Bedser broke into a huge grin as his team-mates congratulated him. Hassett's skills in the stubborn first innings made him a prize wicket of the second dig, indeed of any innings in which he batted.

As Harvey entered the arena, Hutton seemed to examine the pitch as if there were a small sign on it saying, 'Strike here and ball will lift alarmingly'. Bedser then crowded the new man with two more extra-close fielders. He wanted to stop Harvey from getting off the mark in his customary quick fashion. The first ball reared up and slapped Harvey on the forearm. Soon after being hurt, Harvey lashed at a short-pitcher and it raced straight to Tom Graveney at backward short leg, who held his ground and took a sensational catch.

In marched Keith Miller. Bedser crowded him too, knowing that the flamboyant all-rounder would retaliate against such tactics by using the long handle to long-off or wide mid-on. Bedser tore in for a few deliveries at top pace, then lobbed up a juicier ball than intended, which turned into a full toss. Miller (5) obliged by mistiming an attempted six over mid-wicket. Instead, a gentle catch was lobbed to wide mid-on. Benaud came in, attempted a flick to mid-wicket off a leg-cutter, and was bowled round his legs for a duck.

Australia was 5 for 68 and in a Bedser-driven tailspin. He had all 5 wickets to fall for just 22 in 12 overs. He could hardly believe his achievement. These figures were more like those acquired by a schoolboy in house cricket, not in a Test against Australia.

Only the stylish, gutsy Morris (60) resisted as Bedser removed Lindwall and Hill, and Australia was all out for a paltry 123. Bedser's figures in the second innings read 17.2 overs, 7 maidens, 7 for 44. His match figures were 14 for just 99 runs as the game petered out to a tame draw because of awful weather. Has anyone done better, considering the opposition and the conditions, in the history of the game?

Jim Laker's 19 wickets for 90 that followed against Australia at Old Trafford in 1956 would have to rank with Bedser's effort. But Australia's batting order was not as good, the wicket was a specially prepared dust bowl perfect for a spinner, and England was never under threat, having scored 459 in the first innings of the match. Then there is Australian Bob Massie's 16 for 139 at Lord's in 1972, which also looks better on paper. Yet the Lord's wicket and the extra-heavy atmosphere were conducive to swing. On top of that, England's batting line-up in 1972 did not come near Australia's of 1953. You could throw in Lillee's 12 wickets against the Rest of the World in 1971 as a performance to rival Bedser's, but the point remained that no-one had ever done better than he did in that extraordinary Trent Bridge game.

A key to the maintenance of his fine figures in each innings was his durability, even when struggling with his badly bruised foot. Bedser's exceptional strength can be traced back to his youth when he developed a massive constitution for hard work—the sort of stamina at which Bradman marvelled. This plus his outstanding skill as a medium-fast swinger caused Bradman to slot the Englishman into his team as the first change pace bowler—along with Garry Sobers.

Twinned Labours of Love

In 1933, Alec and identical twin brother Eric, not yet 15 years old, both worked in a solicitor's office in Lincoln's Inn Fields on the Thames embankment, London. They used to daydream while watching trams wend their way over Westminster Bridge en route to The Oval at Kennington. The carriages were symbolic of their lives, which they wished would one day take them to The Oval, permanently. The lads from Woking were diligent workers, but they were not destined to toil in grey suits—their ambition was to wear whites and be flannelled fools out in the midday sun, forever.

The brothers were very close. They made a decision that perhaps only twins could: they tossed a coin to see who would continue on as a medium-fast bowler, and who would turn to spinning. They aimed only to play for the same county, Surrey. Separation was unthinkable. Alec won the toss and went on bowling medium-fast. Eric took to off-spin. That most fateful decision was followed by another in April 1938 when the two 19-year-old sons of a bricklayer gave up their safe jobs and joined Surrey. Their aim was to become county professionals, which was enough to fulfil their wildest dreams. Neither believed they would go further than county cricket and would have scoffed at anything beyond it.

Alec made his first-class debut in 1939 against Oxford and Cambridge universities. Labouring work, coaching and a small retainer from the club allowed him and Eric to just make ends meet, until war intervened. The twins were determined to always live and stay together. This led to them both joining the RAF in 1939 and they didn't leave it until 1946 at 27 years of age. On the surface, it seemed that missing seven years of cricket was a personal tragedy, but Alec felt that it made him more mentally mature and physically hardened.

By June 1946 Bedser had taken 46 wickets from 11 games. A Test trial was held at Lord's to decide the team to play against the touring Indians in the first post-war international series. He removed two of England's best-ever batsmen, Hutton and Hammond. It was enough to gain him his maiden Test at Lord's against India.

Bedser opened the bowling from the nursery end, his favourite, which allowed him to make the ball go away with the ground's slope and deliver effective inswingers. It was just such a delivery that caused Vijay Merchant to flick the ball to Paul Gibb close up on the leg-side, giving Bedser his first Test wicket. He went on to take 7 for 49 off 29.1 overs and 4 for 96 in the second innings, giving him 11 for 145 in his debut Test. Even though the Indian batting line-up was not replete with champions, Bedser's effort was a big one. He bowled accurately and shrewdly. His confidence was high when he batted and he even managed to make 30 in a partnership with Joe Hardstaff, who made a typically stylish 205. England won the game by 10 wickets.

At the end of it, Hardstaff told him in private: 'You've booked your passage to Australia (for the 1946-47 Ashes series).'

Bedser was stunned. He had been concentrating on his debut performance. Now such a legend as Hardstaff was adamant about him joining the most challenging tour of all— Australia. To celebrate, Bedser took another 11 for 93 at Old Trafford in his second Test. He had 2 for 60 in the Third Test at his beloved Oval when rain stopped the game, leaving him with a series total of 24 for 298 at 12.41. It was a sensational start to a Test career. As Hardstaff predicted, he was on the boat heading downunder in September 1946.

It was a mixed tour for the medium-pacer. He liked the people and enjoyed the abundant hospitality, but his on-field experiences were not so memorable. Bedser faced Bradman, who was making a post-war comeback against all odds, and a powerful new batting line-up. Bradman was not quite as nimble as pre-war, but his determination more than made up for it.

In the First Test at Brisbane, Bedser had early success,

dismissing new opener Arthur Morris for 2 with the score at 9. But he had to wait another 313 runs before striking again, this time having Hassett caught for 128. By then the damage was done and Bradman went on to 187 in a score of 645. Bedser returned 2 for 159 from 41 overs.

He did worse in the Second Test at Sydney as Australia compiled another mammoth score—8 for 659, with Bradman and Sid Barnes collecting 234 each. Barnes was Bedser's only wicket at a cost of 153 from 46 overs.

He did better at Melbourne in the Third Test, taking 3 for 99, removing the most respectable trio of Barnes (45), Morris (21) and Lindwall (9). Bedser took another 3 good wickets in the second innings: Morris (155), McCool (43) and Lindwall (100). However, he was again expensive. The wickets cost 176 off 34.3 overs.

Bedser's reputation and confidence were given a huge boost in the Fourth Test at Adelaide early in January 1947. He bowled Merv Harvey for 12 and this brought Bradman to the wicket. Bedser had yet to take Bradman's wicket and had been treated harshly by him in the previous Tests in which Bradman had scored 187, 234, 79 and 49. The bowler was 'pumped', knowing that his chances of removing Bradman would be slim once he was settled. Bedser had to strike now. He delivered a couple of inswingers and then a faster leg-cutter.

Bradman remembered it decades later as if it were yesterday.

'It was delivered about three-quarters of the way straight on the off stump,' he said. 'It dipped suddenly to pitch on the leg stump. Then it turned off the pitch and hit the middle and off stumps.'

Was it the best ball Bradman ever faced?

'That's not easy to say,' he replied, 'but it was perhaps the best ball ever to take my wicket.'

This was a supreme compliment to Bedser, considering that Bradman was the most difficult batsman to remove in the history of the game. That delivery headed a list of 547 that caused Bradman's dismissal in his entire career, if 14 run outs and one hit wicket are not included.

In his career Bedser bowled plenty of similar deliveries that missed the off stump by a whisker.

He later added Morris' wicket to take 3 for 97 off 30 overs in his best display in Australia yet. He had a terrific duel with the new Australian left-hand opener, whom he dismissed five times in 8 innings. Morris' scores were 2, 5, 21, 155, 122, 124 not out, 57 and 17.

Bedser finished with 2 for 49 and 2 for 75 in the Fifth Test, giving him 16 wickets at a costly 54.75 and a dose of reality after his heady start against the Indians. In Australia in the Tests he sent down 246.3 overs and was the team workhorse. His renowned physical strength carried him through a summer that was mediocre for him and a disaster for England, who lost the Ashes 0:3.

He wrote in his autobiography, *Twin Ambitions*, that he was disillusioned with Hammond's less than ideal captaincy. Hammond wasn't nurturing or encouraging. He didn't discuss tactics much and he left field placings to the bowler. Like many in the team, Bedser resented Hammond's aloofness to the rest of the team between matches.

Bedser had a further Test against New Zealand on the 1946-47 tour, in which he took 4 for 95, and a short series against South Africa in 1947, where he returned the undistinguished figures of 4 for 233 at 58.25.

Against the Invincibles

The team Bradman brought to England in 1948 looked strong, particularly in batting. Bradman had been impressed by Bedser in Australia and anticipated that he would be even better in England.

Their first encounter on the tour was the Surrey v Australia match at The Oval beginning 8 May. Bradman scored 146 before Bedser bowled him with a glorious delivery. It pitched on leg stump and hit off, and reminded Bradman of the ball that bowled him for a duck at Adelaide in 1947. Australia won the game by an innings and 296 runs, but Bedser's effort in picking up 4—Bradman, Hassett (110), Johnson (46) and Lindwall (4)—for 104 off 40 overs ensured he would be in the England team for the First Test at Trent Bridge, beginning Thursday, 10 June. England won the toss, batted and collapsed for 165. Bedser was second-last man in and managed second-top score of 22.

By the end of the second day, Australia was 4 for 293, Bradman on 130 not out and Hassett on 42 not out. Bedser had bowled well to the very negative leg-side field set by his skipper Norman Yardley, which had reduced Bradman to the slowest scoring of his career. All bowlers concentrated on or outside leg stump. Only off-spinner Jim Laker (3 wickets) and Yardley (1) were successful.

After the day's play, a weary Bedser met Bill O'Reilly, now retired and covering the Tests as a journalist, for a beer at the Black Boy Hotel. Bedser complained that he couldn't get through Bradman by carrying out Yardley's negative directives. O'Reilly told Bedser how effective he had been in bowling to Bradman over the years (a claim not supported by the record). The Englishman didn't have to ask the former great leg-spinner how he thought he could remove Bradman—O'Reilly told him.

'Put in a backward short leg and feed him with inswingers,' O'Reilly advised. 'If you bowl on leg, swinging away, he can ignore it. He won't be able to resist going for something on middle and leg and swinging away. Braddles loves the mid-wicket, square-leg boundary. But if you bowl a quicker one, he may flick it to backward short leg.'

Bedser heeded the advice. He had tried everything else and failed. Why not this? He asked Yardley for a fielder, Hutton, in the new position. Bedser craftily bowled Bradman some innocuous deliveries down leg-side moving away and then bowled one on middle and leg, up enough to entice Bradman into an attacking stroke aiming at mid-wicket. Hutton caught him round the corner for 138. Bedser raised his arm in triumph to O'Reilly in the press box; the former leg-spinner couldn't hide his exuberance. Mentally, wily Bill felt he had been out there, wrestling with the Bowral Boy once more. Forget that Australia was playing the old enemy, O'Reilly would help dismiss Bradman every time.

Bedser added Hassett (bowled for 137) and Ernie Toshack (22) to his victims and ended with 3 for 113 off 44.2 overs with 12 maidens. It was a fair return given Australia's batting line-up, which gathered 509.

Australia needed only 98 to win in its second innings, and Bedser began well by bowling Morris for just 9. Bradman came in and the bowler brought Hutton into short backward square leg again. He tried the same ball as that which brought the first-innings dismissal. Bradman played a similar shot and again mishit to Hutton. He was out for a duck, his first in a Test in England. An elated Bedser had the world's number one batsman twice, the same way in the same match. It had never been done in Bradman's entire career. Bedser ended with 2 for 46, a consolation in an 8-wicket defeat for England.

In the Second Test at Lord's, Bedser was surprised and delighted to remove Bradman twice more—yet again snaffled by Hutton for 38, and then 89 in the second innings when Edrich, diving full length, took a one-handed 'blinder'. It meant that Bedser had now removed Bradman seven times in five successive matches against Australia: in the first innings of the Fourth Test at Adelaide in 1946-47; the second innings of the Fifth Test at Sydney in 1946-47; for Surrey in May 1948;

then each innings in the first two Tests of 1948. There was wild talk provoked by English journalists that Bradman was Bedser's 'bunny', but usually this applied to batsmen continually dismissed early. So far, Bradman had made 187, 234, 79 and 49 in the first three Tests of 1946-47 without Bedser dismissing him. Since then he had made 0 (bowled Bedser) and 56 not out at Adelaide (1946-47); 12 and 63 (caught Compton bowled Bedser); 146 v Surrey (bowled Bedser) in May 1948; then 138, 0, 38 and 89 (all falling to Bedser) in the first two Tests of 1948.

After the bunny remarks, Bradman was never dismissed by Bedser again, hitting 128 v Surrey in June–July 1948; 7 and 30 not out in the Third Test of 1948; 33 and 173 not out in the Fourth Test; and 0 in the Fifth Test of 1948.

In all, Bedser bowled in 15 innings against Bradman to dismiss him six times, but only twice cheaply (the 2 ducks). Bradman notched 6 centuries, including one double, and a further 3 fifties in those 15 knocks. These figures show that Bedser did not have more than an average impact on Bradman when compared with all the prominent bowlers who delivered to him. Nevertheless, Bedser caused him more concern than most in two decades of cricket.

The medium-pacer's 1948 Ashes series saw him collect 18 wickets at 38.22, an improvement on his 1946-47 figures, but still a far cry from his debut series against the Indians. Some critics claimed that his first series was a flash in the pan. Against top-class batsmen, it was said, he couldn't quite deliver the major spells of bowling that win Test matches and series. Bedser was 30 years old and his critics thought they were safe to make these pronouncements. His enormous toiling as England's leading bowler would surely take its toll, even on such a big-hearted character. But the determined Bedser had points to prove yet.

Over the next three series against South Africa away, and

New Zealand and the West Indies at home, Bedser didn't lift his rating. His figures were never near those of his opening series against India. He was relegated to 12th man in the First Test against the West Indies in 1950 in England and in the remaining three games took 11 wickets at 34.27. He had a memorable moment at Lord's in the Second Test when he took 5 for 31 in a pre-lunch session, after beginning the day with figures of 0 for 96. His dominant spells were very few as he encountered the West Indies stars Everton Weekes, Frank Worrell, Clyde Walcott and Roy Marshall at their peak on easy-paced pitches. The tourists won 3:1 and left the England selectors with major problems for the coming tour to Australia for the 1950-51 Ashes series.

A consolation for Bedser was that Surrey won the county championship, thanks in no small measure to his brother. In the final game of the season against Leicester at The Oval, Eric took 12 for 98.

At 32, Bedser felt that this was his last chance to achieve the sort of results that seemed possible in 1946—now nearly half a decade ago—and thus cement a place as one of England's finest-ever bowlers.

The 1950-51 Ashes series was the first not to feature—and be dominated by—Bradman since 1926. England, while not overstocked with top bowlers, was confident of at least doing better than on the last tour in 1946-47.

England was unlucky with the weather at Brisbane again, this time after dismissing Australia for 228, largely thanks to Bedser who took 4 for 45 off 16.5 overs, his best figures against Australia. His haul included Morris (LBW, 25), Harvey (caught behind, 74) and Hassett (bowled, 8)—about the most handsome trio, excluding Bradman, a bowler could snare.

The rain came down and England could only manage 7 for 68 before captain Freddie Brown declared. This desperate early innings termination paid off as Australia fared worse in the sticky conditions, falling apart to 7 for 32 before Hassett too declared, leaving England 193 to win. Bedser revelled in the favourable conditions. His drubbings at the hands of the West Indians just six months earlier were now only bad memories. He took 3 for 9 off 6.5 overs. This time he picked up Morris (caught, 0), Harvey (caught, 12) and Sam Loxton (caught, 0).

A match tally of 7 for 54 was a much-needed boost for Bedser, despite England falling short by 70 runs. The tourists went to Melbourne for the Second Test. The pitch was fast and the atmosphere heavy, just right for the swingers of Trevor Bailey (4 for 40) and Bedser (4 for 37). They both played to the conditions with glee. For the third successive time in an innings, Bedser sent back two of Australia's three best bats-men—Morris (caught, 2) and Harvey (caught behind, 42). The home team struggled to 194. *Wisden*'s reporter was impressed enough to call his bowling 'great'.

England fared little better when it batted, reaching 197, and it was soon up to its bowlers again. Bedser took 2 for 46 as Australia again slumped to all out for 181. This left England with just 179 to win, but the conditions also favoured Australia's bowlers Ray Lindwall (3 for 29) and Bill Johnston (4 for 26). England fell short once more, this time by just 28 runs. Australia was up 2:0 but the home team was by no means superior.

England happily batted first at Sydney, but failed to capi-talise on the opportunity with a mediocre 290. Bedser began well by bowling Morris for a duck—his third cheap dismissal out of four at Bedser's hands. But with Bailey and Doug Wright injured, England's bowling was depleted and too much was left to Bedser, Freddie Brown and Johnny Warr, making his Test debut. Bedser's bag—Ron Archer, Morris, Miller and Lindwall—was a worthy marathon effort as Australia reached 426, with skipper Hassett notching up 145 not out. Bedser conceded 107 runs off 43 eight-ball overs—equivalent to more than 57 six-ball overs and at a rate of less than two runs a six-ball over.

The tourists collapsed for 123 in their second innings, thus giving Australia a win by an innings and 13 runs. England had lost the elusive Ashes for the sixth successive time. Further humiliation was in store at Adelaide, despite Bedser making an early breakthrough by bowling Archer for another duck. Bedser tried to make sure Australia couldn't settle its opening batting positions, but Morris was overdue for runs and he batted like a champion hellbent on restoring his reputation. Morris reached 206 out of 371. Bedser bowled Harvey (43) before he could do damage and finished with the respectable figures of 3 for 74 off 26 overs.

England replied with 272, Hutton carrying his bat with 156 not out. Australia pushed England out of the game with 8 declared for 403 (Bedser 0 for 62) and then won it by dismissing the tourists for 228. Australia now led 4:0.

For the Fifth Test it was off to the fast Melbourne wicket once more. Hassett won the toss and batted, and yet again Bedser made the early breakthrough, putting back Jim Burke, a debut Test century-maker in Adelaide, on the faster MCG track for just 11 at 23. It was Freddie Brown's day for a good haul (5 for 49) and Bedser's turn to mop up the tail, which he did, taking 5 for 46 off 22 overs as Australia struggled to 217. England replied with 320 (Reg Simpson 156 not out), setting up the tourists' best chance for a win. Bedser came to the party early by dismissing Burke for 1 and Morris for 4, and later again ripped through the tail. He ended with 5 for 59 off 20.3 overs, and England was able to polish off the 95 runs, losing just 2 wickets. There was jubilation in the English camp, and it appeared as if they had won a series, not a dead rubber. Bedser was elated. It was his first win against Australia in 15 Tests. He was also well satisfied with his series figures. He took 30 wickets at 16.06, his best Test performance yet, and against top-quality batting.

'Although I never saw S F Barnes,' Bradman remarked, 'this level of performance would have to rank Alec with him.'

Bedser's 1950-51 effort was a big improvement from his 16 wickets at 54.75 in 1946-47. He was overworked on his first tour and delivered far more than any other apart from Doug Wright. In 1950-51 he still bowled 86 more overs than anyone else, but captain Freddie Brown more evenly distributed the work. Bedser could attack in shorter spells to obvious effect. He had also learned to move the ball after it had pitched by cutting across the seam. Bedser himself pointed out that he didn't have Bradman and Sid Barnes to contend with in 1950-51. Yet the Australian batting line-up in 1950-51—Archer, Morris, Harvey, Miller, Hassett—was still strong by world standards. Bedser removed Morris and Harvey five times each in his 30 wickets. (Morris and Harvey were each dismissed eight times in total.)

Phoenix in Royal Blue

England was rejuvenated by that Melbourne win. With more confidence than at any time since the war England met Dudley Nourse's South Africans in England for a five-Test series, beginning at Trent Bridge early in June 1951. Bedser maintained his Australian form and turned on a brilliant performance in South Africa's second innings. He was aided by the fine keeping of Godfrey Evans, who stood up to Bedser's medium-pacers. Evans noticed that batsman Jackie McGlew moved outside his crease when playing shots down the leg-side. In a mid-pitch discussion they decided that Bedser would deliver a slower ball (his fourth) outside leg stump. Evans moved across in anticipation. McGlew missed the ball and fell outside the crease as expected. Evans gathered the ball and whipped off the bails. It was as much the keeper's wicket as the bowler's. Bedser ended with the dominant figures of 6 for 37. England had 186 to chase but were spun out by Athol Rowan and 'Tufty' Mann for 114.

England regained their composure at Lord's after winning the toss and batting first. They scored 311, which was enough. Bedser took a backseat as Roy Tattersall, aided by a wet wicket in the first innings, captured 12 wickets for the match, which England won by 10 wickets. This was followed quickly by the Third Test at Manchester, which was wet and overcast. The dreary conditions were just right for Bedser's swing as he cut a swathe through South Africa's brittle batting, taking 7 for 58 in the first innings. His leg-cutter, which gained him four of the wickets, was deadly and he beat every batsman with it. His stamina allowed him to capture another 5 for 54 in the second innings, giving him 12 for 112 for the match. He also passed 150 wickets in Tests. England was set 139 to win and lost only 1 wicket in achieving the target. This gave the home team a 2:1 lead in the series.

Bedser was less pleased with the easy-paced pitch at the Fourth Test at Headingley. It took four days to complete a little more than two innings and he was happy to see the fifth day washed out. His only consolation in a batting-dominated game was to equal Maurice Tate's Test record for England of 155 wickets.

At the final Test at The Oval, South Africa won the toss, batted and was troubled by Jim Laker's off-spin. He took 4 for 64, while Freddie Brown and Bedser collected 2 each. South Africa reached an ordinary 202. England replied with 194, and Laker, with the pitch turning, took 6 for 55. South Africa collapsed for just 154. This left England with another chase— this time 163, which it made with 4 wickets to spare. England won the series 3:1, fulfilling the hopes and aspirations of the nation after the promise of the last Test in Australia. For the second successive time Bedser was the best bowler for the duration of the series, taking another 30 wickets at 17.23 apiece. His last 12 Tests, including two in New Zealand after the Australian tour, in a nine-month period had yielded 62 wickets at 16.50 each. His 1951 season in England was his best yet as he took 130 first-class wickets at 15.56, surpassing his 130 at 24.42 in 1947.

But there were even better things to come for this tireless 33-year-old.

Better Late

The Bedsers continued to star for Surrey in 1952 under its new skipper Stuart Surridge. Eric scored 1,723 runs at 35.16 and took 70 wickets at 21.85 in one of the best all-round records in county cricket. Alec missed nine matches for the county but showed what a champion he had become by taking 117 wickets at 16.11. He was hampered early in the season by a hip injury but paced himself well enough to be selected in a new-look England under Len Hutton, the first professional ever to be appointed captain. Fred Trueman, the young Yorkshire speedster, joined Bedser in opening the bowling, and over-shadowed his more experienced partner against India at Leeds in the First Test and during the Second at Lord's. England won both games comfortably. Bedser took four sets of 2 wickets—8 for 192 in all. Trueman did twice as well, taking 15 for 298.

Surrey had four players—Peter May, Jim Laker, Tony Lock and Bedser—in the Test at Manchester, the third of the series. Hutton set the tone by scoring a century and declaring at 9 for 347. Again Trueman was the key speedster as he rolled India in its first innings, taking 8 for 31. India slumped to all out for 58. Bedser, who took 2 for 19, found good form in the second innings, with 5 for 27 (while Lock took 4 for 26) as the tourists fell apart again, gathering just 82. England won the match comfortably, taking their lead in the series to 3:0. After South

Africa the previous season, England had the taste for Test wins, but was robbed of another victory by rain in the fourth and final game of the series at The Oval.

Bedser ripped through the Indians on the rain-affected pitch, taking 5 for 41, slightly better figures than Trueman's (5 for 48), as India capitulated under unfamiliar conditions for just 98.

Although Bedser became England's number two opening bowler for the first time in his Test career, he still took a remarkable 20 wickets at 13.95. He sent down a backbreaking 1,185.4 overs (296 maidens) and took 154 wickets at 16.42 for the 1952 season—a performance that would rank as one of the best in first-class cricket in the 20th Century. And all at the not-so-tender age of 34 years.

Bedser proved that he had reached the height of his powers and that his bowling had matured. His performances had been sustained from November 1950 through to September 1952, a 22-month period. However he would not be satisfied until he had been part of a winning Ashes combination. Time was running out. Bedser reckoned that 1953 had to be the year.

Bedser's Peak

England looked at the 1953 Australian tourists and acknowledged that the team's backbone of Hassett, Morris, Harvey, Miller, Lindwall and Johnston was still formidable. There would be a terrific scrap for the Ashes. Australia's Bill Johnston was set back by injury. England didn't have Trueman for the first four Tests. Illness, injury, poor form and national service kept him out.

1953 was Bedser's year and he gave everything for England and Surrey. He struck a psychological blow for England in the drawn First Test at Trent Bridge by taking 14 wickets for 99 runs.

Hutton lost the toss at Lord's in the Second Test and Australia batted steadily. Bedser couldn't get much swing in the lighter, sunnier Lord's atmosphere. He relied on guile and the skill of Evans behind the stumps. Bedser bowled one between Morris' bat and pads, which put the left-hander off balance and made him fall forward of the crease for a split second. It was enough for Evans, who whipped off the bails. Bedser later trapped Harvey (59) LBW and had the injured Hassett (104) caught. Australia's late-order batsmen, led by Alan Davidson (76) helped the tourists reach 346. Bedser sent down 42.4 overs with 8 maidens and took 5 for 105. England replied with 372 (Hutton 145, Graveney 78 and Compton 57).

Bedser took 3 for 77 in Australia's second innings of 368 (Miller 109, Morris 89 and Lindwall 50) and reached the magic figure of 200 Test wickets. His best effort in the second innings was to bowl the ever-dangerous Harvey for 21 and thus maintain an upper hand over Australia's number three. England managed to hang on for a draw when 50 runs shy of the target and with just 3 wickets in hand. Bedser now had 22 wickets in the two Tests, the same number as he had against India in the first two Tests of 1946. Bedser would have been content with that number for an entire series against Australia, but, barring injury and fatigue, which was setting in after two years of non-stop cricket, he had three more Tests and up to six innings in which to bowl.

In the first innings of the Third Test at Old Trafford Bedser snapped up Harvey for the fifth successive time in the series, but not before the dashing left-hander had scored 122. He also got rid of Morris (1), Miller (17), Hole (66) and Archer (5), giving him another grand Aussie haul and the figures of 5 for 115 off 45 overs with 10 maidens. Australia made 318 and England replied with 276. Morris, delivering the spinners that promised so much in his youth, bowled Bedser for 10 runs. He was still 15 wickets behind Bedser in their personal duel.

The rain killed the game but not before Australia collapsed in the sensational last 65 minutes of the match to be 8 for 35 at the end of play. Bedser took another 2 for 14 off four overs with 1 maiden (Johnny Wardle took 4 for 7). He now had 29 wickets.

The three Tests had been drawn and pressure mounted in the Fourth at Headingley. Hassett won the toss and sent England in on a pitch that may have retained some moisture. Lindwall (5 for 54) promptly bowled Hutton for a duck in front of his home crowd, and this set a pattern as England collapsed for 167. Australia was dogged in response, but Bedser did the damage once more, taking Morris (10) for the 17th time in Tests, and fellow opener Hassett (37). Bedser went on to take 6 for 95 off 28.5 overs with 2 maidens as Australia climbed to 266, which put them 99 ahead. Despite the big bag, the medium-pacer was not happy. He felt that giving away 3.5 runs an over was sinful under the conditions. Nevertheless, he passed Clarrie Grimmett's world-record number of Test wickets (216), which was immensely satisfying and against all odds. Bedser's late start and years of ordinary returns after his Indian beginning had made him a long shot to becoming the world's greatest wicket-taker. For a lad who dreamed of playing for Surrey at best, Bedser had travelled a hard road to the top.

England fared better in the second innings with 275, leaving Australia to get 177 in a shade under two hours. When the tourists looked likely to reach the target, Trevor Bailey shut the gate by bowling wide down the leg-side to a packed leg-side field. The tactics destroyed the game as a spectacle but saved England as Australia lost four wickets in reaching 147, just 30 short. Bedser's sole wicket was Harvey LBW for 34. He now had 36 wickets with one Test to play, at his beloved Oval. Maurice Tate's record of 38 wickets in an Ashes series was in his sights.

For the Fifth Test England was strengthened by the return of Trueman (4 for 86 in the first innings). Bedser again dominated the opposition's early order, who had never settled against his swingers throughout the series. He removed Morris LBW (16) and Hassett (53) caught behind and this helped keep Australia's first innings score down to 275. Hassett's wicket drew Bedser level with Tate. When he caught and bowled Ron Archer, the world record was his. Bedser's figures were 3 for 88 off 29 overs with 3 maidens. England's answer was 306 (Hutton 82, Bailey 64). Lock (5 for 45) and Laker (4 for 75) ran through Australia for 162, leaving England 132 to win, which they reached with 8 wickets in hand. The Ashes were England's after two decades, and the nation rejoiced.

'It was the greatest satisfaction of my life to be a member of the England team that carried off the Ashes,' Bedser said.

He was the main reason England won, taking a world-record 39 wickets at 17.48 each. He secured 162 first-class wickets for the season (eight more than in 1952), his best-ever total, and at the most economical rate of 16.67.

Bedser had an enormous influence on Surrey winning seven successive championships from 1952 to 1958. In each of the first six years he took more than 80 wickets at a cost of less than 19. *Wisden*, Bedser himself, Trevor Bailey (one of 17 players to share the new ball with him) and Bradman all thought that Bedser was at his peak from 1950 to 1954.

'The quality of his bowling on all types of pitches and under varying conditions was as near to perfection as I have encountered,' observed Bailey.

Bedser's international career came to an abrupt and disappointing end in 1955. He began the 1954-55 tour of Australia at 36 years old and rated as the world's best bowler. But he encountered ill health, brought on perhaps by the continual grind of cricket at an age when most bowlers of his type have long ago put their feet up and become spectators.

Bedser's main problem was painful and debilitating shingles early in the tour. He played in the First Test at Brisbane though he was still unfit, and ended with 1 for 131 off 37 overs and 4 maidens. His only wicket was Harvey, whom he had caught at 162. England lost by a whopping innings and 154 runs, and Bedser was dropped for the Second Test at Sydney. Hutton preferred the potency of speed men Frank Tyson and Brian Statham, in part to counter Australia's Lindwall and Miller, who had given so much trouble to England for eight years after the war. Bedser's illness had impacted on his form and fitness, and now his place in the side. After England won in Sydney by just 38 runs, Hutton decided not to change the team for the Third Test at Melbourne on a pitch that would have aided Bedser's bowling.

Bedser, fitter and with his shingles subsiding, thought he would be back in the team in place of Appleyard or Statham, who took 5 wickets in Sydney and bowled well in supporting Tyson, who took 10 wickets. He was stunned to learn of his omission when he read the team list pinned up in the dressing room. It upset Bedser that Hutton, for whom he had the highest regard, did not tell him face-to-face. (Hutton later admitted he erred in not personally telling the bowler who had done the most of anyone to help preserve his record as a successful England skipper.) The bowlers, led by Tyson, kept doing well, pushing the tourists to a 3:1 Ashes victory. Bedser could not regain his place. He played one more Test at home in the summer of 1955 against South Africa, as a late replacement for the injured Statham. At 37, and with England now well served by Statham, Tyson, Lock, Laker and Trueman there was no place for him.

His Test record read 236 wickets at 24.89 runs apiece. He sent down 1,730.3 overs to get them with a remarkable 560 maidens—almost one in three overs delivered—making him not only one of the great strike bowlers of all time, but one of the most economical as well.

Despite his lapse downunder and the termination of his Test career, his form did not fall away. Bedser remained a Test-standard player relegated to the county championship and out of favour with the national selectors. In 1955, he collected 144 wickets at home for 19.11 each, hardly a noticeable slide from the peak of his strike-power in 1953. He continued to dominate the championship and Surrey was most pleased to have him full-time as it cleaned up championship after championship. In England in 1956 he took 96 first-class wickets at 20.31; in 1957 he took 131 at 16.56; in 1958, when restricted by injury, and 40 years old, he took 48 at 17; in 1959 he took 91 at 24.26; and in his final year of top cricket, 1960, he took 67 at 25.80.

Alec Bedser could well have carried on for several years, but at 42 years of age and after a career spanning 22 years, it was time to hang up the boots. He took 1,924 first-class wickets at 20.41 runs each. They were harvested from 15,346.4 overs—with 4,406 maidens.

The Bedser twins invested their Surrey benefits in an office equipment company that had become most profitable by the mid-1960s. In 1962 Alec became an England selector and remained so for 23 years. For 13 of those years he was chairman of the panel. He also managed tours of Australia, New Zealand and India, and became an MCC and Surrey committee member. In 1987 he became President of the Surrey club, a position that forced him to give up his long career as a Test selector. He was later knighted for his enormous service to the game.

Don Bradman's choice at number nine brought both enormous skill and tactical intelligence to the team.

CHAPTER 12

TIGER
OF SPIN

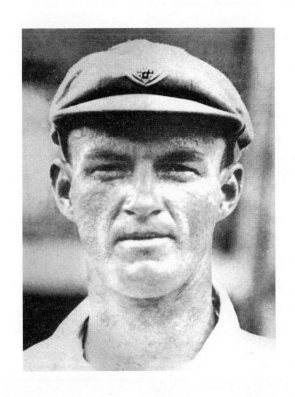

WILLIAM JOSEPH O'REILLY

10

(Australia)

20 December 1905—6 October 1992

Follow-through of Grace and Strength. Alec Bedser demonstrates his balance and force after delivery.

The Bedsers and Friends. Don Bradman meets his good friends Alec (left) and Eric Bedser at Adelaide airport during the 1950-51 Ashes tour of Australia. The other man is C. A. Middleton, chairman of Australia's then Board of Control. England won the last Test of the series, the first time Alec experienced victory over Australia.

The Swarm of Bees. Don Bradman described Bill O'Reilly as coming at the batsman like a swarm of bees. His height allowed him to extract good bounce, and he delivered at just under medium pace. These factors made him the hardest of all spinners to keep out.

Opposite: The Nottingham Sevens. Alec Bedser receives the plaudits coming off the Trent Bridge ground during the First Test of the 1953 Ashes series. He took 7 for 55 and 7 for 44 in the drawn game.

Above: Striding Out. This side-on shot taken during a New South Wales v Victoria game shows Bill O'Reilly's exceptional stride.

Left: The Don and Tiger. In 1976, Don Bradman and Bill O'Reilly walk from the Bradman Oval at Bowral for the last time together. Whatever their differences, Bradman regarded O'Reilly as the best bowler he ever faced or saw play in 80 years of cricket.

Round-arm Revival. Clarrie Grimmett's round-arm delivery reminded older fans and cricketers of a style more typical of the 19th century than the 1920s and 1930s.

Left: Capped and Courageous.
Clarrie Grimmett always
bowled wearing a cap. He
had to persevere more than
most players before entering
Test cricket at the age of 32.
He made the most of his 12
years at the top, taking 216
wickets at 24.21.

*Below: They Seek Him Here,
They Seek Him There.*
Grimmett was variously
known as 'Scarl', after the
Scarlet Pimpernel, the Fox,
because of his cunning ways
with the ball, and simply
'Old Grum'. Here, he
delivers a ball that rises above
eye level and drifts down into
the batsman's 'blind spot', a
Grimmett specialty.

Hammond's Drive. Don
Bradman judged Wally
Hammond as England's most
forceful and best batsman.

Below: In His Prime. Wally Hammond strides out to bat during the Third Test of the 1936-37 Ashes series in Melbourne. He was 33, and England's best bat of the 1930s.

Above: Grinners Are Good Tossers. Wally Hammond and Don Bradman (straight from his stockbroking office) watch the spinning coin before the England versus South Australia game of October 1946. Hammond won the toss. A frail Bradman struggled his way to 76 in 150 minutes in his first post-war match after a long illness.

Left: Two Great Rivals. Bradman and Hammond greet each other in a cordial moment. They were the two major rivals and biggest scorers of the cricket world for 20 years, yet Bradman said their personal rivalry was overplayed.

> *'He was the greatest bowler*
> *I ever faced or saw.'*
>
> SIR DONALD BRADMAN

Bill O'Reilly marked out his run to open the bowling for Australia against England in the Second Test at Melbourne in the bodyline series of 1932-33. It was unusual to attack with a spinner—but O'Reilly, known as 'Tiger' for his ferocious approach to bowling, was no ordinary spinner. He had the reputation of being the best deliverer of leg-spin, top-spin and the wrong'un at such speed that at times he was not far off medium pace. Now the burden was on this country-raised schoolteacher to turn the game around for his country. In the first innings, 64,000 spectators at the MCG saw Australia dismissed for 228. Don Bradman, playing in his first innings of the series, had first ball pulled a short delivery from Bill Bowes onto his stumps. His duck had stunned the crowd, and the nation. Now Australia's bowlers had to perform against a low score on a docile pitch. England's batting line-up was one of its best ever—Sutcliffe, Wyatt, Hammond, Nawab of Pataudi, Leyland, Jardine, Ames and Allen. Larwood at number nine could make runs and wasn't a regular bunny. Sutcliffe, Hammond and the Nawab were coming off centuries in the First Test won by England by 10 wickets.

The 27-year-old O'Reilly was under pressure. He had come late to Test ranks, taking 10 wickets in three Tests—7 in two Tests v South Africa in the previous Australian summer.

Suddenly the burden of being a key strike bowler was his. Yet the 191 cm (6 ft 3 in), lanky, athletic bowler, who had started with Wingello in the New South Wales country and then the North Sydney Cricket Club, was ready. He had supreme self-confidence. O'Reilly's aggressive, intelligent approach to his cricket was something special.

He opened steadily in the Melbourne Test, imparting little spin but bowling accurately. At 30, after bowling mainly leg-breaks and wrong'uns to both openers, he squeezed a top-spinner into Bob Wyatt's pads for an LBW decision. Paceman Tim Wall then bowled Wally Hammond for 8. O'Reilly pinned the Nawab back on his stumps for several overs. It was the best way to play this leg-spinner, the English rightly thought. The problem was, it was a tough way to score. The Nawab began to lose patience. Sensing this, O'Reilly sent him down a fast leg-break. The Nawab danced, but to the bowler's tune. The ball spun past his bat and Bert Oldfield stumped him neatly. England was soon 4 for 98 as Wall had the stubborn Herbert Sutcliffe (52) caught. Six runs later, Wall brought the biggest cheer for the day from the huge crowd when he had the England skipper, Douglas Jardine, caught behind for 1. Moments later, Wall bowled Leslie Ames and England was 6 for 110.

O'Reilly kept the pressure on, bowling Larwood (9) and finally removing Gubby Allen (30) as England was all out for 169.

O'Reilly walked off the MCG to a standing ovation. His 5 for 63 off 34.3 with 17 maidens was a fine effort. It thrust him into the limelight at a moment when Australia was desperate for a hero—anyone—to fight against Douglas Jardine and his talented troupe. Despite his gregarious, sometimes blustering Irish nature, O'Reilly was not going to get a swollen head. He set high standards for himself and this was just a first major attainment, in what he hoped and expected would be a long career for Australia.

Australia responded poorly in its second innings, except that Bradman this time played a great innings and remained 103 not out in a total of 191. This left England 241 to make to win. The odds were with the tourists. The pitch seemed to be holding up well and was still good for batting despite the dominance of the ball in the three innings so far. At the end of the third day, England was 0 for 44 with Sutcliffe, in attacking mood, on 33 not out and Maurice Leyland, opening instead of Wyatt, subdued on 10 not out.

England now had plenty of time for victory. Australian captain Woodfull decided that O'Reilly was his best bet at the beginning of the fourth and what was expected to be the final day. In his second over of the morning, he bowled Sutcliffe (33) with a fast wrong'un. Without addition to the score (53), Wall bowled Leyland (19). In the space of a few deliveries the game's momentum had shifted. England was still 198 short of victory with 8 wickets in hand. Woodfull brought on Bert 'Dainty' Ironmonger, then 49 years old and still a more than handy left-hand, first-finger spinner. His slow-medium deliveries had the Nawab (5) and Jardine (0) caught and back in the pavilion with the score at 70.

The game's complexion had now changed dramatically. England had 6 wickets in hand and another 181 to make. Chances for a win were about even. But O'Reilly changed all that in a devastating second spell by having Hammond (23) and Voce (0) caught by O'Brien, and Ames (2) caught by Fingleton. He was well supported by Ironmonger, who had Allen (23) stumped and Larwood (4) caught. England crashed to all out for 139, giving Australia a win by 111 runs.

Once stumps and bails had been souvenired, O'Reilly—5 for 66 off 24 overs with 5 maidens (10 for 129 for the game)—led Australia off the ground once more. The appreciative Melbourne crowd gave him a tremendous send-off.

'I felt 10-feet tall,' O'Reilly remarked. 'It was the first such reception (for me) in a Test and we had levelled the series.'

This game marked the beginning of a secure spot for O'Reilly in the Australian team, which he did not relinquish until his retirement in 1946.

A Lesson for the Teacher

O'Reilly's other sporting love through his late teens was athletics—especially the long jump, which was then known as the hop-step-and-jump. He became a member of athletics club Botany Harriers when he moved to Sydney from the small country town of Wingello, 166 km southwest of Sydney (not far from Bradman's home town of Bowral). It helped the young O'Reilly when he turned to spin bowling. His angular frame and long, loose limbs gave him the appearance of an over-heated electric fan, but he had the balance and rhythm to direct the ball with unerring accuracy.

He began a two-year course as a trainee teacher in 1924 and played in the Moore Park Saturday morning competition, building a reputation as a big wicket-taker. Moore Park had produced several champions, including Victor Trumper, Alan Kippax and Arthur Mailey. O'Reilly played for the David Jones XI for two seasons and topped the bowling averages. He bowled pace at first but turned to spin and developed a slower, well-concealed wrong'un. O'Reilly's grip was unorthodox. He held the ball closer to the palm than the fingers. This curtailed his spin but, because of his strong wrists, gained speed and accuracy. The unusual style also allowed for greater and more effective changes in pace. O'Reilly flighted the ball deceptively, and his height helped him exact lift from the pitch, especially with his faster ball.

Each summer the young student returned home for two months' vacation and played with Wingello in the Berrima

District competition. In December 1925, the end of his second year at college, O'Reilly took the train home but was taken off some stops early so he could play for Wingello against Bowral at Bowral. He had been seconded to counter a local young batting sensation whose name was Don Bradman. O'Reilly had already heard of him.

Bowral won the toss and batted. O'Reilly was given the new ball and bowled an opener in his first over. The diminutive figure of Bradman, then 17 years old, walked out to the wicket, his pads seeming to flap against his stomach. It was up to O'Reilly to knock over this emerging local star and uphold Wingello's good name in this battle with rival Bowral. He was ready and confident. His quick leg-breaks would bounce high on the coir matting, which always favoured spin.

O'Reilly's first ball to the new man was pulled off the back foot through mid-wicket for 4. The next ball was lifted first bounce over the mid-on boundary. O'Reilly was stunned. In his second over, he pitched up more and drew Bradman forward. Bradman took 3 twos off him with superb placement. The spinner's third over was his best. Bradman nicked a fast-turning leg-break pitched on middle stump. It flew low and fast to Wingello captain, Selby Jeffrey, at slip. He spilled the tough chance. O'Reilly gesticulated furiously, not at the respected Jeffrey, an Anzac veteran, but at his own ill luck. In the fifth over, with Bradman on 29, O'Reilly bowled a well-flighted top-spinner. The batsman mishit and the ball just squeezed past Selby's outstretched hand. Bradman would not give another opportunity for two hours of the most remarkable batting anyone on either side, or among the several hundred spectators, had witnessed. Bradman chopped and carved all of Wingello's bowlers to pieces. O'Reilly responded, Bradman noted, 'like a disturbed hive of bees. He seemed to attack from all directions.'

On that hot December afternoon, Bradman was the beekeeper, hitting O'Reilly for 4 of 6 sixes. The spinner's length was destroyed as the pint-sized batsman danced down the wicket and swatted his deliveries through and over the arc from square leg to mid-on. He even used his feet to position the ball through gaps on the off. O'Reilly's anger turned to resignation and finally defeat as Bradman smacked his first century, then a double. His last 50 included 48 in boundaries—4 sixes and 6 fours. His 234 not out took him 165 minutes.

O'Reilly left the ground demoralised and thankful that he had other sports to play, as this would surely finish his promising cricket aspirations. He had to bowl to this dynamo the following Saturday, on the Wingello pitch. The thought depressed him all week ... but what a difference seven days make.

O'Reilly opened the bowling again and, to his dread, it was Bradman, ready to advance his score another hundred, he was facing. O'Reilly let go his orthodox leg-break on leg stump. Bradman moved forward. The ball spun past the bat and crashed into the top of the off stump. O'Reilly was thrilled. His self-confidence returned in a flash. Yet it would not be fully restored until years later when he truly understood the force he had encountered from the little hamlet close to his.

O'Reilly began his teaching career in Sydney in 1926. Within that year, he played his first game in first-grade cricket with North Sydney. It was against Balmain, which featured the dashing young teenage batsman Archie Jackson. This elegant player already had a big reputation so O'Reilly was wary, the Bradman experience still fresh in his mind. His chance to bowl to Jackson came in Balmain's second innings. The spinner concentrated on line and length, forcing Jackson to defend right back on his stumps. Jackson, unlike Bradman, took no liberties with him. O'Reilly snared 37 wickets at 17 runs apiece for the season. His best effort, 6 for 25, was against Northern Districts, and it included a hat trick. He also took 5 for 82 against Paddington. No batsman found him easy or dominated him, and, at 21, O'Reilly was already marked down by selectors and commentators as a future state and Test player.

In the following 1927-28 season, O'Reilly was selected to play in his initial first-class match, for New South Wales against New Zealand in Sydney. He took 2 for 37 from 10.6 overs, and 1 for 53 off 16 overs. This was followed by his first Shield game against Queensland at Brisbane. Rain ruined the match and he went away with the figures of 0 for 43. He played against Tasmania at Sydney and took 4 for 35 off 8.6 overs and 0 for 21 off 5. He was relegated to the New South Wales Second XI for a couple of matches. In one, against Victoria at Sydney early in 1928, he took 0 for 46 off 18 overs, and 3 for 42 off 16 overs. (Bradman also played for New South Wales in this game, scoring 43 and 8.)

O'Reilly continued his good form in first-grade cricket for North Sydney. According to North Sydney's yearbook, O'Reilly was 'the most promising bowler the club has turned out in many years'. He took 14 wickets at 24.12 before the New South Wales Department of Education transferred him to Griffith, 700 km from Sydney, because he was 'a nuisance', presumably as he took time off to play cricket. The move ruined any chance he had of playing for Australia during the 1928-29 tour by England. It also robbed him of a place in the 1930 squad sent to get the Ashes back.

He returned to Sydney early in 1931 to teach history, English, geography and business principles at Kogarah Intermediate High School. He'd been three years in the cricket wilderness with limited opportunities to play the game against quality opposition. However, during that three-year hiatus he kept bowling and working on his wrong'un and other difficult balls. He didn't bother with the flipper, which he thought was a waste of time.

'I didn't need one,' he said often.

He was 25 years old and needed to consolidate. He took 29 wickets at 14.72 for North Sydney in the last few months of the 1930-31 season, too late to force his way back into the state side. O'Reilly had to wait until the next season. He wasn't selected for the opening game of 1931-32 but was chosen for the next against South Australia in which he took 1 for 61 and 1 for 20.

O'Reilly was taking bags of wickets in Sydney first-grade competition but he needed a good haul in a state game to give the Test selectors, who were keen to bring on a leg-spinner, confidence he could go one step further. He provided them with excuses to pick him in a game against Victoria at Melbourne in which he took 5 for 22 off 9.1 overs and 2 for 112 off 35.7 overs with 6 maidens. O'Reilly was a shock bowler in the first innings and a stock bowler in the second. His all-round performance stayed with the selectors, who picked him for the Fourth Test against South Africa at Adelaide beginning 29 January 1932. Australia had won the first three Tests.

Into the Test Arena

O'Reilly was 26, and making the most of the limited opportunities presented to him. Australia's pace bowling was weak, with Stan McCabe, a medium-pace trundler, opening the bowling. The spinners were dominant in South Africa's first innings. O'Reilly bowled 39.4 overs with 10 maidens and took 2 for 74, while Grimmett dominated with 7 for 116 off 47 overs with 11 maidens. O'Reilly was understudy to Grimmett, and he bowled with fine control and no batsman could get on top. He went for less than two runs an over.

South Africa scored 308, and Australia replied with Bradman hitting a fine double hundred. O'Reilly came to the wicket with the score at 8 for 215, with Bradman on 227 not out. They put on 78, with O'Reilly contributing 23, an impressive debut Test effort with the bat. Bradman was 280 not out when O'Reilly departed, and just missed his third triple century in Tests, with 299 not out in a score of 513. South Africa hit 274 in its second innings and again Grimmett, taking a further 7 for 83 off 49.2 overs with 17 maidens, overshadowed O'Reilly (2 for 81 off 42 overs with 13 maidens).

O'Reilly's performances were enough to gain him selection at Melbourne for the Fifth Test, even when the selectors added Bert Ironmonger to the side. Australia, playing without an injured Bradman, managed just 153 (of which O'Reilly hit another creditable 13) on a rain-affected pitch. South Africa fared even worse, managing just 36. O'Reilly and Grimmett were not required as Laurie Nash (4 for 18) and Ironmonger (5 for 6) ran through the visitors. It was the same story in South Africa's second innings, with Ironmonger taking 6 for 18 as South Africa crumbled to all out for 45. Woodfull gave O'Reilly a chance this time and he found the treacherous pitch to his liking, taking 3 for 19 off 9 overs with 5 maidens.

His overall returns for the two Tests—7 wickets for 174 at 24.85—were enough for him to make the side again for the Ashes series against Jardine's team in 1932-33.

The First Test was at Sydney and Woodfull won the toss and batted. England, for the first time ever, employed 'fast leg-theory', where a paceman bounced the ball at the ribcage and head of the batsman. If well executed, this bowling usually led to one of three results: the batsman would take evasive action; he would defend and risk being caught in a packed close leg-side field; or he would step away and attempt to make runs on the off-side. Whichever way, the style increased the chances of being out. Most of the Australians (Bradman was ill and missed the game) succumbed to these tactics, except for McCabe, who held up Larwood and Voce with one of the greatest batting displays ever in Test cricket.

The eighth wicket fell at 300 (McCabe 137 not out) and O'Reilly, full of trepidation, made his way from the dressing room to bat against England for the first time. His skipper, Woodfull, told him not to get hit. O'Reilly obliged. Larwood trapped him LBW for a duck and he left the wicket unscathed, to both his and his captain's relief. Tim Wall stayed with McCabe (187 not out) and Australia reached 360.

England replied with 524 (Sutcliffe 194, Hammond 112, Nawab of Pataudi 102) and O'Reilly stood up well to the pressures and rigours of an Ashes Test. He took 3 for 117 in a marathon spell off 67 overs with 32 maidens. Australia collapsed for 164 to the force of the 'leg-theory' tactic—known after this game as 'bodyline'—giving the tourists a 10-wicket win. The English had decided to counter O'Reilly by 'going defensive' and turning over the strike when facing him. A team meeting had decided that his fast leg-breaks and disguised wrong'un were too dangerous to take on.

O'Reilly's stocks went up in the second bodyline Test at Melbourne—his fourth—in which he took 10 for 129. Had there been a man-of-the-match award, he would have just pipped Bradman, who scored a dashing century against Larwood, Voce and Bowes.

O'Reilly opened the bowling in the Third Test at Adelaide after Jardine had won the toss and batted. The England skipper (3) was soon bowled by Wall, who then took a catch from Sutcliffe (9) off O'Reilly. Wall got one to jump off a good length to have Hammond (2) caught behind and leave England 3 for 16. However, Leyland (83) and Wyatt (78) restored England before O'Reilly struck again and bowled Leyland. England crawled to 7 for 236 at stumps. They played O'Reilly with the caution of the First Test, but he was well satisfied with his performance on a dull day. England went on to 341 thanks mainly to Paynter (77), and O'Reilly finished with 2 for 82 off 50 overs with 19 maidens. Wall took 5 for 72.

Australia was attacked by Larwood at his most ferocious in front of a crowd that went close to rioting after Woodfull received some fearful blows. On the third day, Oldfield (41) held England up until Larwood cracked his skull with a bouncer which the batsman tried to hook. Oldfield was carried off to hospital. The home side was all out for 222. Resentment and bitterness had now been generated between the sides.

In its second innings, England consolidated with 412. O'Reilly, for the third time in four innings, had the best figures, taking 4 for 79 off 50.3 overs with 21 maidens. Australia crumbled for 193, with Woodfull carrying his bat, 73 not out, and Bradman on a *too* dashing 66. This gave England the Test by 338 runs.

O'Reilly was Australia's outstanding bowler so far in the series with 19 wickets at 21.42. He entered the Fourth Test buoyed by his good form but apprehensive about the workload he would have to carry because of Australia's weak attack. The Australian selectors had omitted Grimmett, with whom O'Reilly enjoyed bowling.

Woodfull won the toss and batted. Vic Richardson (83), Woodfull (67) and Bradman (76) batted well to help Australia to 340. England's reply towards the end of day two was slow, with Jardine the main offender. He took more than 90 minutes to score one run.

O'Reilly was the pick of the bowlers for the fourth time in five games, taking 4 for 120 off 67.4 overs (equivalent to 90 six-ball overs) with 27 maidens. His haul included Jardine (46), Sutcliffe (86) and Leyland (12) as England compiled 356. It was his longest bowling stint yet. Australia crumbled again to Larwood in the second innings and was all out for 175, giving England a puny target of 162, which they reached with 6 wickets in hand. O'Reilly took 1 for 65 off 30 overs with 11 maidens.

One night during the game, Jardine invited O'Reilly to join the England team's dinner. Not being a batsman with any grievances or bruises because of bodyline, he took up the invitation. O'Reilly said in his biography, *Tiger*, that he saw it as a chance to observe this 'Cromwellian' character at close quarters.

In the final Test at Sydney, Australia managed 435 with an even effort in which six batsmen scored between 42 and 85. At last, Australia's wafer-thin attack, made even lighter by Grimmett's continued omission, had something to defend. England demonstrated the hold they had on the series by making 454, a lead of 19. O'Reilly picked up the openers, Sutcliffe (56) and Jardine (18), whom he had bamboozled throughout the series, and later added Wyatt (51). His figures of 3 for 100 off 45 overs with 7 maidens showed his reliability.

Despite the efforts of Woodfull (67) and Bradman (71) at the top of the order, Australia fell apart in its second innings due to pressure from Voce and the guile of left-arm spinner, Hedley Verity. Australia's score of 182 left England just 164 to win, which they reached with 8 wickets in hand. Under the strict discipline of Jardine the tourists had won the Ashes back with a 4:1 thrashing.

O'Reilly took 27 wickets for the series at 26.81 apiece. He sent down 383 eight-ball overs and conceded an economic 722 runs. Only Larwood with 33 wickets at 19.51 did better. O'Reilly and Bradman were easily Australia's best performers in that sorry Ashes series. The spinner had his best season of cricket, taking 62 first-class wickets at 19.95.

History Lessons

At the end of the 1932-33 season O'Reilly had a steady job and a place in the national team. May 1933 was as good a time as any to marry his true love, Molly Herbert. Their first home was in Hudson Street, Hurstville, Sydney where a young Ray Lindwall and his mates would try to catch O'Reilly's eye playing street cricket.

The leg-spinner began the 1933-34 season with high hopes for a trip to England for the 1934 Ashes. He was troubled early in the season by pulled rib muscles and fared poorly in a Test trial game, which was also a testimonial match to Don Blackie and Bert Ironmonger, between V Y Richardson's XI and W M Woodfull's XI. O'Reilly took 0 for 78. O'Reilly's rivals—Fleetwood-Smith, Grimmett and Ironmonger, who was retiring—fared little or no better. O'Reilly had just five Shield games to prove himself, and secured his place on the boat to England by his performances in two of them. He took 13 for 111 against Queensland and 9 for 50 in one innings against Victoria (12 for 142 for the match). His first-class figures, 38 wickets at 22.63, were consistent with the previous year. It was clear now after three first-class seasons in succession that O'Reilly was a three-in-one: a strike bowler who could open, a stock bowler who could keep batsmen under control, and a fierce spinner who could turn a game on a conducive pitch. Only three batsmen at grade, state or Test level had ever mastered him in at least one innings—Bradman for Bowral and St George, Stan McCabe at Mosman, and Gordon's Ray Robinson—with only Bradman having his measure on most occasions. These were three exceptional batsmen in the history of the game. (Bradman regarded Robinson as one of the finest batsmen, in style and technique, he had seen.)

The tour of England in 1934 was a dream come true for O'Reilly, not just because he was to play an Ashes series in England. His Irish-Catholic working-class roots would not allow him to love the English, but he loved history. After the five-weeks at sea, O'Reilly was in an excellent frame of mind when the RMS *Orford* docked at Southampton.

Early in the tour the team was invited to Windsor Castle

where they met Queen Mary and King George. At a function in the early 1960s attended by McCabe, Bradman and others, O'Reilly said that when he met Queen Mary he couldn't help thinking how difficult it would be being married to her and 'coming home at 2.00 am'.

'Difficult Bill, to imagine you married to an old queen,' McCabe quipped.

O'Reilly took a great interest in the relics at the Castle. He and Stan McCabe were able to inspect the musket ball that killed Lord Horatio Nelson at the Battle of Trafalgar.

'Don't show it to Clarrie (Grimmett),' McCabe said, 'he'll try to bowl it.'

With his knowledge of history replenished, O'Reilly proceeded to Trent Bridge, Nottingham, for the First Test and a chance to make his own name, a little more modestly, in history. Woodfull won the toss and Australia batted evenly with eight batsmen contributing between 20 and 99 to reach 374. When England replied with 268, O'Reilly retained the control he had over the opposition in the bodyline series, sending down 37 overs (16 maidens) and taking 4 for 75. His bag contained Hammond (25), Hendren (79) and Ames (7). Grimmett did better with 5 for 81. Woodfull declared Australia's second innings at 8 for 273, leaving England 380 to make to win. After an hour some English optimists began to think they could save the game. But at 51, O'Reilly had Sutcliffe (24) caught. From then on there was a steady procession of batsmen back to the pavilion until England was 9 for 137. Time was ticking away. The end of play, and the match, was looming. O'Reilly had 3 wickets and Grimmett 3. Woodfull crowded the last two batsmen, Verity and Mitchell. O'Reilly and Grimmett were on, appealing for LBW's. There were now just 10 minutes left. O'Reilly trapped Mitchell LBW and England was all out 141—238 short.

'Grimmett and O'Reilly overshadowed all else,' England's

former Test all-rounder Percy Fender said. He hadn't seen finer bowling by slow bowlers on a wicket that wasn't wet. O'Reilly's remarkable figures, his best yet in a Test, read 7 for 54 off 41.4 overs with 24 maidens. Grimmett took 3 for 39. The spinners had taken all 10 second-innings wickets and 8 in the first, giving them all but 2 to fall. O'Reilly's match figures were 11 for 129.

In the Second Test the firmer Lord's wicket allowed England to score 440, with Leyland and Ames both scoring centuries. O'Reilly took just 1 for 70 off 38 overs with 15 maidens. He was not penetrating, yet no England batsman could take control of him. They simply defended, using their pads and turning over the strike. Australia had crumbled to 8 for 273 when O'Reilly came to the wicket. It needed just 17 to avoid the follow on. Arthur Chipperfield was in form at the other end. Verity was bowling his left-arm spinners, which turned in from the off to O'Reilly, who batted left-handed. When Australia was six runs short of its target, O'Reilly went for some heroics and tried to heave Hedley Verity into the members' pavilion Long Room, but was bowled for 4. Then Verity trapped Wall LBW. Australia was all out for 284 and 6 runs short of saving the follow on. Verity, the destroyer, took 7 for 61.

O'Reilly was pondering, helplessly, what he could have done on the Lord's wicket, which was beginning to turn. He blamed himself for the next miserable period in which Australia (118) again collapsed to Verity, who took 8 for 43, giving him the sensational match figures of 15 for 104. O'Reilly was left to wonder what might have been. It was another lesson well learnt.

It was one-all as the teams marched on to Old Trafford. England won the toss and batted, and were sailing along nicely but slowly on the dead wicket in the extreme heat of early July when O'Reilly struck. He had Walters (52) caught at short leg by Darling to make England 1 for 68. Next ball he bowled Wyatt. Two for 68. Hammond came in. The Gloucester champion drove him for 4, then next ball O'Reilly clean-bowled him too. O'Reilly had 3 wickets in four deliveries and England was 3 for 72. He had delivered one of the great overs in Test and Ashes history.

England made a recovery, with Sutcliffe and Hendren taking the score to 149, until O'Reilly broke through once more, having Sutcliffe caught for 63. Thereafter it was a long time between wickets as Leyland and Hendren dug in and added another 191 runs. Mid-morning on day two, O'Reilly broke through again and caught and bowled Hendren for a patient 132. England was on top with 5 for 340 when Leyland found a new partner in Ames for another crushing stand, taking his score to 142 of 482. O'Reilly collected his sixth successive victim when he had Leyland caught for a powerful 153.

England declared at 9 for 627, with O'Reilly's final figures being 7 for 189 off 59 overs with 9 maidens. Even in a massive total like this, the leg-spinner was still a dominant force.

Australia's reply was limited as Bradman and Chipperfield had throat infections. Yet the tourists made a brave response, with McCabe (137) in touch and nearly every Australian contributing. Bradman (30) left his sickbed long enough to string out the innings. He lasted 66 minutes and faced 51 balls.

O'Reilly, with a strong sense of déjà vu, came to the wicket when Australia was 8 for 419 and 59 short of avoiding the follow on. This time he would not try to bat beyond his means. There would be none of the premature slashes for glory he had displayed at Lord's. After his mighty bowling effort against the odds, he was determined not to let it be in a losing side. If Australia had to follow on, it could lose the game and the series. He and Chipperfield, also out of his sickbed and dry-retching in the heat, struggled to push the score up to 454 before Chipperfield was caught for 26 off Verity. Right at the critical moment of the series, O'Reilly used every ounce of his limited batting skills to get behind each ball. He was not going to be dismissed without a battle. Tim Wall joined him and they clawed their way to 478 and avoided the follow on. Australia reached 491. O'Reilly, unconquered on 30, had played the innings of his life.

As it turned out, his performances with ball and bat saved Australia. O'Reilly, a perfectionist, felt he had redeemed himself after his batting failure at Lord's and the lost opportunity to fight back in that Test.

The Third Test fizzled out to a tame draw after England declared at 0 for 123 with Australia at 1 for 66 at the close. For the second time in two Tests, O'Reilly was Australia's player of the match, while Maurice Leyland performed best for England.

It was on to Leeds for the Fourth Test. If Australia were to win back the Ashes lost in the bodyline series, they had to avoid defeat in the final two Tests and win at least one of them. England had to either draw both games or win one. The series now hinged on the form of Australia's batsmen, in particular, one player: Bradman. He had been laid low by a mystery illness that had left him looking gaunt. On top of that, he was carrying some injuries and had a throat infection. Nevertheless, he had shown flashes of his former brilliance. So far he had scored 955 runs at 53.05, which brought him down to the level of the next best five batsmen playing in that 1934 England season. O'Reilly and the rest of the tourists bemoaned the fact that Bradman was performing at about half his usual rate, which was roughly twice as good that season as everyone except Bill Ponsford.

'He was the key,' O'Reilly said. 'The other batsmen had chipped in with useful scores through the series, but his revival was needed if we were to secure the coveted Ashes. Our chances were next to nought if he did not fire up.'

Bob Wyatt won the toss and batted. O'Reilly, as was becoming his wont, broke through the openers by having Keeton (25) caught by Oldfield at 43. The first two sessions saw him and Grimmett rout England, which was all out for 200 soon after tea. O'Reilly managed 3 for 46 off 35 overs with 16 maidens, once more demonstrating his accuracy and economy on an unhelpful wicket in perfect weather. Grimmett took 4 for 57.

At stumps Australia was in trouble at 3 for 39. The next day, Bradman returned to form at the appropriate time and galloped to 271 not out in a day, accompanied for much of the way by Ponsford (181) in a series-shattering partnership of 292. Bradman had overcome his mystery illness, later diagnosed as peritonitis, in a supreme effort for his country. At times he hit fours rather than expending his limited energy by running. He went on to a triple century (304) on the third morning and Australia reached 504. The lead was 304—significantly, Bradman's score, which graphically highlighted that he was the difference between the two teams.

'The facts were blatant and barefaced,' O'Reilly said. 'When Don batted to his usual standard we could not be beaten, provided everyone else in our team made a maximum effort.'

Rain saved England at 6 for 229. O'Reilly had 2 for 88 off 54 overs with 25 maidens. Grimmett had 3 for 72. The game was drawn, although Australia took much comfort from Bradman's superhuman effort at the crease, and the fact that the team was holding form as the vital timeless final Test at The Oval loomed.

Time for Victory

First there was another minor battle to be fought against

Nottingham. The team arrived by train at 9.00 pm to a hostile crowd. This was the home county of Larwood, Voce and Arthur Carr, the Notts skipper, who was happy to trial bodyline sporadically from 1929 to 1932. Carr dropped out of the game as did Larwood, who had been snubbed by the MCC selectors because he justifiably refused to apologise to them for carrying out Jardine's orders to bowl bodyline at the Australian batsmen. Only Voce was left of that intriguing triumvirate. He bowled bodyline in two overs of Australia's second innings, after tea. Bad light stopped play for the rest of the day. That night, Woodfull told the county's officials that if Voce played any more during the match, the Australian team would go back to London. Voce then went missing on the last day of the game, with a supposed leg injury. The crowd didn't believe it. They hurled verbal abuse and hooted at the Australians. The game ended in a draw.

With this disturbing experience behind them, the Australians went on to The Oval on 18 August to play the 1934 Ashes decider.

Woodfull won the toss and batted. Brown fell early, bowled by Clark, which brought Bradman to the wicket to join Ponsford. They put on a world-record second-wicket stand of 451. Bradman was out shortly before stumps for 244. Ponsford went on to 266 and Australia to 701. All of Australia's bowlers contributed to restricting England's innings to 321, with O'Reilly taking 2 for 93 off 37 overs with 10 maidens. Woodfull did not enforce a follow on. There was no need in a Test with no time limit, and with Bradman, McCabe and Ponsford to bat again.

Bradman (77) and McCabe (70) put Australia beyond all reasonable reach of England as they led the charge to a second innings of 327 and a lead of 707. No-one had managed even half that in a fourth-innings chase in a Test at that time. Led by Grimmett (5 for 64), the Australian bowlers rolled a despondent England for 145. O'Reilly took 2 for 58 off 22 overs with 9 maidens. The Ashes and the series went to Australia 2:1.

O'Reilly had taken 28 wickets at 24.93 in the Tests. His first-class season in 1934 saw him take 109 wickets at 17.04. He was the dominant bowler of the series and the scourge of the less-equipped counties.

Not too long after returning victorious from England, Molly O'Reilly gave birth to their first child, Patricia. It capped off a fine, memorable year for O'Reilly, which turned sour at the end when he decided that he would have to retire from cricket rather than harm his chances for advancement within the education department. The crisis was averted when Sydney Grammar made him an offer to teach and play any amount of cricket he wanted, at half-pay for every day he was absent. At 29, O'Reilly's physique and stamina suggested he had even a decade of top cricket in front of him. His 1934-35 season was reduced to two first-class games because of his temporary 'retirement', but it didn't harm his chance to tour South Africa in the following season. He was selected in the squad under 41-year-old Victor Richardson who had been made captain following Woodfull's retirement.

The Springboks had been weakened by the deaths of talented medium-pacer Neville Quinn and fine wicket-keeper batsman captain, Jock Cameron. They were no match for the Ashes-hardened Aussies, even without Bradman, who made himself unavailable for health reasons. In December 1935, O'Reilly took 8 wickets at Durban in the First Test (3 for 55 and 5 for 59) and was Australia's best bowler. A man-of-the-match award would have been a toss-up between him and McCabe, who scored a slashing 149. Australia won by 9 wickets. In the Second Test, played at Johannesburg at Christmas in 1935, O'Reilly was the best bowler of the first innings, taking 4 for 54. The wicket was perfect for batting.

South Africa's Dudley Nourse hit 231 and McCabe, in one of his three great innings, hit 189 not out. The game was drawn with Australia on 2 for 274, and 125 short of victory. Early in the New Year, in the Third Test at Cape Town, Australia batted first and made 8 for 362 declared (Brown 121, Fingleton 112) and then rolled South Africa for 102 and 182. Grimmett managed 2 hauls of 5 in each innings, while O'Reilly backed him, taking 4 for 74. Australia won by an innings and 78 runs.

The two spinners were rivals for wickets, but each fed off the success of the other, putting continual pressure on the opposition. They moved through their overs quickly, ensuring that the batsmen had no let-up but had to face a ball every 20 seconds. Both were unerringly accurate and the South Africans were left with no margin for error. One frustrated heave, any attempt at an unorthodox push to avoid the field, or any loss of concentration, would spell trouble. The O'Reilly and Grimmett combination that helped defeat England in 1934 consolidated as a great force in Test cricket.

In the Fourth Test at the Wanderers Stadium in Johannesburg in mid-February 1936, O'Reilly dominated the Springboks' first innings, taking 5 for 20 (delivering 21 overs with 10 maidens), while Grimmett had the figures in the second with 7 for 40. Australia's 439 (Fingleton 108) was enough to easily defeat South Africa, who only managed 157 and 98. In the Fifth Test, Grimmett took another 7 for 100 in restricting South Africa to a first innings of 222. Australia's reply was 455 with Fingleton scoring his third century for the series. South Africa made 227 in their second innings with all 10 wickets falling to the spin combination. Grimmett took 6 for 73 and O'Reilly, reduced to a support role in the last two Tests, secured the other 4 for 47 off a remarkable 40.1 overs with 18 maidens. Australia won by an innings and 6 runs, making it a 4:0 whitewash. O'Reilly kept up his consistent standards, taking 27 wickets at 17.59, but was forced to play second fiddle to Grimmett, who returned the world-record figures of 44 wickets at 14.59.

Disillusion

O'Reilly was selected for the First Test at Brisbane in 1936-37 under Bradman, his third captain in three Test series, and without his great bowling partner Grimmett. Initially, he didn't mind being skippered by his old nemesis, but he was miffed about the dropping of Grimmett, whom he generously regarded as the 'best leg-spinner in the world'. O'Reilly felt that his omission left him with too much of a personal bowling burden and Australia in danger of being unable to seriously penetrate. It was an understandable sentiment coming after Grimmett's sensational effort in South Africa and his amazing success in combination with O'Reilly.

At Brisbane early in December 1936, England scored 358 (Leyland 126). O'Reilly was the pick of the bowlers, taking 5 for 102 off 40.6 overs with 13 maidens, and cleaning up the tail. Australia replied with 234, Fingleton scoring his fourth successive century in Tests, and Voce taking 6 for 41. In England's second innings, Frank Ward, who had replaced Grimmett, was the best bowler, taking 6 of the top eight batsmen for 106, while O'Reilly went wicketless, taking 0 for 59 off 35 overs with 15 maidens. Ward took 2 for 138 in the first innings and was loose, probably because of nerves. Yet he removed two fine batsmen, Leyland and Ames, giving him 8 wickets for 244 for the match. He was the most effective Australian bowler of the game, but didn't match Grimmett.

Australia collapsed for a miserable 58 (Voce 4 for 16, Gubby Allen 5 for 36) on a wet wicket—its second for the game—and lost the match by 322 runs. O'Reilly, Fingleton and Grimmett now began grumbling about Bradman's capacities as captain. This was unfair and mischievous. The weather, not Bradman's efforts, was the telling factor in England's win, as it was in the Second Test at Sydney. England was lucky enough to again bat first, build a big score—6 for 426 declared, thanks to Hammond hitting 231 not out—on a good wicket, and then watch a thunderstorm turn the wicket into a sticky.

O'Reilly took 1 for 86 off 41 overs with 17 maidens. No batsman dared take liberties with him. No-one could remember a four being hit off the spinner, but there were plenty off Ward, McCormick and McCabe. Australia was 7 for 31 when O'Reilly arrived at the wicket. He had nothing to lose, and had on his mind the incentives offered by the producers of Wolffe's Schnappes, who put up £5 for every six, and a cigarette company who gave £50 to anyone who hit 3 sixes. He wielded the bat with great vigour, launching himself at everything, connecting sometimes. He hit 3 sixes, made 37 not out of Australia's total of 80, and collected £65. The wicket dried out and when Australia followed on, Fingleton (73), Bradman (82) and McCabe (93) all contributed but not enough to challenge England, who won by an innings and 22 runs.

The knives were out for Bradman for leading Australia to two defeats. O'Reilly and Fingleton pushed for Stan McCabe to replace him. The weather god that had been unfair to Bradman and Australia in Brisbane apparently thought matters should be evened out in the Third Test at Melbourne in the New Year. Bradman won the toss and batted, even though it had been wet overnight. Australia struggled to 6 for 181 when rain stopped play. It was wet again overnight. Bradman let the score reach 9 for 200 and then pushed England out to bat on a sticky. No-one, except perhaps Hobbs and Sutcliffe, could have done better than Hammond (32) and Leyland (17) in handling the atrocious conditions, which are inconceivable today with covered wickets. Sievers took 5 for 21 and was supported by O'Reilly, who was almost impossible to play. He took 3 for 28 off 12 overs with 5 maidens as England capitulated, losing 9 for 76.

England captain Gubby Allen declared when he saw that Bradman was telling his bowlers to keep the last few batsmen at the wicket. Bradman didn't want his team to bat on the deteriorated strip. When Australia had to bat, Bradman sent O'Reilly and Fleetwood-Smith into open because he thought they were the batsmen least likely to hit the ball. Unfortunately O'Reilly was capable of making contact—he was caught and bowled first ball for a duck. Ward, who had not been called upon to bowl in the first innings, was sent in. He lasted a few minutes. Then rain ended the day's play. The next day, Sunday, was a rest day.

On Monday Australia's upside down batting order struggled, with Bradman (270) and Fingleton (136) doing the most to push Australia to 564. England started the fourth innings of the game chasing 688. Ward started England's fall by dismissing Worthington (16) at 29. The two key spinners, O'Reilly (3 for 65 off 21 overs with 6 maidens) and Fleetwood-Smith (5 for 124), steadily moved through England until their score reached 323 (Leyland 111 not out). Australia won by 365 and England led the series 2:1.

Straight after the Third Test, the Australian Board of Control summoned O'Reilly, Fleetwood-Smith, McCabe and O'Brien before it at the Victorian Cricket Association rooms and reprimanded them for drinking, lack of fitness and team spirit, and insubordination. Someone at the board had overreacted. All these cricketers liked to relax with a beer, but only one of them, Fleetwood-Smith, was given to drunkenness and then more after he had retired from the game.

O'Reilly asked if the four of them were being held responsible for all the allegations. They were told 'no' without qualification. He asked why they were being spoken to and no-one on the board could give an answer. O'Reilly left the meeting feeling glum. First he had lost Grimmett as a partner, then England had won the first two Tests, and now he felt humiliated. The fun was slipping out of the game.

Nevertheless O'Reilly turned up at Adelaide for the Fourth Test. Bradman won the toss on 30 January 1937 and batted in the heat. Again, Australia failed to score well in the first innings, reaching 288 (McCabe 88). England replied with fight, but O'Reilly snared Hammond (20), the most dangerous English bat ever on Australia wickets, and went on to deceive Wyatt (3) with a wrong'un to have him caught. His figures were the best at 4 for 51 off 30 overs with 12 maidens. England reached 330.

Australia, or at least Bradman (212), replied and reached 433, leaving England 392 runs for victory. They fell 148 short, mainly due to Fleetwood-Smith (6 for 110), who bowled Hammond (39) with what Bradman described as 'a glorious, sinuous ball'. O'Reilly took 1 for 55. Though he was not as penetrating as in previous innings, he still tied up one end, putting increased pressure on the batsmen, who had long ago given up attempting to attack him. This was the third successive series in which he controlled and dominated England's finest. They had no serious answers to him, and could only rely on tight defence and, as ever, turning over the strike with right- and left-hand combinations where possible.

The series was 2:2 when the teams assembled in Melbourne a month later for the Fifth and final Test. O'Reilly was in a very good mood. Molly had given birth to a son, Peter, a week before.

Bradman won the toss again and made 169 in great partnerships with McCabe (112) and Badcock (118) as Australia hit a thumping 604. Astute captaincy by Bradman, erratic but dangerous pace from Laurie Nash (4 for 70) and superb spin by O'Reilly (5 for 51 off 23 overs with 7 maidens) combined to reduce England to a mediocre response of 239. O'Reilly was the star once more, capturing Hardstaff (83), Hammond (14), Leyland (7) and Wyatt (38)—the heart of England's batting.

Bradman didn't hesitate to enforce the follow on and England had no answer to O'Reilly's tactical bowling. He seemed to have a problem ball for every batsman, having thought through their weaknesses long ago. His 3 for 58 off 19 overs with 6 maidens were fair figures but did not do his form justice as England fell apart for 165 (Fleetwood-Smith 3 for 36).

Bradman with the bat and O'Reilly with the ball were the two key players in Australia's eventual 3:2 Ashes win. They were far from mates off the field but they put aside their differences in combat for their country.

England for the Last Time

O'Reilly's form continued through the 1937-38 season in the build-up to the England Ashes tour. He took 64 first-class wickets at 12.24 including five 5-wicket bags and one sensational performance against Bradman and South Australia in December 1937 at Adelaide. New South Wales batted first and scored 337 (McCabe 106). In South Australia's response, O'Reilly took 9 for 41 off 33.6 overs with 12 maidens, his best-ever return in first-class matches.

The clash between O'Reilly and Bradman ranked as one of the great contests in cricket history. While O'Reilly unsettled, contained and defeated all the other bats, Bradman rose to the occasion, going onto the back foot and placing the ball through the well-set field, or dancing forward to drive him either side of the wicket.

'He was at his peak in experience and form,' Bradman said, 'and one of the best challenges I ever had.'

'I would have given back five of them (the South Australian

wickets) for his wicket before he got going,' O'Reilly said.

He eventually snared Bradman, caught by Charlie O'Brien for 91. New South Wales collapsed for 104 in its second innings, leaving South Australia 225 to make for victory. They started well with a 100-plus first-wicket stand between Badcock and Bradman before O'Reilly had him a second time, caught Chipperfield for 62. Normally undemonstrative after taking a wicket, O'Reilly held his hands above his head like a victorious boxer. He had never before taken Bradman twice in a game. The dismissal lifted the New South Wales team and they crashed through South Australia for 191, O'Reilly leading the way with 5 for 57 off 20 overs with 8 maidens. New South Wales won by 33.

The 1938 England tour was not a happy one for O'Reilly. Apart from missing Grimmett, he felt that England had 'cooked' the Test wickets to nullify his spin. He had a good build-up to the Tests, including 8 for 104 v Surrey, 6 for 65 v Hants and 6 for 22 v Gloucester.

At Trent Bridge in the first innings of the First Test in June, England reached 8 declared for 658 (Paynter 216 not out, Barnett 126, Hutton 100, Compton 102).

'The wicket was made to last forever,' O'Reilly grumbled.

O'Reilly took 3 (including Edrich and Hammond cheaply) for 164 off 56 overs with 11 maidens. Australia replied with 411 (Stan McCabe scored 232 in his greatest innings) and was forced to follow on. They managed to steer clear of defeat with 6 for 427 (Bradman 144 not out, Brown 133).

At Lord's, England won the toss again and made 494 (Hammond 240), with O'Reilly the best of the bowlers, taking 4 for 93 off 37 overs with 6 maidens. His wickets once more included key batsmen Paynter (99) and Compton (6). Australia's response looked likely to fall well short until O'Reilly, at 7 for 308, joined opener Bill Brown, who was approaching his double century. O'Reilly clubbed 42 in 44 minutes, including 2 towering sixes, before being bowled by Farnes. Brown reached 206 not out and carried his bat as Australia reached 422. O'Reilly took 2 for 53 (Hutton and Ames before they got started) off 29 overs with 10 maidens in England's 242. The lead was 312. Australia was 6 for 204 (Bradman 102 not out) when the game finished in a draw.

The Third Test at Manchester was washed out without a ball being bowled.

A less disgruntled O'Reilly commented wryly in his book *Tiger* that the wet weather had apparently interfered with preparation of the pitch for the Fourth Test. At last the Australians had a wicket they could exploit. England won the toss for the third successive time and batted. O'Reilly managed turn early and troubled everyone. He bowled Edrich (12) and Compton (14) and later captured Hammond (76), the only Englishman to command respect. O'Reilly's final figures, again the best of the Australians, were 5 for 66 off 34.1 overs with 17 maidens. England could only reach 223 and this gave the tourists their big chance. But only Bradman (103, his third century in the three Tests played) seemed ready to take advantage of the opportunity as they staggered to 242. It was up to O'Reilly once more and he set up his country for victory for the second time in the match, taking another 5 for 56 off 21.5 overs with 8 maidens. His bag this time included Hardstaff (11), Hammond (0) and Compton (15) in England's paltry 123. Australia lost 5 for 107 in attaining a win, the only one in the series so far.

Bradman lost the toss at The Oval for the fourth time and England batted. Hutton was missed twice before he was 50 off McCabe and Fleetwood-Smith. He went on to a world-record 364 as England climbed to 7 for 903 in the timeless Test.

'Would Hutton have made a score like that with Grimmett bowling in tandem with me?' O'Reilly often asked rhetorically in the decades after the Test. 'No way.'

Bradman was bowling, a rare event, when he went over on a weak ankle in one of O'Reilly's deep foot marks and fractured a tibia. This left Australia without a serious answer to such a big score. O'Reilly still bowled well, taking 3 for 178 off a record 85 overs with 26 maidens. At no point did an English bat attempt to take the game to him and attack. The same story had now been repeated in four successive Ashes series. The batsmen defended, went onto the back foot, used their pads and tried to get up the other end. Facing O'Reilly for a complete over seemed a dangerous thing to do. He would beat you at least once, and it might mean a wicket would fall. In the four Tests he took 22 wickets at 27.7. Despite most pitches not being conducive to spin, he was Australia's dominant bowler for the fourth time in five Test series.

Australia without Bradman and Fingleton, who was also injured, made 201 and 123. England's win by an innings and 579 runs was the biggest margin in Ashes history. It levelled the series 1:1. The consolation for O'Reilly was that the Ashes stayed with his team.

War Stops Spin

In 1939, after five happy years at Sydney Grammar, O'Reilly went to work as secretary to the Lion Tile Company, where he remained for the next 35 years. Work commitments and a knee injury reduced his 1938-39 season to three first-class matches. In 1939-40 he took 55 wickets at 15.1 and, with Grimmett, continued to be the best performer with the ball in the country. The 1940-41 season was much the same. He took another 55 wickets, this time at 12.43. By this time the war was under way and O'Reilly, 35, saw the end of his career looming. Unless the war ended quickly—and that seemed impossible—there would be no more tours of England for him.

O'Reilly bobbed up after the war for one final Test against New Zealand at the Basin Reserve, Wellington, late in March 1946, at the age of 41. He showed that age had not curtailed his skills, taking 5 for 14 and 3 for 19, but his knees were suffering. He looked wistfully at Grimmett who had survived at the top until nearly 50 years of age, but knew he could not follow him. Symbolically, he threw his boots out of the dressing-room window at Wellington at the end of the Test.

In all, O'Reilly had taken 144 Test wickets at 22.59 in 27 Tests. He scored 410 runs at 12.81. He won almost all encounters with the world's great batsmen in a career spanning two decades. His most telling victories were against the greatest English bat of that period, Hammond, whom he dismissed seven times for 26 or less. England's left-handed Maurice Leyland troubled him and was tough to penetrate, and Jack Badcock and Lindsay Hassett seemed up to the task of tackling him in state games. The only batsman to dictate terms to him numerous times was Bradman, with whom he had first-class encounters in 10 matches and 17 innings. Bradman scored 1,194 runs at an average of 91.84 (4 centuries, 2 double centuries, highest score 251 not out) and O'Reilly took his wicket six times. They also clashed in country and first-grade cricket in Sydney. The story there was much the same, and there was no doubt who O'Reilly considered the best batsman of all. In first-class cricket O'Reilly took 774 wickets at 16.60. He scored 1,655 runs at 13.13.

After retiring from first-class cricket O'Reilly became a respected journalist. Controversial Melbourne businessman John Wren offered to match all the newspaper contracts O'Reilly had picked up, including one with London's *Daily Express*, if he would make a comeback in the 1946-47 Ashes series, but he was not physically up to it. O'Reilly's pungent features appeared in *The Sydney Morning Herald* and *The Age* until 1992, the year he died. Sometimes they were a little too punchy and had to be toned down after fierce confrontations on the phone with *The Age*'s legendary editor Graham Perkin. No-one else would stand up to O'Reilly.

One of O'Reilly's last features was on a tubby blond leg-spinner named Shane Warne who was making his debut in a Test against India at Sydney in January 1992. In a generous yet perceptive critique, considering Warne's figures were 1 for 150, O'Reilly concluded: 'I am prepared to accept him with open arms to the important spin society.'

The old spinner had been annoyed by the subjugation of spin to pace in the preceding 20 years. He yearned to see a top-quality leg-spinner restore the art to its former pre-eminence. O'Reilly would have been thrilled to know that the novice performer, on whom he had just passed judgment, would be ranked by Bradman and other good judges alongside O'Reilly and Grimmett as the best leg-spinners the game had ever seen.

CHAPTER 13

THE FOX

CLARENCE VICTOR
GRIMMETT

II

(Australia)

25 December 1891—2 May 1980

> *'Clarrie Grimmett was the best genuine slow leg-spinner because of his great accuracy and control.'*
>
> SIR DONALD BRADMAN

Australia's captain Herbie Collins tossed the ball to Clarrie Grimmett lurking almost unnoticed at mid-off. The date was 28 January 1925, the second day of the Fifth Test of the 1924-25 Ashes series, and the venue was Sydney. All eyes turned to the little bloke who bowled with his cap on. He looked calm, and he was. Grimmett was 33 years old and this would be his first over in Test cricket. He had waited over a decade for this moment, travelling from his native New Zealand to Sydney, Melbourne and Adelaide in search of recognition from Test selectors. He had played far too long at club and Shield level waiting for four wise men to acknowledge what hundreds of batsmen who had faced him, and tens of thousands of spectators who had seen him, already knew: he was the best purveyor of the art of leg-spin bowling that the world had ever seen.

He measured out his run, his movements dainty yet definite. Even in 1925 there was something old-fashioned and almost comical about his chest-on run-in and near round-arm delivery. He could have been an old park cricketer used to figures of 1 for 100. Yet no batsman was seen laughing when a Grimmett ball hit the deck. He had all the deliveries in the leg-spinner's arsenal tucked up his sleeve. His target was one of the world's best left-handers, Frank Woolley. Grimmett knew he could put the ball on a pinhead, but he could not be sure how such an elegant champion would deal with it. Especially a left-hander—they adored those leg-spinners turning into the middle of their bats. They would go on the back foot and wait, or push forward, hitting with the spin into their favourite area in the arc between square leg and mid-on. Grimmett dished up the conventional leg-breaks in his first over and Woolley dutifully pushed into the on-side for singles.

At the commencement of his second over Grimmett had 0 for 4. Woolley was on 47, one artistic drive away from another 50, a milestone he had reached often. Woolley would not take kindly to delays caused by this Test tyro's spinners, they frustrated him. Nevertheless, Grimmett could not rely on a rash, nervy whoosh from this batsman. He had a basic plan, based on his memory of a Victoria v MCC game four-and-a-half years previous. Grimmett had delivered a wrong'un to Woolley, who seemed to have picked it but, in his hurry to show the bowler he had not been fooled, mishit to cover, where two fieldsmen hesitated about who should catch it. The ball had plonked harmlessly on the MCG grass a few metres from the shamefaced fieldsmen. Grimmett knew that an experienced star such as Woolley would remember the incident, would have read much in the Australian papers about Grimmett's wrong'un, and would be on the lookout for it. That was what Grimmett wanted—to keep the champion guessing and worrying about when the expected wrong'un would come. And Grimmett, living up to his nickname of 'the Fox', would not give it to him.

Woolley looked for the wrong'un, straining his eyes to see a different movement of hand and wrist. Subconsciously his bat drifted towards his off-side, away from his pads, as he readied himself for the inevitable. Grimmett dished up several slow but not innocuous leg-breaks, which Woolley thrashed to cover with style. He didn't score a run but there was absolute timing in his smooth, high follow-through. He was showing he was on top, intent on demolishing the new boy. Then Grimmett delivered an 'ordinary' leg-break—one that didn't turn as much but instead pushed through a fraction faster. It was in line with off stump, nicely up for the cover drive. Then it swerved, apparently a fraction more than the normal Grimmett delivery. It hit the pitch and threaded its way between Woolley's driving bat and pad to clean-bowl him.

Woolley's dismissal for 47 left England at 5 for 96. Jack Gregory dismissed Hendren (10) and opened up the tail further for Grimmett, who trapped the next two batsmen, Hearne and Whysall, LBW with a specialty: the dipping top-spinner. Then after a short stay of execution he lured Roy Kilner from his crease with a pitched-up wrong'un. The ball again dipped, Kilner missed and Bert Oldfield removed the bails for a swift stumping. Jack Ryder bowled the stubborn Tate (25) and England skipper Arthur Gilligan heaved at a regular leg-break, missed and was also stumped. England was all out for 167 in reply to Australia's 295 (Ponsford 80, Kellaway 73, Oldfield 65 not out), with Grimmett taking 5 for 45—a brilliant debut effort, equivalent to a batsman making a century. Australia made 325 (Andrews 80), leaving England 454 to make to win—an improbable target at any time, made nigh impossible by this new spinner.

In England's second innings, Grimmett delighted in cajoling the great Jack Hobbs a fraction forward of the crease, enough for Oldfield's third eye-blink fast stumping for the match. It began Grimmett's run-through of the hapless opposition who were unused to such wizardry. He round-armed down a succession of big-turning leg-breaks interspersed with top-spinners, the occasional wrong'un, and the very occasional flipper. His second innings bag of 6 for 37 included Hobbs, Sandham and Hearne (LBW to the top-spinner), Hendren (caught Oldfield), and Whysall (Oldfield's fourth stumping)—a useful collection in any era. Grimmett's 11 for 82 was one of the finest Test debuts ever. It satisfied thousands of Australian cricket fans and a few perceptive journalists across the nation who nodded a collective 'We told you so' to the tardy national selectors. Clarence Victor Grimmett had at last reached the high plane, for which he always felt destined.

Early Years

At 13, Grimmett was ordered to bowl leg-breaks by his Mount Cook Boys' School, New Zealand, sportsmaster, Dimp Hempelmann, who had faced him in the nets and pronounced him as 'more than promising'. Grimmett preferred to bowl fast but that changed in a big junior game in 1905 between Wellington Schools and Wairarapa Schools. He reluctantly opened the bowling under orders to bowl leg-breaks and took 6 for 5 and 8 for 1 (14 wickets for 6 runs). Grimmett never bothered with pace again, realising that he had a special gift with the spinning ball.

In March 1905, a few months after he wiped out the schoolboy opposition, he sneaked into the Basin Reserve, Wellington, to watch the already legendary Victor Trumper play in Monty Noble's side against a New Zealand XI. It was obvious to the young Grimmett that the great cricketers of the era were in Australia. If he were ever to reach the heights the game could offer, he would have to migrate there. This seemed an impossible dream to the 13-year-old, and if anything it thwarted his impulse to play competitively. What was the point if he could never reach the standards he had seen at Basin Reserve? However, YMCA officials who knew of his talent talked him into playing for their Boys League team. At 15, he took a job as sign-writer. Three years later he was selected to play for the Wellington B team, then two years after that he was given a long-overdue boost into the Wellington XI in the Plunket Shield. Grimmett was 20 and kept the dream of top cricket alive by listening to the stories of Australian Jack Saunders who captained Wellington. He told tales of playing with Trumper, Warwick Armstrong, Joe Darling and Monty Noble. They were gods of the cricket world and Grimmett badly wanted to follow in their footsteps.

New Zealand selectors began a dimwitted trend that would dog Grimmett for much of his career by failing to choose him to tour Australia in 1913-14. An international team including Trumper, Englishman Jack Crawford and the peripatetic Arthur Mailey came to New Zealand in 1914. Grimmett grabbed the chance to bowl to Trumper when the tourists played Wellington. He didn't take a wicket and managed just one over to Trumper. It was a big moment for Grimmett. He thought Trumper was the best batsman he ever saw and maintained that view for the rest of his life.

The visiting team was happy to give instruction to the Wellington players so Grimmett approached Mailey and asked him how he bowled his wrong'un. Mailey bowled a couple into the nets and then walked away without a word of advice. There was a lesson in this slight by Mailey. It made Grimmett realise that some people took the attitude that you should never give a sucker an even break. Perhaps Mailey sensed Grimmett's skills could develop beyond his. The New Zealander may well have even expressed the desire to play in Australia. His plans for it were already under way.

The Big Wide Land of Opportunity

In May 1914, only a few months after the game against Trumper and Co, Grimmett arrived in Sydney by boat with his mother Mary and sister Eva (his father had long ago split from the family).

Grimmett's innate modesty prevented him from telling any-one he had played first-class cricket in New Zealand, and he started playing in the Sydney club's third grade. He took 12 for 60 against University and was soon elevated to the seconds, then the firsts, ironically against Arthur Mailey's Redfern at the SCG. The newcomer remained calm and hid his excitement. He made a huge start by rolling the opposition, taking 7 for 32 and 5 for 33. Mailey (3 for 45) bowled well but not as brilliantly as Grimmett. He went through the 1914-15 season taking 28 wickets at 10.64 runs apiece. World War I began in 1914, and Shield cricket was suspended in February 1915. Even if the Shield hadn't been suspended he would not have been able to squeeze in front of Mailey, who would maintain his place as long as he continued to return good figures.

Times were bleak. Victor Trumper died on 28 June 1915 and Grimmett joined the 20,000 mourners at his funeral parade through Sydney. He played out two more seasons taking lots of wickets and heading nowhere. At the end of 1916-17 he was 25 years old and depressed that he had yet to play first-class cricket in Australia. Just when he was feeling that he had made a mistake leaving New Zealand, he was selected in April 1917 to play in Syd Gregory's XI v Monty Noble's XI at the SCG. In what was virtually a state trial game, he took 3 for 79. Mailey took 3 for 102. The happy-go-lucky, very popular Mailey was your millionaire's spinner. He pitched it up, spun it hard and aimed often at catches in the outfield. He could be loose and was occasionally dealt with in buying wickets. Grimmett was of a different persuasion. His line and length were perfect. He could hit stumps blindfolded and once did in the nets at Sydney to prove a point. The little New Zealander, a tad over 165 cm (5 ft 4 in) was a will-o'-the-wisp who kept his own counsel at all times and was an observer rather than a showman. He gave nothing away off the field and less on it. Batsmen were never sure how he would bowl. They always feared that he had some scheme, some hidden plan. Not surprisingly he gained a second nickname 'Scarl', for the Scarlet Pimpernel. Batsmen sought to destroy him everywhere but none succeeded.

A week after his first unofficial state tryout he was selected to play for New South Wales against St George in an incestuous Sydney event. Grimmett this time took 5 for 18, Mailey 4 for 22. Unfortunately for Grimmett these returns were not quite enough to put him in a position to replace Mailey. His former captain, Jack Saunders, suggested that he flee New South Wales because Mailey was too popular and entrenched in the state side, a certain block to Grimmett's advance. Grimmett saw the writing on the wall and moved on, this time to Melbourne. He began with Saunders' old district club, South Melbourne, in 1917-18 and took 40 wickets at 14.4 a piece. By November 1918 the war was over and state competition games were once again played. Grimmett was chosen but underbowled. He was relegated to the state seconds for the rest of the 1918-19 season and played against the New South Wales seconds and Victorian country teams, securing in all these games 30 wickets at under 20 apiece.

The 1919-20 season began well with Grimmett marrying Elizabeth Egan, whom he had met soon after arriving in Melbourne. On the field he took his usual swag of club wickets—40 at 20.8—but was ignored by state selectors. He moved his home to Prahran and was forced to play for that club. In the 1920-21 season, he took a massive 67 wickets at 14.95, but was once more overlooked for state selection. Grimmett was now 29 and it was becoming increasingly unlikely that he would cement a state spot, not because of a Mailey stopping him but because of the incompetence of the Victorian selectors.

Grimmett built a full-sized turf pitch in his backyard so that he could bowl in any spare time he had, and trained a fox terrier to fetch the balls. He trained all year round, playing baseball sometimes in the off-season. His fanatical, obsessive efforts were rewarded when he was selected to play for Victoria against Johnny Douglas' MCC team, but he had a poor, unlucky game. He took 3 for 160, had several catches dropped and was injured when balls struck him on the knee and split his spinning finger. It was a setback, but while Clarrie had life in those deft spinning fingers he would not give up.

He turned 30 during the 1921-22 season, in which he took 39 wickets at 14 apiece. Still the Victorian selectors overlooked him. In 1922-23 he stepped up a notch and took 60 wickets at 11.52, and followed this up in 1923-24 with 54 at 12.12. He and wife Elizabeth had a son, Victor, in December 1922. Grimmett had dominated club cricket in Melbourne for five seasons running—the last four at Prahran netting 258 wickets—and had had only one first-class match. He got a second chance when selected for Victoria against South Australia at Adelaide in the last game of the season. He took 1 for 12 in the first innings and then showed how great he was by taking 8 for 86 in the second innings.

The Adelaide Club noted Grimmett's performances and made him a seductive offer to move again. At 32 he quit Victoria and moved to Adelaide to play for the Adelaide Club, and took a sign-writing job for £10 a week at Harry Lyons Pty Ltd.

Clarrie's Last Throw

This was the last throw of the dice. Adelaide had long been the final stop for bowlers on the road to oblivion—or glory in the case of Jack O'Connor and Bill Whitty of Sydney, who both went on to play for Australia. At last sanity prevailed among state selectors and Grimmett was chosen to play for South Australia, where he began taking wickets as if he were still playing club cricket. Seven bags of between 4 and 7 wickets propelled him into the Fifth Test of the Ashes series of 1924-25. He took 11 wickets and less than two weeks later, just to demonstrate it was no fluke, against the departing MCC team took 1 for 40 and 7 for 82. In the entire season he took 49 wickets at 22.03. Clarence Victor Grimmett had arrived at last at the first-class level, and with a vengeance.

He followed up his serious debut season at the top with 59 wickets at 30.41. He was more expensive but just as destructive as ever, snaring six hauls of 5 wickets and three of 10. It was easily enough to ensure him a place in the 1926 tour of England with Herbie Collins' team. Grimmett, at 33 years, and after 14 years in the cricket wilderness, was receiving the accolades he was due. Mailey was selected in front of him for the first two Tests in England, but felt Grimmett's ambitious breath on his neck after the third game against the counties (Oxford) when he took 6 for 28. Grimmett followed with 6 for 87 against Yorkshire and other good performances every time he took the field. The first two Tests were drawn and Mailey was struggling. The selectors chose them both for the Third Test at Headingley. Grimmett took up where he left off in his first Test 16 months earlier by taking 5 for 88, dismissing Sutcliffe caught and bowled (26), and running through the tail. Mailey took 2 for 63. Grimmett outbowled Mailey for the fourth successive innings when he took 2 for 59 as opposed to Mailey's 0 for 80. This game was also drawn and the selectors, desperate for a win, decided to retain both Grimmett and Mailey for the Fourth Test at Manchester. Mailey did better, taking 3 for 87, while Grimmett returned 1 for 85, but the rain-affected game was another draw. The series was now down to a shoot-out at The Oval in mid-August.

England won the toss. Mailey, the big spender, sent down 33.5 overs and returned a commendable 6 for 138, going for 4.5 runs an over. He tossed the ball up and encouraged his opponents to strike out. Grimmett sent down the same number of overs and took 2 for 74. He was twice as mean as his spin partner but not as penetrating. England reached 280. Harold Larwood made his debut in Australia's first innings, taking 3 for 82. With Tate (3 for 40), he held Australia to 302. Grimmett slowed England's advance by showing rare prowess with the bat, notching 35 before being bowled by Maurice Tate. A fine opening stand by Hobbs (100) and Sutcliffe (161) of 172 helped push England's second innings up to 436.

Grimmett, his very name sounding parsimonious, delivered 55 overs and 17 maidens while returning 3 for 108—an economy rate of under 2 runs an over. Mailey bowled a lot less (42.5 overs) in taking 3 for 128, for an economy rate of 3 an over. In this Test skipper Collins used Grimmett as a stock bowler to hold up one end, while attacking with the rest from the other. Larwood completed his impressive debut, bowling at about 160 km per hour (100 miles per hour) with 3 for 34, and with Rhodes (4 for 44) cleaned up Australia for 125. This gave England the game by 289 runs, and the series 1:0. The Ashes had gone home to England.

Grimmett and Mailey took 27 wickets of the 41 to fall in the series, but their partnership was to be short-lived. Mailey retired from Test cricket at the end of the tour, leaving the number one spinner's spot with Grimmett. He tackled the new season with verve but was distracted off the field by a business failure. He had been making ends meet with sign-writing, cricket coaching and writing articles, but, like all cricketers, was on the lookout for a business that would set him and his family up for life. He invested in a fashion store in the heart of Adelaide known as The Big Store, which failed. With the help of South Australian cricket officials, who hated the idea of Grimmett leaving the state, he found a job with Stevens and Rowe, a sports equipment wholesaler. His off-field troubles caused him to be a little wayward. His

30 wickets through 1926-27 for South Australia went for 34.33 apiece.

Bradman: First Encounter

In 1927, Grimmett faced the young Don Bradman in his debut first-class game for New South Wales in Adelaide. It was mid-December 1927 and 36°C (96°F). Bradman respected the spinner as the finest leggie in the world, and Grimmett knew of the tyro's reputation as an up-and-comer to watch. Bradman was not then perceived to be in Archie Jackson's class, but had to be thwarted early in case he used his skills in a showcase debut innings against South Australia, and Grimmett in particular.

Bradman came in at the fall of the fourth wicket (Kippax had retired because of heat exhaustion) when the score was 250. It was a good time to bat, with the bowling side under pressure in the heat, but first up he had to face Grimmett, who could bowl brilliantly in murderous heat or a mudslide.

Grimmett had six balls left of a standard eight-ball over. Bradman took block. Grimmett didn't move a fieldsman, but the novice bat put his hand up to stop the leggie wheeling in. He noted every fielder's position and then leant over his bat, ready. The first ball was a standard leg-break, well up. Bradman stayed in his crease, stretched forward and blocked it. The second ball was identical. Bradman this time danced down the wicket and smashed it to cover. No run. He looked good. Very good. But Grimmett thought he seemed a fraction too eager to stamp his mark on him, the 36-year-old veteran, twice Bradman's age. Grimmett varied his line to just outside leg stump to test the new man and was astonished to see him move his back foot swiftly into position as the ball spun across him. Bradman heaved into the delivery against the spin, rolling his sinuous wrists to powerful advantage. The ball went straight to the ground and sped to the pickets. Grimmett frowned, not from despair—he would never give away that emotion—but with interest. The sight of Bradman's audacious aggression and unorthodoxy early in an innings encouraged all bowlers. 'He'll be another notch on the belt,' Grimmett probably thought, like O'Reilly before him.

Now the leg-spinner's step became sharper. The fieldsmen clapped encouragement. If they could get this junior swashbuckler out, New South Wales might collapse and they could all slump back to the dressing room for a well-earned drink. Grimmett gave him another ball just outside leg stump, but this time with more loop and bounce. Bradman used his feet and drove to mid-on. He blocked the next ball. Grimmett tossed another one up on the leg and the batsman was drawn forward with alacrity. He stroked the ball for 4 between mid-wicket and mid-on. Grimmett had the rare experience of being thumped for 4 twice in a first-class over. He displayed no emotion, but strode to his place at mid-off deep in thought. Bradman had appeared vulnerable, but no ball even challenged him. The big crowd didn't know it, but they had just witnessed the first encounter between the best bat of all time and one of the best spinners ever. Bradman went on to make 118 and Grimmett failed to remove him. The evening after Bradman's debut century, Grimmett invited him and a few other members of the New South Wales team to his home and displayed his talents by performing a tennis-ball spinning exhibition on a tabletop. It impressed his audience. It may well have mesmerised them, for in the second innings, Grimmett gained some measure of revenge when he bowled Bradman with a top-spinner off his pads for 33 and took 8 for 57 in a withering display that won the game for South Australia.

As with O'Reilly, Bradman had cast a psychological hold on the star bowler that he would try to maintain over the next decade of confrontations. Grimmett dismissed him only thrice in their first 17 contests. He removed him for the fourth time in their 18th encounter after an exciting battle when Bradman scored 76 on a wearing pitch. In their 19th, a Testimonial game and Test trial—Vic Richardson's team v Bradman's—in October 1936, Bradman announced his right to captain the country with a thunderous 212, thrashing O'Reilly and Grimmett to all parts of the SCG. At the end he was heaving at everything and threw his wicket away to Grimmett. The bowler dismissed him in the second innings for 13 when Bradman's team was cruising to a 6-wicket win.

In all 24 encounters where Grimmett bowled to him at the first-class level, Grimmett snared Bradman eight times (these scores appear in brackets): 118, (33), 2, 73, 5, 2, (35), 175, 47, 2 run out, (84), 258, 23, 0, 56, 97, 1, (76), (212), (13), (17), (29), 8 and 20. Bradman's average for these innings was 59.82, which is a little misleading considering he threw his wicket away on four occasions. Nevertheless, Grimmett did better than any other bowler against Bradman. Hedley Verity snared him 10 times, with Bradman's average 74.23. Bedser removed him eight times, with Bradman averaging 92.93. Larwood removed him seven times with Bradman's average 87.34.

Grum's Glory

Grimmett was selected in an Australian team to make an unofficial tour of New Zealand early in 1928. He had not been home for 14 years and was determined to make it a triumph. He took 47 wickets on tour at 12.64 apiece. In the 'Tests' he took 3 for 85, 0 for 15, 6 for 47 and 3 for 52. In his best games against Wellington, Dunedin, Canterbury and Auckland he captured two hauls of 7 wickets and two of 6. This gave him great pride, and all the commentators delivered high praise.

That success launched him into the 1928-29 season in which the MCC toured Australia to defend the Ashes they had won in 1926. Grimmett was more settled now. The South Australian Cricket Association backed him with various deals and benefits worth £60 a month and he began playing for the Kensington Club.

Once the selectors' last choice or an afterthought, Grimmett now was the most prized bowler in Australia. In fact, with Jack Gregory breaking down with knee problems and Kellaway retiring, the cupboard was almost bare. Clarrie's slight, sinewy shoulders were expected to carry an unfair load in 1928-29. How he would have liked O'Reilly to bowl in tandem with him against England's outstanding batting line-up of Hobbs, Sutcliffe, Hammond, Woolley, Hendren, Jardine and Chapman. But the New South Wales Education Department had sent O'Reilly bush. Blackie and Ironmonger's support was worthy but not strong enough to challenge the foreign talent.

The Australian team was old and tired. Not even the injection of new boy Bradman for the First Test at Brisbane in November 1928 was enough to make any impression on the MCC juggernaut that had thumped its way from Perth. They thrashed Australia. Bradman made 18 and 1 and was dropped. Grimmett sent down 40 overs in taking 3 for 167 in the first innings (England 521, Hendren 169) and another 44.1 overs in the second innings (England 8 for 342), taking 6 for 131. His second bag included Hobbs, whom he trapped LBW for 11, Hendren for 45 and Chapman for 27.

In the Second Test, Australia batted first and made 253, just two more than the brilliant Hammond who was at his early career peak and did the most in an otherwise even effort to lift England to 636. Grimmett's only real joy was the wicket of Hobbs (40) again, who in his declining seasons had trouble picking the leg-spinner. Grimmett ended with 2 for 191 off 64 eight-ball overs, equivalent to more than 85 six-ball overs. Australia showed more spine in the second innings, reaching 397 (Woodfull 111, Hendry 112), but it wasn't enough.

England sailed to an easy 8-wicket win.

Australia batted first in the Third Test at Melbourne and made 397 again with Kippax (100), Ryder (112) and the restored Bradman (79). England fought hard and clawed their way to 417, the dynamic Hammond hitting another fine double hundred. Grimmett, in another marathon stint, delivered 55 overs and 14 maidens in taking 2 for 114. In the second innings, Australia, bolstered by the now unstoppable Bradman (112) and the reliable Woodfull (107), reached 351. The batsmen were not letting the country down, but when it came to bowlers the team was under-manned. Grimmett, at 37, was being called upon to be the main stock bowler, not something that suited his abilities or age. After overnight rain the wicket was sticky for England's second innings, and should have been right for Grimmett, but Hobbs (49) and Sutcliffe (LBW to Grimmett for 135) played one of the best opening stands in the history of cricket, putting on 105. It was such an inspirational effort that the rest of the England team lifted for an improbable but mighty win by just 3 wickets. Grimmett's other wicket was Jardine (33), whom he bowled. Overall it was an unsatisfactory performance by the Australians who were now beaten 0:3. The Ashes were England's to have and to hold.

England carried their fine form into the Fourth Test at Adelaide. Grimmett lifted his rating in front of his home crowd but again couldn't stop Hammond, who settled in well and went on to 119 not out as England made 334. Grimmett bowled his best for the series, taking 5 for 102 from 52.1 overs, picking up Sutcliffe (64) and Jardine (1).

Australia went out with its strongest batting line-up for the series and opened with Archie Jackson, who stroked a fine 164 in his Test debut. He helped the home team up to 369 and into the lead on the first innings.

England began shakily before Hammond (177) and Jardine (98) worked up a big reply with a third-wicket stand. After

Hammond reached 30, skipper Jack Ryder brought on Grimmett. He deceived Hammond with a top-spinner, which Ryder spooned back as a catch on the on-side. Grimmett took a side-step to snaffle it. The non-striker, Jardine, made what appeared to many observers to be a deliberate blocking move. Grimmett couldn't tell if Jardine had made the move reflexively or on purpose. Regardless, it was effective. Grimmett didn't think of appealing under the hardly used and controversial obstructing the ball rule, but one of the umpires said later that had Grimmett appealed, Hammond would have been given out.

That incident aside, the batsmen gave little away in amassing a stand of 262. Grimmett went from his best to his least effective bowling stint for the series, returning 1 for 117 as England reached 383 and a lead of 348.

Australia now had a frightening fourth-innings target that no team in the history of Test cricket had achieved anywhere near. Yet with the fearless young bloods, Jackson and Bradman, to bat there was a feeling of hope. Australia may well have been victorious had Bradman not been run out for 58. Australia fell 12 runs short.

Grimmett was the only bowler to retain his place for the Fifth Test and was surrounded by a new set of companions—Wall, Hornibrook and Oxenham—to take on this formidable edifice of English batting. They did no better than the squad at the beginning of the series, England amassing 519 and Grimmett having another lean time with figures of 0 for 40. Bradman (123) and Woodfull (102) led the charge in response as Australia reached 491, just 28 short. Grimmett, who liked to dispense advice to batsmen at any opportunity, scraped together a surprisingly stylish 38 not out in an important final-wicket stand of 59 with Hornibrook (26). These runs were vital in a series where the two teams' scoring capacities had converged noticeably in the last three Tests. Thanks to

Australia's strengthened batting line-up there was now nothing between the teams.

Wall's refreshing speed (5 for 66) and Grimmett's guile (2 for 66) held England to 257. Hobbs (65) once more fell to the spinner as did Hendren, whom he bowled for 1. That left Australia with the more manageable target of 286 to win, which they did.

Grimmett was Australia's best bowler, taking 23 wickets but at a cost of 44.52 apiece. He needed support so that his captain could use him more as a surprise bowler, not someone with whom the batsmen became familiar. His first-class figures were better. He took 71 wickets at 34.25, with five 5-wicket bags. In the following season, 1929-30, a trial year for the 1930 Ashes tour of England, Grimmett cemented his place with 82 wickets at 23.69. He had improved by 20 runs a wicket from his Test effort the previous year, and by 10 runs from his last first-class performance.

Apart from the Tests, Grimmett's most gripping game was in Adelaide against New South Wales just before Christmas in 1929. In New South Wales' second innings Grimmett bowled brilliantly, dismissing Fairfax (46), Jackson (82), Bradman (84), McCabe (70), Allsop (73) and two others to return 7 for 136.

'Grimmett bowled magnificently,' Bradman recalled just on 70 years later. 'Some of the balls he delivered that day (24 December) were the most difficult I ever played.'

'He had everything going, particularly the wrong'un, which was unusual. He preferred the top-spinner to deceive, but he was getting so much turn he employed the wrong'un more on this particular occasion. But it wasn't just turn. He was flighting them beautifully, getting drift. It was a fine display of the art of wrist-spinning.'

Why was it unusual for him to employ the wrong'un?

'He didn't have a great wrong'un. Consequently he didn't

use it that much. Clarrie's wrong'un was easy to pick. He couldn't disguise it very well. His main ball was the leg-spinner without too much turn on it. He had a very good top-spinner and a good flipper. He tended to bowl the flipper more as he got older. His strength was his capacity to bowl with tremendous control. He was very accurate. I once saw him take a wet ball and deliver five overs without one loose delivery.'

Did he bowl any flippers that day in Adelaide?

'Yes. He delivered his complete repertoire.'

How was Bradman out?

'LBW to a top-spinner.'

Plumb?

'I wasn't umpiring,' Bradman replied with a chuckle, 'but I would say so, yes.'

Grimmett looked forward with nervous anticipation to his second England tour. He was 38 yet as fit as anyone in the team except perhaps the young Bradman who was 17 years his junior. Grimmett continued to practise with the enthusiasm of a teenager and left Australia with Woodfull's squad ready to be recognised as one of the great spinners of all time. His decade-late start had made him even more determined to set new records.

1930—Unsung Hero

From the first game of the 1930 season against Worcester Bradman with the bat and Grimmett with the ball served notice to all England that Australia intended to win back the Ashes. Bradman hit 236 and Grimmett took 4 for 38 and 5 for 46 to finish off the job. In his next game, Grimmett took 7 for 46 against Leicester, followed by 2 for 17 and 3 for 57 against Essex. Then in a game against Yorkshire at Sheffield in mid-May, Grimmett did something that took the cricket world's eyes off Bradman. According to *Wisden*, coming on with the score at 46, Grimmett 'bowled with wonderful accuracy and varied his break and flight with delightful ingenuity'. It was needed, even if the pitch was rain-affected. Yorkshire had the strongest batting line-up of the counties with Holmes, Sutcliffe, Oldroyd, Leyland, Barber, Mitchell, Robinson, Wood, Macaulay and the old-stager Wilfred Rhodes batting at number 10. Grimmett sent down every ball he knew and took all 10 Yorkshire wickets for 37. He clean-bowled four of them, while number two keeper Charlie Walker stumped three, and three others were caught. It was the third time an Australian had taken 10 in an innings in England, Howell performing the feat in 1899 and Mailey in 1921. Bradman could not top that unless he scored a triple century—statistically as rare as taking 10 wickets—which he failed to do though he did play brilliantly that day according to *Wisden*.

Both players continued on their merry way in May, Bradman collecting 1,000 before the month was ended and Grimmett mowing down every county in his path with further big bags of 5, 6 and 7 wickets (twice) against Lancashire, Surrey, Oxford University and Hampshire. Grimmett was overshadowed by Bradman, especially given Bradman's magnificent innings of 252 not out in 267 minutes against Percy Fender's Surrey team. But in the cold analysis of winning and losing, Grimmett and Bradman were equally important to Australia's success in the Tests. Someone had to get the runs at a rate that would allow Australia to dismiss the opposition twice—that would be the 21-year-old Bradman. But no matter how many runs the tourists piled up, they still had to dismiss the opposition twice to win. Overlooking this simple fact was Australia's undoing in 1926 and 1928-29. Bradman had yet to prove himself in the Tests in England and the spectre of the proven Hammond, who had slaughtered Australia's bowlers in the previous Ashes contest, made Woodfull and his men apprehensive.

England won the toss in the First Test at Trent Bridge and batted. Woodfull brought Grimmett on at first change with the score on 63 and Hammond batting. Grimmett dished up nine leg-breaks and then slipped in the cunningly disguised top-spinner. It trapped the champion LBW for 8 and the Australians were relieved. The leggie then caused a sensation by luring Woolley from his crease to have him stumped for a golden duck. Three runs later he bowled Hendren for 5. Chapman (52) helped his team recover to 270 over two rain-affected days, with Grimmett taking 5 for 107. The Australian batsmen let Grimmett down on a tough, wet wicket by only notching 144.

When Grimmett went out to bowl again Australia was 126 in debt. Hobbs and Sutcliffe launched England's second innings with an opening stand of 125. Grimmett finally removed Hobbs, stumped by Oldfield the same way he had been in Australia. In came the bothersome Hammond to face Grimmett, whose length was now perfect to a centimetre. Once more, Grimmett cleverly served him up several leg-breaks. Each one was calibrated to spin a fraction less than the last, and Hammond's eyes were out on stalks trying to pick that damned toppie. Grimmett refused to bowl it and instead each ball reduced the spin with the leg-break action. Then, just at the right moment, he pushed through a much faster, fuller ball on leg stump, which hardly turned at all and trapped Hammond back on his stumps, dead in front. He was on his way for 4, again artfully deceived by a true magician.

England made 302, and Grimmett took 5 for 95, giving him 10 for 202 for the game—equivalent in batting terms to a century in both innings. Australia had 429 to make to secure victory. In the pre-Bradman era this would have been a nigh-impossible task in the fourth innings of a Test on a pitch that was much more a bowler's delight than a batsman's, but the English fans were beginning to realise that this new batting star might just do it. Australia reached 6 for 316 with Bradman on 131 and Robins bowling his leg-breaks. The batsman received a terrific wrong'un and was bowled off stump.

Grimmett would have loved the ball, one of the best Bradman ever faced.

'I still have nightmares over it,' Bradman told me seven decades later. 'I was well set. We had 113 to win and four wickets in hand ...'

After Bradman was out the next three wickets fell cheaply and Australia was all out for 335. England won by 93 runs.

Between the Tests, Grimmett continued his rampage against the counties taking 6 for 24 and 1 for 35 against Surrey at The Oval. In the Second Test at Lord's England made 425 with the dashing young Indian Duleepsinhji stroking 173 before Grimmett had him caught by Bradman. Grimmett took just 2 for 105 but his second wicket was even more significant for the fate of the Ashes. Hammond was on 38 and looking set, yet wary of the leg-spinner, who this innings bowled the top-spinner often, varying it with the leg-break. Just when Hammond was looking comfortable picking both deliveries, Grimmett hurled up a wrong'un to match Robins' at Trent Bridge, and bowled him. Grimmett had dismissed Hammond before he could do any damage in three successive innings.

Australia's reply was a whopping 6 declared for 729, with Bradman playing his technically perfect innings of 254 and Woodfull battling on for 155. Now, for the first time in several Tests, Grimmett could play the millionaire and not worry about bowling tight. There was plenty in the bank. He turned profligate and tossed the ball higher, causing the batsmen to mishit. He bowled Hobbs for 19 and forced Woolley back on to his stumps. He had Hammond caught for 32 and Hendren for 9. Chapman made 121, but England was all out for 375. Grimmett the destroyer had taken 6 for 167. This time the batsmen didn't let him down—they lost 3 wickets getting the

72 runs needed for victory. The series was 1:1. If Grimmett was Australia's best player at Trent Bridge, Bradman took that honour at Lord's.

Grimmett continued creating mayhem against almost every county, taking 6 for 75 and 5 for 58 against Yorkshire at Bradford. Mid-season he was taking scalps with more alacrity than Geronimo.

The team stayed in Yorkshire for the Third Test in July, when the weather was better. Woodfull won the toss and batted. Australia was 3 for 458 at stumps with Bradman on 309 not out. He went on the next day to 334 in 375 minutes, hitting 46 fours. Australia rattled up 566 against a strong bowling attack led by Larwood, Tate and Geary with Tyldesley, Hammond and Leyland in support. The speed of Bradman's massive run accumulation set most matches up for the bowlers. Grimmett contributed a gritty 24, taking inspiration from Bradman's organised genius and Woodfull's determination.

Hobbs and Sutcliffe set off on the long chase on a good wicket and saw off Wall, a'Beckett, McCabe and Hornibrook. The score reached 53 and these two looked settled. No-one had troubled them. Woodfull brought Grimmett into the attack a little belatedly, but to immediate effect. He sent down a quicker leg-break to Hobbs (29), who now could be labelled his mature bunny, and the opener edged it to gully where a'Beckett took a stunning catch. Grimmett then had Sutcliffe (32) caught by Hornibrook. The leggie's double breakthrough made England vulnerable, especially with the out-of-sorts Hammond at the wicket, but Grimmett couldn't remove him this time. Hammond went on to make 113 and helped England to 391, with Grimmett mopping up the tail. Grimmett ended up with 5 for 135 off 56.2 overs, acting first as an attack bowler, then an end-plugger for long spells, and finally a lower-order destroyer. After him, the Australian bowling looked ordinary, although a'Beckett was accurate and steady. England batted again in deteriorating weather. Grimmett put a stop to Hammond (35) again by beating him with a fast leg-break, which was nicked to Oldfield. Grimmett had now dismissed him five times for low scores or uninfluential knocks in the three Tests played. If Grimmett could claim him and Hobbs as bunnies, then no greater pair in the history of the game to that point had been mesmerised by one bowler. England struggled to 3 for 95 and a draw.

Ten days later at Manchester, the weather shortened the Fourth Test. Grimmett failed to take a wicket in England's only innings of 8 declared for 251, but showed his batting capacities once more with a fighting 50 out of 345. His batting had a certain flourish, not at all like a tail-ender.

Grimmett wanted to play every game, eager to make up for his lost decade. At Taunton, he toyed with the Somerset side, taking 3 for 38 and 7 for 33, and followed it up with 8 wickets against Glamorgan.

In the deciding Fifth Test at The Oval, England batted first and put in a firm bid for retaining the Ashes. However, Grimmett's form was the best in his career so far, and he could not be denied or kept out. He cajoled Duleepsinhji (50) into a dip that ended in a catch to Fairfax. Then he swung the game back Australia's way by bowling Leyland for 3. Hammond, seemingly unable to come to terms with his run of outs against Grimmett, looked uncomfortable coming in down the order to face him. It was no surprise to see him bowled by McCabe for 13. England nevertheless was on top at the end of day one with 5 for 316, Sutcliffe on a solid 138 not out. The next day Grimmett stepped in and aided Fairfax in wrapping up England's innings at 405, which kept Australia in the game. Grimmett took 4 for 135 off 66.2 overs. Once more he was the main bowler, delivering twice as many overs as the others.

Australia responded with 695. Bradman was dominant with 232 and well supported by Ponsford with 110 and four others who reached 50. England's spirit was broken and they struggled to 251, Hornibrook taking 7 for 92 and Grimmett 1 for 90. Australia won by an innings and 39 runs, and took the series 2:1.

Those most responsible were Bradman and Grimmett. Bradman scored 974, a Test record that still stood at the beginning of the 21st Century, at an average of 139.14. Grimmett took 29 wickets at 31.89. Over the entire 1930 England season Grimmett took 144 at 16.85, snaring 15 five-wicket hauls and five 10-wicket hauls. Bradman scored 3,170 runs at an average of 99.06.

Years of Plenty

The West Indies toured Australia in 1930-31 and Grimmett continued where he left off in England. He enjoyed the chance to bowl to a new squad of cricketers who had never seen a bowler with his control and surreptitious skill. In the First Test at Adelaide he took 7 for 87 from an innings of 296. In the second innings he bowled the fine West Indian batsman Learie Constantine and grabbed another 4 for 86, setting up Australia for a 10-wicket win. Kippax scored 146 but Grimmett would have been player of the match with 11 for 173.

In the Second Test at Sydney he took 4 for 54 in the West Indian score of 107, but in the second innings of 90, Hurwood and Ironmonger had done the damage before he came on, and Grimmett took 1 for 9. Australia won a second time by an innings and 172 runs. Ponsford gave the best performance of the match, hitting 183 in Australia's only innings of 369. In the Third Test at Brisbane Bradman scored a masterly 233 from 558, and this time Grimmett did the rest, taking 4 for 95 (West Indies 193) and 5 for 49 (West Indies 148) for an overall 9 for 144. Australia won by an innings and 217 runs. The tourists were often put out due to impatience, for they had never faced someone so accurate or cunning. If Grimmett saw them coming down the wicket at him he was happy; if they went back on the stumps, sooner or later he would deceive them with turn or no turn at all. Oldfield was often part of the act, stumping several batsmen without fuss or exuberance. The combination was so quietly lethal that spectators were often unsure of the method of dismissal. Oldfield would gently tap off a bail, and the batsman would be on his way.

At Melbourne in the Fourth Test, Ironmonger upstaged his bowling companions by taking 7 for 23 and 4 for 56 on his home wicket. Grimmett picked up 2 for 46 and 2 for 10. Bradman's 152 would have put him in contention for player of the match. Australia won by an innings and 122 runs, their fourth successive win.

In the Fifth Test at Sydney, Grimmett was the best of the Australian bowlers, taking 3 for 100 as the West Indies declared at 6 for 350. Australia's reply was a weak 224 and Grimmett picked up just 1 for 47 when the tourists declared again at 5 for 124. Australia made 220 in its second innings to lose by 30 runs, and win the series 4:1.

Grimmett's series figures were 33 wickets at 14.94 apiece, enough to suggest he was the best player of either side, Bradman included. He was just as effective in the Shield competition, taking another 36 wickets at 19.52. In all, he took 74 first-class wickets at 19.14. In the 1931-32 season, which included a tour by South Africa, he had much the same figures. He had a reputation for being just as effective on good wickets as bad. He was never ineffective or out of the game, and could come on and dismiss a troublesome opener or wrap a tail with equal facility.

The Springboks were another team who had never faced a bowler of Grimmett's calibre, and it showed in every Test they played in Australia. At Brisbane in the First Test Bradman set the tone with a terrific double hundred from 450 and South

Africa were shot out for 170 and 117. Ironmonger again managed the rare feat of overshadowing Grimmett with 5 for 42 (from 170) and 4 for 44 (from 117). Grimmett's contribution was such immaculate line and length that he went for a little more than one run an over, taking 2 for 49. In the second innings he played second fiddle to Wall (5 for 14), taking just 1 for 45. Australia won by an innings and 163 runs.

In the Second Test at Sydney in December 1931 Australia won by an innings and 155 runs. Grimmett hit his straps in that Second Test, being the best of the Australians with 4 for 28 and 4 for 44 from South Africa's 153 and 161. Bradman (112) and Rigg (127) set up the win. McCabe's 4 for 13 in South Africa's first innings and 79 with the bat out of Australia's only innings of 469 made him a contender for the best performer throughout the contest. Then again, so was Grimmett with 8 for 72 over the two innings.

At Melbourne for the Third Test, Australia was bundled out for 198 and South Africa gleefully took advantage, compiling 358. Grimmett held up one end, sending down 63 overs (23 maidens) for 2 for 100. If these figures were calculated in relation to six-ball overs, Grimmett sent down 84 at just above one run an over. Not a wet ball, nor an attempted onslaught, nor a slow-turning wicket could reduce his efficiency.

Bradman (167) and Woodfull (161) led the charge in the second innings to compile 554. Then Grimmett turned attacking match-winner, taking 6 for 92 off 46 overs with 14 maidens as South Africa was dismissed for 225, giving Australia a win by 169 runs.

At Adelaide in the Fourth Test, Grimmett produced the best bowling figures ever attained in an Adelaide Test. The tourists batted first, scoring 308, and Grimmett beguiled every batsman, taking 7 for 116. Bradman then carved his way to 299 not out to take Australia to 513. Grimmett responded with 7 for 83, giving him match figures of 14 for 199 and allowing his team to coast to a 10-wicket win. Who would have been judged man of the match? Surely a player who cracks one off an unconquered triple century would be unbeatable, yet such great bowling twice in a game might have pipped even Bradman's sensational feat.

In the Fifth Test at Melbourne, neither of these champions had any impact. Bradman was out injured, which showed in Australia's score of 153 in the second innings of the match on a rain-affected pitch. South Africa was sent back for 36 and 45. Grimmett was not even needed as Laurie Nash (4 for 18) and Ironmonger (5 for 6) cleaned up the tourists in the first, and Ironmonger (6 for 18) and O'Reilly (3 for 19) did the damage in the second.

Australia won the series 5:0, mainly because of Grimmett with the ball (capturing 33 wickets at 16.88), and Bradman with the bat (hitting 806 at an average of 201.5, the best ever in a five-Test series).

Grimmett had a slump in the 1932-33 bodyline Ashes series against England. In the three Tests he managed only 5 wickets at 65.2 before he was dropped for the last two games. However, his first-class season was still a very good one as he took 55 wickets at 28.67.

Grimmett felt the pressure of serious competition for his Test place for the first time since gaining it in 1924-25. O'Reilly had cemented his spot with an excellent 1932-33 Ashes series, and it meant that Grimmett would have to convince selectors that Australia needed at least two leg-spinners. The left-arm unorthodox spinner Leslie 'Chuck' Fleetwood-Smith from Victoria was now also emerging as a challenger.

Grimmett did well enough in 1933-34 to secure his berth on the boat to England for the 1934 Ashes tour, taking 66 first-class wickets at 21.83. His bowling in 1926 (105 wickets at 17.68) and 1930 (144 wickets at 16.85) would have made it hard for selectors to deny him a third tour. Moreover, Australia's pace attack of South Australia's Tim Wall and Victoria's Hans Ebeling was not penetrating.

More in '34

The selectors decided to take three spinners to England— Grimmett, O'Reilly and Fleetwood-Smith, who ended up missing all the Tests but played a useful support role by taking 106 wickets against the counties for the tour. Grimmett, with O'Reilly at the other end, snared 5 for 53 and 5 for 27 in the first game at Worcester. He kept this form up in the First Test at Trent Bridge beginning on 8 June 1934, taking 5 for 81 in England's first innings of 268, in reply to Australia's 374 (Arthur Chipperfield 99, in his debut). Grimmett removed the openers, Walters (52) and Sutcliffe (63), as well as Leyland, whom he deceived with a slow leg-break that the batsman popped back to him to be caught and bowled.

Woodfull declared Australia's second innings at 8 for 273, giving Australia a big lead of 379. On the last day, England was batting to save the game with Grimmett and O'Reilly destined to do the bulk of the bowling in tandem. Woodfull decided to switch ends, giving Grimmett the River End, which seemed to be more conducive to spin. O'Reilly, delivering from the pavilion end, had the last laugh, taking 7 for 54 as England crumbled to be all out for 141. Grimmett took the rest with 3 for 39, including Hammond (16), whom he lured forward for a stumping by Oldfield, and the Nawab of Pataudi (10). Grimmett's match figures were 8 for 120 against O'Reilly's 11 for 129. Combined, they removed all but one English wicket for the match, which was won by Australia by 238 runs.

England had the better of the weather at Lord's in the Second Test, batting first for 440 (Leyland 109, Ames 120) and bowling on a sticky to send back Australia for 284 and

118. Australia's spinners were ineffective, with Grimmett taking just 1 for 102 from 53.3 overs. It was Hedley Verity's match—he had the sensational figures of 15 for 104. Grimmett had another ordinary Test at Old Trafford, taking 1 (Ames for 72) for 122 off 57 overs, while O'Reilly took 7 for 189 off 59. O'Reilly took the wickets at a cost of 3 runs an over, while Grimmett put a clamp on matters at the other end, going for about 2 runs an over. No matter how many wickets he took, Grimmett was most economical, always able to tie up a batsman at one end, thus allowing pressure to be applied at the other.

He was back with O'Reilly at Headingley for the Fourth Test, taking 4 (Wyatt and Ames among his victims) for 57 as England reached a poor 200. Australia's reply of 584 (Bradman 304, Ponsford 181) should have given them victory, but rain intervened and England hung on to be 6 for 229 in their second innings at the end of the match. Grimmett took 3 for 72, again removing Wyatt and Ames, and adding Keeton to his bag. His 7 for 129 were the best figures for the match. Bradman's effort against the odds and in bad health was the best individual performance of the series. Yet the holder of the Ashes was still to be decided at The Oval, with the teams locked at 1:1.

Bradman (244) and Ponsford (266) lifted once more for the big one as Australia reached 701 in the timeless encounter that in theory could run until Christmas. England fought hard to make inroads into the massive target, but the pressure from Grimmett—the perfect bowler in a game of attrition and patience—wore England down to be all out for 321. Grimmett took Sutcliffe (38), Wyatt (17) and Leyland (110) as he conceded 103 runs off 49.3 overs. Woodfull refused to send England in again and Australia made 327 in its second innings, leaving England another huge tally—708—to make to win the series. The home side was demoralised, and not in the best state of mind to face the trickeries of Grimmett. He lifted as Bradman and Ponsford had, removing Sutcliffe (28), Wyatt (22) and Leyland (17). Grimmett took 5 for 64, finishing off his opponents (on 145) with glee and giving Australia the Ashes after the debacle of 1932-33. He took 25 wickets at 25.7 in the Tests, and during the tour captured 109 wickets at 19.80, taking 5 wickets on 10 occasions and 10 wickets once, in the first match at Worcester.

Grimmett—or 'Old Grum' as everyone knew him then— was now 43 years old, but he certainly didn't show his age on the field, ending the series with the same haul of wickets with which he began it, and with the same vigorous application of his exceptional skills he had displayed for a decade.

Grimmett returned to Australia and kept up his high wicket-taking at first-class level in 1934-35, taking 58 wickets at 20.94. He was picked for a tour of South Africa and on that trip, at 44 years of age, he sampled his first beer after much cajoling by Bill O'Reilly. He was a moderate drinker from then on, and it didn't hurt his bowling. He began modestly in the First Test at Durban in mid-December 1935, taking 2 for 48 and 3 for 83 in a comfortable 9-wicket win. O'Reilly took 8 wickets and their combined success looked set to have an impact on another series. This was confirmed at the Wanderers Stadium in the drawn Second Test as Grimmett took 3 for 29 and 3 for 111, and O'Reilly another 5. In the Third Test at Newlands, O'Reilly took a further 5 for the match, while Grimmett took 5 for 32 and 5 for 35. Grimmett was the player most influential in Australia's win by an innings and 78 runs. His 10 for 67 was followed by 10 for 110 (3 for 70 and 7 for 40) back at the Wanderers in the Fourth Test. O'Reilly, who for the third successive game took 5 wickets in all, was forced into a supporting role once more.

In the final match at Durban, Grimmett took 7 for 100 and 6 for 73, giving him match figures of 13 wickets for 173, and

Australia the series 4:0. His overall Test figures were 44 wickets at 17.03. This placed him third in the record book behind Sydney Francis Barnes' 49 at 10.93 for England on the mat in South Africa in 1913-14, and Jim Laker's 46 at 9.60 against Australia in England in 1956.

The Australian selectors thought that the opposition in South Africa was not strong so any big wicket hauls against them would be ignored in selecting the side to play a much more powerful England team under Gubby Allen. The selectors decided that a Test trial in the form of a testimonial match between a Vic Richardson XI and a Bradman XI in October 1936 would help sort out the team to play for the Ashes in 1936-37. This was a little unfair as Grimmett and O'Reilly would have to bowl to Bradman while Frank Ward, Grimmett's rival for a Test place, would face Bill Brown and McCabe. Richardson's side batted first and Ward ran through them, taking 7 for 127 in a total of 363 (Brown 111, McCabe 76, Oldfield 78). Bradman's side hit 385 in reply thanks to the skipper being in his most devastating form. O'Reilly tied up several batsmen early in the innings but then Bradman (212) got going and smashed him and Grimmett out of the attack, not once but several times each. Grimmett's figures were 4 for 146 off 20.7 overs. Bradman forced him off his normally immaculate length and then lifted and stroked him to every point of the compass. Ward looked the superior bowler. He took another 5 for 100 in the second innings as Richardson's team collapsed for 180, leaving Bradman and Co just 159 to make to win, which they did with 6 wickets to spare. Grimmett took another 3 for 82, giving him 7 for 228 against Ward's 12 for 227. Had Bradman batted against Ward it would have been a different story. Ward, known for his spin not his economy, would have fared worse than Grimmett.

Two weeks later Bradman and his fellow two selectors had a further chance to study and compare Ward and Grimmett in a

South Australian state game against Victoria at Adelaide. Ward took 6 for 107 in one innings while Grimmett failed to impress. Bradman, in his customary direct manner, told Grimmett that he had 'lost his leg-break'. It hurt Grimmett, though he admitted relying on using a greater variety of deliveries, including the flipper, than before. Age was another factor said to be against Old Grum. Ward, his rival, was 16 years his junior. The selectors were also coloured by Grimmett's poor showing during the 1932-33 series when the Englishmen were last out in Australia.

The three selectors dropped Grimmett from the Australian team and replaced him with Ward, who had once played with The Don at St George in Sydney. In the First Test Ward took 8 wickets and justified his place. But thereafter he didn't perform well enough and was dropped after the Third Test.

Grimmett was bitter about being dumped. It affected his efforts during the entire first-class season and he played below top form, taking 48 wickets at 30.06, including just one 5-wicket bag. In 1937-38 he played in another Test trial game to help the selectors decide who would tour England in 1938. The game was a combined testimonial for him and Vic Richardson. This time Grimmett bowled Bradman with a leg-break for just 17 and was overjoyed, telling Richardson: 'That'll teach the bugger.'

Richardson was not as thrilled. He wanted the attendances to be big and with Bradman out so soon they might be smaller. In the end they each received £1,028 and Grimmett took 3 for 39, while Frank Ward, back in contention for the 1938 tour, took 4 for 71.

Grimmett captured another 41 at 20.60 during 1937-38 with 2 hauls of 5 wickets, but it wasn't enough to impress the selectors. He was denied a fourth tour of England. O'Reilly, Fleetwood-Smith and Ward were chosen. At 46, Grimmett's Test career seemed over—and too early, according to good judges. Still, Grimmett was not done yet. In 1938-39, at 47, he helped South Australia under Bradman to another Shield victory, taking 73 wickets at 22.65. Had World War II not intervened the great little champion spinner may well have been good enough to return for one last bout of Ashes cricket. He told writer Neville Cardus it was a pity that conflict in Europe had begun because he'd 'been working on a new type of delivery'.

Clarrie Grimmett was the first cricketer to reach 200 Test wickets, and ended with 216 Test wickets at 24.21, a record at the time. In first-class matches he took 1,424 wickets at 22.28, including 127 five-wicket bags, and 33 times snared 10 in a match.

He coached for some time after retiring from first-class cricket in 1941 at the age of 50. Later in life he sold life insurance. His first wife died in 1968 and he remarried in 1971.

Whatever their differences, Bradman had no hesitation in selecting Clarence Victor Grimmett in his World XI, a fitting tribute to a battler who had to wait far too long to prove he was a champion.

CHAPTER 14

ENGLAND'S
FINEST

WALTER REGINALD
HAMMOND

12

(England)

19 June 1903—1 July 1965

> *'During his era Wally was undoubtedly England's greatest cricketer.'*
>
> SIR DONALD BRADMAN

Ted McDonald, the sinewy, powerful Australian quick playing for Lancashire, was in a fierce mood. It was 19 August 1925 and this Dennis Lillee of his day had just removed two Gloucester batsmen for 20 with controlled brutality. A young, impressive physical specimen named Walter Hammond strode to the Old Trafford wicket with a grace and confidence that suggested he was somebody to be reckoned with. In fact, he had only scored one hundred, admittedly a big one against Middlesex. There had been something of the careless cavalier in his stroke-play that had seen him dismissed early in an innings. He had shown the kind of form often exhibited by young blades intent on quick destruction of bowlers: a drive here, a cut there, perhaps a wallop for 6 over square leg and then, whoops, *out*—usually caught in the deep. Such players stayed a season or two at county level then dropped out. Hammond was 22 years old and could either go the way of the could-have-beens or on to Test cricket.

It was the mean-looking McDonald's first full season in county cricket and he was making impressions everywhere, not the least on batsmen's ribcages. He was the fastest bowler of the era and was backed up by the treacherous ambitions of Cecil Parkin and Dick Tyldesley, who had knocked over the young Hammond before.

The new man took block. McDonald uncoiled his magnificent action, the best ever seen, with an ease that could fool someone who had never faced him before. The first ball was full in length. Hammond stepped into it with an unexpected authority that bordered on arrogance. It flew hard to mid-off and left the fielder wringing his wrist. No run. The second ball was meant to put Hammond on the back foot. And it did. But instead of being left in fearful disarray like scores of batsmen facing McDonald this summer, Hammond rocked backed and hooked him one bounce to the fence backward of square leg.

An over later he played a similar stroke forward of square. McDonald was seething. Tyros were supposed to show fear, not form, against him. The Australian let go a volley of accurate bullets. Hammond intermittently dispatched him to the white pickets. If McDonald had a weakness it was losing his cool at such moments, which were as rare as penny blacks. He was not used to being treated with such defiance and contempt, and banged the ball in shorter and harder. As the sessions and bowling spells came and went, McDonald showed unmatched stamina, but his control was gone. As Hammond responded with crunches beyond the field's reach, the speedster was left with just unscientific, indeed uncharacteristic, brute force. Many deliveries were directed at the batsman's head. McDonald wanted to maim this upstart, send him off legitimately, or on a stretcher. Hammond, in the kind of hooking mood that would be seen on very few occasions for the rest of his career, would not oblige McDonald, crashing his way to 250 not out in a 330-run partnership with A E Dipper that took 238 minutes.

England's selectors took note. Such a performance against the very best bowling combination in the country meant the young Hammond might just be a Test champion in the making.

Once an Athlete

Wally's father William was a bombardier in the Royal Garrison Artillery and before World War I was stationed with his wife Marion and Wally in Hong Kong for three years and Malta for three years. Thus young Wally's very early years were spent in happy sun-filled places. Even from a young age he showed a great love of games in contrast to a loathing for anything even vaguely academic.

At the age of six Wally had to face a tougher life that would in turn shape his attitudes, ambitions, drive and single-mindedness. His father was stationed in France and Wally was sent as a boarder to Cirencester grammar school. His mother had two reasons for this move. First, she felt that he needed a masculine influence, and second, the school was noted for turning out farmers and she thought that the physical Wally would be suited to life on the land.

Wally's father made it to the rank of major but was killed in action just before the end of the war, when Wally was 15. Wally developed into a more sombre, laconic type. He loved cricket, tennis, football and athletics. He was better than most at all sports, but was superior at cricket—a natural at strokeplay, bowling and fielding. All champion bats are remembered for something at school. Wally belted 365 in a house match, which was to be his highest score in any form of the game. Yet house cricket performances like this meant next to nought, with bowlers as slipshod at delivering the ball on the pitch as fielders were at stopping shots. The one significant clue to come out of his school effort was that he very much liked staying in the middle to crunch bowlers. More impressive was his ability to carry his bat through several innings against other schools. His agility, athleticism and raw skills were in evidence. Two other characteristics—determination and ambition—would soon be apparent.

At 17 Hammond finished school and entered the real world. In the next few critical years he would either be noticed by county cricket officials or consigned to a farm labourer's tough life. Hammond, with his square-shouldered stride that registered a raw elegance of bearing, seemed destined for a richer existence. His self-possessed gait when walking out to bat or field bespoke confidence, and this influenced others around him. He was a doer not a talker. Rather than beat his chest he set about methodically murdering bowlers with a style not seen on English fields, save for perhaps Grace and Hobbs, two of the greats of all time.

Hammond joined Gloucester in 1921 and in his second season (1921-22) was selected to play against Warwick Armstrong's all-conquering Australians. In June, just shy of his 18th birthday, he was thrown in against the second-greatest team ever to tour England (Bradman's 1948 Invincibles being the best). A very unconfident Hammond was bowled by Hendry for 1 and took 0 for 53 off 7 overs. He had to endure severe punishment from Charlie Macartney and Warren Bardsley.

'Watching Charlie that day taught me much about foot-work,' Hammond later told Bradman. 'He was the best batsman in the way he moved his feet, used the crease, and for speed (of footwork), that I had ever seen.'

Hammond told Bradman how he went into the nets straight after watching that innings to try to emulate the Australian star, and continued to do so for weeks until he felt he had improved. The apprentice Hammond was a silent learner, an absorber. He knew every stroke in the cricket manual, but set his mind on improving his steps at the crease with all the diligence of a ballet dancer. At first he occasionally got in a tangle, especially moving down the track to spinners, but eventually his footwork would become a hallmark of his superior talent, along with his mastery of most strokes.

He was up for another lesson in August of 1921 when he faced the Aussies again. Macartney danced his delightful rhythms with Bardsley once more and they both went on to make powerful centuries. Hammond was only given 3 overs this time and was belted for 23. Then he had to face the fearsome Syd Gregory and Ted McDonald, who formed one of the best fast-bowling combinations of all time. Gregory was at him first and uprooted a stump for a duck. Hammond walked back to the pavilion wondering if he was ever going to be able to take on the old enemy from the antipodes. Arthur Mailey, the big-turning Sydney leg-spinner, compounded Hammond's insecurities in the second innings by bowling him for 1 on his way to a 10-wicket haul.

In 1922, 18-year-old Hammond again strode into the Gloucester side. His county championship debut was inauspicious as he faced yet another fine speedster, Arthur Gilligan of Sussex, who also bowled him. Hammond may not have been making runs against the great bowlers of the time but he was developing much resilience. In his second game, at Lord's against Middlesex, he made 32. It was an impressive knock against quality opposition, and young Walter Reginald seemed to be on his way. His progress was temporarily held up by the cricket supremo Lord Harris, of the MCC, who dictated that because the young man was born in Dover in Kent, which was Lord Harris' county, he had to serve a qualification period that did not allow him to play for Gloucester for the rest of 1922. This was cruel legal pedantry brought on by Kent's pique at not having secured the young champion. It meant he missed a vital stage of development as a cricketer at an age when others, such as Bradman, had worked their way into the Test arena.

In May 1923, and now legal after a two-year residency qualification, he burst out of the blocks with a century against Percy Fender's Surrey at Bristol, his initial first-class hundred. It took four hours, but it was all class. No-one who saw it was in any doubt that Hammond had Test potential. He followed it up in the same game with a second-innings knock of 92. Not only did he have a quality technique, he had the right temperament too. Two such innings in one match showed he was hungry, in fact famished, and that he had something of the determined mongrel in him necessary to force the bowlers to submit. Gloucester pushed him into opening the batting, which distracted him for a few games, until he crashed scores of 90 and 99 in even time. Yes, he was getting out due to callow excitement, but what a wake he was leaving behind him after these carefree cameos.

Hammond's figures for 1923 reflect his status as a promising all-rounder. He made 1,421 runs at an average of 27. His 18 wickets were collected at a cost—41 runs apiece, but he took 21 catches and fielded brilliantly. He was still only 20, a boy among hardened professionals, but few of them had better statistics.

Wisden said he was 'one of the best professional batsmen of the future' and that he was 'irreproachable in style'.

Slow Progress

Hammond wanted to make quick progress, but wet fields and black days of no play made 1924 a frustrating year. He managed 120 against Somerset in June and later 96 against Oxford, but generally he was in too much of a hurry, wafting, hooking and driving at balls he shouldn't have. It seemed that *Wisden*'s proclamations had put too much pressure on him. Nevertheless he salvaged much for his team and himself in the last innings of the season when he made a blistering 174 against Middlesex, which stopped them winning the County Championship. Hammond came of age in this innings, ruthlessly going for the bowlers' jugulars with a magnificent array of off-side strokes. They looked technically perfect and authoritative, and were struck with a power that Bradman later remarked was megawatts above everyone of the era.

'You have to think of Viv Richards in the modern era to imagine someone comparable,' said Bradman.

1924 ended with Hammond averaging 30.22 from 1,239 runs with 2 centuries and 4 fifties. He took 29 wickets at 26.72 and held 30 catches.

Hammond missed the tour of Australia in 1924-25, and went backwards at the beginning of the hotter, drier 1925 season, making 7 runs in 5 innings. In May he scored just over a hundred runs, woeful for a player capable of 10 times that. His misery with the bat continued into June, but he compensated by taking a lot more wickets and catches, which boosted his flagging confidence. In the middle of the season he finally struck form with the bat, making 121 against Kent at Maidstone in quick time on a dangerous wicket. In that same game he took 7 wickets and 2 catches. There was no question that Hammond had both guts and skill—it was a matter of combining these two and checking any silly adventurism. Against Derby he hit 76 and took 5 for 57. In August he played the most dazzling innings of his career to that point with 250 not out against Lancashire and Australia's Ted McDonald. He ended the season with 1,818 runs to his name at an average of 34.30, with 3 centuries and 9 fifties. His average had crept up steadily: 27, 30 now 34. He took 68 wickets at 29.46 and held 65 catches. At 22, Wally Hammond had arrived as a serious all-rounder in first-class cricket, but he knew, and so did the Test selectors, that his batting was what would make or break him.

Early in 1926 he toured the West Indies, who did not yet have Test status. His average moved up to 45, boosted by 238 not out in five hours. It was his third big, important knock after his 174 against Middlesex in 1924 and his 250 not out against Lancashire.

Late in the tour he was stricken with a mystery disease brought on, it was said, by a mosquito bite to the groin region. It could have been this or blood poisoning or a strange West Indian venereal disease—even a combination of all three. Whatever it was, it had a debilitating impact on Hammond, who ended up in a Bristol nursing home facing death. He recovered after a year but was depressed about missing the entire 1926 season and a Test series against the visiting Australians. Hammond had missed two cracks at Ashes Tests, first due to bureaucratic malice and now illness. His team-mates noticed that the mild cheerfulness he had once displayed had dried up. He was withdrawn, and the word 'moody' was used to describe him for the first time. How his pent-up ambition and lonely near-death experience would manifest at the wicket was anyone's guess.

He managed to channel his darkened temperament into a torrent of runs in May 1927. It began with a century at Gloucester then a pair of centuries against Surrey at The Oval. He reached the coveted 1,000 in May. Beating the freezing, wet weather was perhaps as much a feat as defeating the bowlers.

After his illness the mysterious Wally was transformed into a true champion. It was obvious to all who saw him play at Old Trafford again against Lancashire and McDonald. In the first innings he drove the Australian demon speedster for 5 bound-aries—3 on the off, 1 straight and 1 on the on—in succession from the first over of the first morning. McDonald exacted belated revenge by having Hammond caught behind for 99, but in the second innings Hammond made all the bowlers submit, as he stroked and drove his way to 187 in 180 min-utes.

Bowlers from every county were now paying for Hammond's lost time. He was meaner and more purposeful in everything he did. It was as if his illness had made him focus on staying at the crease longer in order to dominate the game. His defence was tighter; his bat was closer to the pads than ever before; and he eschewed the hook and was judicious about which ball to cut. If anything, he was cutting late, with a grace and precision displayed by few in history. He refused to drive at anything too wide, whereas in the past nothing seemed too distant. For accumulation he employed the leg-glance, which he had once ignored as effete. Another of his more delicate developments was a beautiful shot picked off the toes. He began using a pulled drive rather than the hook—a safer shot if you had the eye. Always good off the back foot, he began driving harder in this position than ever before. Only a player with his muscular shoulders and forearms could penetrate a field so proficiently while hovering on a back leg. Hammond turned what was usually a defensive stroke into an offensive one, arguably with greater effect than anyone before or after him save for Viv Richards.

Greater circumspection allowed Hammond to stay at the wicket longer so that he could deliver unparalleled off-side strokes and straight drive more often per innings. More time at the wicket also saw him gain confidence in lofted drives. In long stays at the crease he began indulging in golf-like drives with long carries through and over the field—shots that would be dangerous if the batsman were not settled in, but calculated minor risks if he were set and capable of laser-like precision.

In 1927, Hammond was a new man and better cricketer, ready for anything. It showed in his season's figures. His average shot up to 65 from an aggregate of 2,825 runs. It was enough to secure him a tour of South Africa, and he made his Test debut at the Old Wanderers in Johannesburg at Christmas 1927, at the age of 24. There were few fireworks early in the game and he took 0 for 21 off 8 overs in South Africa's first innings. He came in to bat at number four after century-makers Sutcliffe and Tyldesley had set the scene nicely for him.

He scored 51, a most satisfying start to a Test career. Buoyed by this, he swung the ball prodigiously in South Africa's second innings, taking 3 wickets for no runs in 23 balls and ending with 5 for 36. England won by 10 wickets. He continued to display his all-round skills at Cape Town a few days later with 43, 14, 3 for 53 and 2 for 50. England won again, this time by 87 runs.

At Durban in the Third Test Hammond failed to take a wicket in a drawn game, but hit 90. Surely a big Test hundred would come soon, most observers opined. It wasn't to be in the Fourth Test where he managed a start in both innings (28 and 25) and took 3 for 62 and 1 for 20.

England was without Tate and Larwood for the entire tour and lost George Geary to injury in the Second Test, causing an inordinate burden to fall on Hammond. After a wearying county season and his illness a year earlier he struggled as the South African tour wore on. He was making runs but not with the sparkle of the county season. He took 1 wicket at Durban in the last Test and made an unremarkable 66. The tour finished in early February and Hammond was able to put his tired feet up in Bristol for a vital two months before the 1928 county season and a tour by the West Indies for their first-ever Test series.

A rested and rejuvenated Hammond amassed another 2,969 runs at 69 as the season unfolded. He took 84 wickets at 23 runs apiece, compared with 20 wickets at 44 in the previous season. He also snaffled 78 catches.

Hammond commenced his first Test on English soil on 23 June 1928 at Lord's. The West Indies players were mediocre opponents, not much above middling county standard despite having a good, fast attack. Hammond made a respectable 45 but with Larwood and Tate back in the national team he was not called upon to bowl much and claimed just 1 wicket in a crushing win by England. He snared another wicket in the

Second Test at Old Trafford and notched 63. A solitary victim fell again at The Oval in the final Test and he made just 3. Hammond's promise of 1927 and 1928 in the county games was not apparent in the Tests. He was now 25 years and had yet to score a Test century. Former Test skipper Plum Warner came out often in his defence, believing it was a case of 'just you wait and see'. Unfortunately for England fans, Hammond's burgeoning as a Test star was not for their eyes. It was to come 20,000 km away in Australia during the 1928-29 tour.

The Awakening of Wally the Great

Hammond was in terrific company on that first tour down-under. The batting order, perhaps the strongest ever to line up for England, read: Hobbs, Sutcliffe, Hammond, Jardine, Hendren and Chapman. Tyldesley and Leyland, champions both, could not squeeze into the early Tests. Hammond cruised to a form-finding 145 in four hours at Adelaide in the second game of the tour, and found the faster, bouncier Aussie wickets to his liking. When the squad reached Sydney for the New South Wales v MCC match, he was in fine fettle. He and Hendren figured in a huge partnership of 333 before a slightly built fellow delivering ordinary leg-breaks had Hendren caught in the deep. Hammond decided that this kid should be taught a lesson and smashed him out of the attack. Then in the next over, the same unknown who had just been banished from the bowling crease figured in a freakish bit of fielding. He flung himself to his left to grab the ball, then wheeled right to throw down the stumps with Hammond halfway down the pitch. Hammond was annoyed with himself for getting out at 225. He felt a triple century was in the offing. In the dressing room he asked Hendren who the fielder was that ran him out.

'They say he's the best fielder in Australia,' was the reply.

'Name's Bradman. Don Bradman.'

'Bradman,' Hammond repeated, making a mental note to be careful of this young kid's arm. 'He got you out, didn't he?'

'Yes,' Hendren replied, 'he got both of us.'

Hammond thought nothing more of the incident until he saw Bradman bat. The boy with the nervous grin made 87 and later 132 not out to save New South Wales from defeat. Hammond thought there were both promise and flaws in the 20-year-old's technique. Though England dominated the game, Bradman scored 229 for the match for once out, compared to Hammond's 225. It was a minor point, but the beginning of a colossal two-decade struggle for supremacy between these two cricketing giants.

For the entire 1928-29 season Hammond's reputation was second to none though he started slowly in the Test, failing to take a wicket in the First Test at Brisbane, and being dismissed for 44 and 28 in England's huge 675-run win. At Sydney he came to the crease at 1 for 37 in reply to Australia's 253 and methodically went about constructing his first Test century, making it a double. Admittedly the Australian attack was the weakest in 30 years without McDonald and Gregory. Nevertheless, Hammond's dissection of Grimmett, Ironmonger, Blackie and Nothling was cool and professional. He stayed at the wicket for nearly eight hours and hit 30 fours. England won the game by 8 wickets.

In the Third Test at Melbourne Hammond went on to a consecutive double hundred, this one exactly 200 in 398 minutes with 17 fours, a feat never achieved before in Tests. Not unnoticed, especially by the big Melbourne crowds, were Bradman's performances. It was his second Test and he scored 79 and 112. He was not yet the answer to the indomitable Hammond, but then no-one—not even the more experienced Hobbs, Sutcliffe, Hendren or Jardine, who had started the season with three successive centuries—could hold a candle to the Gloucester man that summer. However, there was a noticeable levelling of the teams in that Third Test, which England won by a slim 3-wicket margin thanks to the finest opening partnership (Sutcliffe 135 and Hobbs 49) ever seen on a sticky.

At Adelaide in the Fourth Test Hammond further cemented his place in sporting history by notching 199 not out and 177. This made him only the fourth player to score a century in each innings of a Test. He became the second player in history to score 4 centuries in one series after Herbert Sutcliffe did it in 1924-25. Hammond's 779 runs in 5 innings became a record for England v Australia Tests. His mighty efforts in both innings of the Adelaide game gave England victory when it should have lost. Only a run out of Bradman on 58 robbed the home team of its first victory of the series. Again, astute observers noted the levelling out of the teams. The inclusion of Archie Jackson (a great 164 on debut) and Bradman had stiffened the home team's batting backbone. They lost by just 12 runs.

At Melbourne in the final Test Hammond 'failed' with 38 and 16, taking his tally for the series to an incredible 905 at 113 runs an innings, a record that most thought would last for decades. His inability to score big again saw Australia cruise to a 5-wicket win thanks mainly to the cool resolve of Bradman who hit 123 and 37 not out.

Hammond took the boat home triumphant, a true hero for having played the biggest part in bringing back the Ashes under the leadership of the jolly and jubilant Percy Chapman. Big crowds greeted the tour party at Dover, where a civic reception was held, then again at Victoria station, where Londoners mobbed them. Hammond was the man they cheered most.

He had been at his absolute peak through the home summer of 1928 and on through the blistering Aussie summer of 1928-29. His desire for more runs was insatiable, and he was determined to keep his well-earned reputation as the world's best bat. Could he keep his marvellous form into the 1929 season and a five-Test series against South Africa?

Before finding out, he was married in April to Dorothy Lister, the daughter of a rich Yorkshire textile merchant. Many were surprised as the 25-year-old Wally had a reputation for playing the field. He began the season where he had left off in Australia with 18 and 138 not out, and English fans expected to celebrate the blossoming of his career. It wasn't to be. In the three other Tests he played (injury kept him out of one) he scored 8, 5, 65, 0, 17 and 101 not out. His average for the series was 58.66, which was excellent—and, as it turned out, close to his career average—but did not live up to the expectations of the fans, who hoped he would average a hundred, as he had done in Australia. His bowling was steady yet not penetrative and he seemed content to let the rest of England's strong line-up of Larwood, Tate, White, Robins and Geary roll their arms over before him.

Hammond's 1929 season was almost up to the higher standard he set in 1927 as he hit 10 hundreds and averaged 64.63 from 2,456 runs. He took 28 wickets at 34.93 and snaffled 36 catches.

All England hoped, indeed expected, he would repeat his 1928-29 antipodean form against Woodfull's tourists in 1930. The Australian bowling, weak in the last series, didn't look any better. Their batting strength was less easy to predict as their squad contained plenty of new faces, including that Bradman, about whom there had been much speculation. Most English observers, including Percy Fender and Neville Cardus, were betting he would not have much impact on English wickets. He was too unorthodox, flawed and too keen on dangerous shots square of the wicket. Only one person disagreed, and that was Bradman, who let his blade do the talking. His technique may or may not have been flawed but he floored every county in the run-up to the Tests.

Grimmett ruined Hammond's chances of repeating his 1928-29 series by snuffing him out cheaply four times in the first two Tests. Hammond couldn't pick Grimmett's top-spinner. He came back for 113 at Headingley but was upstaged by Bradman who made 334. Grimmett got Hammond in the second innings for 35, thus snaring him five times in six innings. Hammond scored just 13 in the Fourth Test, and 13 and 60 in the Fifth Test at The Oval. Australia won the series 2:1.

Hammond's Test series aggregate was 306 and he averaged 36, whereas Bradman notched 974 and averaged 139.14, toppling Hammond's record of 1928-29. Bradman's world record has stood since then. All those close to Hammond knew that being superseded by Bradman affected him deeply. There can be no doubting Hammond's skill, character and strength of mind. He was just unfortunate to come along at the same time as someone with even greater skill and powers of concentration who would have dominated any era. Being eclipsed by Bradman in 1930 didn't make Hammond curl up and die, far from it. He was only 27 and he would fight on.

Hammond ended the 1930 season with 2,032 runs at an average of 53.47. He took 30 wickets at 30.93 and took 31 catches. He toured South Africa in 1930-31, scoring 49, 63, 57, 65, 136 not out and 75, before failing only in the last three innings with 15, 29 and 28. His aggregate was 517 and he averaged 57.44, again close to the overall figure he would end up with after two decades at the top. He took a few wickets and in one spell managed 2 for 9 off 11 overs. He seemed to eschew his bowling in favour of his batting, especially with England well served by other bowlers during this period.

Hammond was off the boil in the rotten wet 1931 season when New Zealand visited England. He scored 1,781 at just 42.40 an innings. Still, he took 47 wickets at 31.00 and held 46 catches. He carried his ordinary batting form into most of the three Tests, but showed at The Oval with 100 not out in as many minutes that he could turn on scintillating performances when he had a mind to and Lady Luck was running his way. The Kiwis were gallant in their first official Tests overseas, but no match for the might of England. Hammond faced greater challenges in the fiercely competitive county matches, where he returned to his higher aggregate range (2,528) and got closer to his overall average (56.18). He took 53 wickets at 27.98 and took 50 catches.

In a prelude to another tour of Australia, England had one Test against India at Lord's in 1932. Hammond managed 35 and 12 with the bat but played a useful part in England's 158-run victory by taking 3 for 9 off 5.3 overs. He may have been reluctant to roll his arm over, but he could still be effective at Test level.

Bodyline Blues

Hammond played a low-key role during the bodyline tour under Douglas Jardine. In the First Test at Sydney, when he opened his account with 112, he looked as if he could give the unspectacular Australian attack a pounding as he did in 1928-29, but subsequent scores of 8, 23, 2, 85, 20, 14, 101, and 75 not out, while commendable, were mortal. He could easily have turned 2 centuries into 4 given his last not-out innings and the way he was proceeding towards three figures in the fateful Third Test at Adelaide. He was into the 80s, it was late in the afternoon and Bradman was bowling his innocuous leg-spinners, a most unusual sight at this level. Ames had just joined Hammond at the batting crease. Hammond made a point of walking down the wicket to the new man and telling him not to relax against this part-timer.

'Can't lose another wicket tonight,' he instructed. Bradman overheard.

'I thought I had nothing to lose by tossing up a leg-break, hoping that Wally would be tempted to loft me,' Bradman said, 'although his remark to Les Ames demonstrated that he probably would not. In any case, I over-pitched. Wally seemed to be caught in two minds for a fraction of a second and was bowled. I think he probably was heeding his own advice, which got him tangled up with the instinct to give such a delivery full treatment.'

Wally stormed off in high dudgeon. Ames had never seen him so angry. Getting out to such a ball was always a moment of shame for any batsman, but for Hammond to fall this way to Bradman compounded the horror.

Did the Don derive satisfaction from this dismissal?

'Considering it temporarily got rid of England's greatest bat, I most certainly did,' he said.

Jardine threw the ball to Hammond to bowl more often than he would have liked under the hot southern sun, yet he did not let the team down, taking the impressive wickets of Stan McCabe and Victor Richardson for 37 in the First Test, and 3 for 21 (including Richardson's wicket again) in the second innings of the Second Test at Melbourne. He was not called on to deliver 'fast leg-theory', which succeeded at maiming Australia's batsmen and nullifying Bradman. The Don was reduced to an average of 56.57 for the series—in effect, the value of one great batsman such as Hammond rather than two. Hammond didn't join Gubby Allen and the Nawab of Pataudi in publicly protesting against Jardine's directives, but he wasn't happy with them and said so privately. However, he was relieved to see that Bradman's figures for the series (396 at 56.57 in four Tests) were much the same as his own (440 at 55 in five Tests). There would be no snide chipping and chiding about his inferiority to Bradman, at least during this Ashes series. While The Don's averages and aggregate were cut in half, the great game was also reduced in stature. Australian cricket administrators and politicians protested but the MCC, without the benefit of instantaneous communication, remained ignorant of the impact of events 20,000 km away.

Hammond rejoiced at being part of a team that was met at the docks and at Victoria station by jubilant England fans who needed something to make them feel proud again during the Great Depression. The Ashes had been brought back in a ruthless yet superb campaign. Hammond, with a tour average similar to that in the Tests, could claim a substantial part in taking the Ashes. The Aussies could squeal all they liked, but the series had been won by methods within the rules of the game as they stood.

Before the team returned to England they played a couple of Tests against a very weak New Zealand team. Hammond, still hungry for big scores at the end of a tiring tour, hit 227 in the First Test at Christchurch, and 336 not out at Auckland in the Second. These knocks did wonders for his Test average, and the triple hundred broke Bradman's record of 334, adding a touch more humiliation for the Australian. However Hammond knew his triple hundred wasn't worth much in reality because of the weak New Zealand opposition. It was a world away from scoring even 50 in an Ashes Test. Like his rival Bradman, Hammond did not go in for stodgy, boring run accumulation. His 300 came up in 288 minutes, the fastest in Test history, with the last century coming in just 47 minutes. Hammond sailed away laughing from those idyllic New Zealand isles with a Test average for the two games of 563.00, which, for what it was worth, was the highest ever for a Test rubber.

Reality struck on his return home. After the celebrations, he had to face the quick West Indians Martindale and Constantine in the summer of 1933. They had read about the success of bodyline and decided to deploy the tactic themselves. With the fabulous Larwood laid low with injury after his superhuman effort downunder, any English retaliation would be limited. England won the First Test at Lord's easily by an innings and 27, Hammond contributing a modest 29. In the Second Test at Old Trafford, a drawn game, he faced bodyline and was hit on the chin by a fierce Constantine bumper that left him bleeding and shaken. Not long afterwards, he was caught in the leg-trap fending off the speedster for 34. Only Jardine, showing his iron grit when struck himself, was able to withstand the barrage in scoring a magnificent 127. It was his last hurrah for England. The MCC now understood why Australia's complaints had merit. Jardine was replaced as captain for the Third Test and would never play for England again. Hammond, still uncomfortable against this kind of intimidation, was softened by the quicks, then dismissed by spinner V A Valentine for 11. Despite the West Indian approach, England won again, prompting Jardine to say bodyline was nothing to complain about.

Hammond made it known that if bodyline was the way cricket was heading, with every team choosing Neanderthal pacemen to brutalise opposing bats, then he wanted no part of it. He threatened to retire.

Meanwhile, back in the counties, he went about slaughtering fairer bowlers, amassing 3,323 at 67.81, top of the averages for the first time in his career in England. At age 30, King Wally of England was performing at the height of his powers. However, with the Australians coming again in 1934, he wore his crown uneasily. He had to face one of the best—if not *the* best—spin combinations of all time in Grimmett and O'Reilly.

In May he was stricken with a bad back but made the First Test at Trent Bridge, only to be dismissed by O'Reilly, caught for 16, in the first innings and by Grimmett, stumped for 16, in the second. He breathed more easily knowing that his mysteriously ailing *bête noir*, Bradman, was himself not in touch. Australia won its first Test since Bradman had begun playing without him scoring a century. England won the Second Test at Lord's, but Hammond, quick to get up the other end to avoid O'Reilly, was removed by Chipperfield for just 2. Wally's mood grew blacker with the only compensation being Bradman's further puzzling failures of just 36 and 13.

In the Third Test at Old Trafford O'Reilly bowled Hammond for 4 in a magic over in which he took 3 wickets. Bradman went down for just 30, due to the lingering peritonitis that had wasted him to a gaunt figure and a severe throat infection that kept him confined to bed when he wasn't batting. The drawn game left the series wide open at 1:1. Scribes scratched their heads at the simultaneous decline of the world's two most outstanding batsmen, who had been missing in action in nine innings between them. Something had to give at Headingley in the Fourth Test. Hammond batted in England's first innings and, after surviving a combined onslaught from the spinners, got a beauty from paceman Tim Wall and was bowled for 37. In the second innings he was run out for 20. Timing had always been a forté of Bradman's, and in Australia's only innings he overcame illness and doubt at precisely the right moment, hitting 304. Although the game was drawn, it demoralised England.

In the Fifth Test, Hammond fell for the one and only time to Hans Ebeling for 15, and then O'Reilly, who caught and bowled him for 43. Bradman soared on to 244, and with Ponsford (266) set up England for destruction in the second innings when Grimmett took 5 for 64.

Australia took the 1934 Ashes series 2:1 and Wally retreated to the county games, where he had been in his best form all season. Commentators were mystified by his inability to turn it on in the Tests, but Woodfull, ever mindful of Hammond's enormous skills, had laid traps for him everywhere. If Jardine and now Bob Wyatt had used the catchcry 'let's get Bradman',

Australia was equally keen to stop Hammond. Woodfull had every captain's dream of a bowling duo who could put constant pressure on Hammond, coming at him every 20 seconds with guile and skill. There was nowhere to hide from Grimmett and O'Reilly. Their variety was wide and deadly, a batsman possibly receiving eight or even 10 types of delivery inside 2 overs. For five gruelling Tests in the 1934 series, Hammond faced these two at their peak. He could be excused for a poor series as anyone in the history of cricket would have been disadvantaged against O'Reilly and Grimmett.

Black Dog Years

Hammond sailed off to the Caribbean with hopes of recovering his Test form, but only succeeded in maintaining his figures against teams who were below Test level. He netted 789 runs at 56 an innings. His best effort was 281 not out against Barbados, a typical Hammond thundering double century.

In the Tests beginning in early 1935 his top score was 47 and he could average only 25, though to be fair, the weather conspired against him. The conditions suited more stubborn players who were content to drop a dead bat on everything and slacken their wrists for hours rather than a player like Hammond. England went down 1:2 to a West Indian side flush with speedsters such as Constantine, Martindale and Hylton. From that series on, the West Indies never looked back.

A few days after being under the Caribbean sun, Hammond braved a bitterly cold April and padded up for another season for Gloucester and England in a five-Test series against the improving South Africa. He was fatigued from the continual grind of first-class cricket and preoccupied by a range of things from tonsilitis, through to problems with the new LBW law, according to which you could be out even if the ball pitched outside off stump. Gone was the unbridled enthusiasm of his youth. Wally Hammond, approaching 32 years, had done it all twice over on the cricket field. Hammond's jowls grew more lugubrious in this period, he was keen to bowl and he became more and more withdrawn. A new chum at the club was unlikely to find Wally inviting him for a rollicking introductory night at the local pub. An old associate in the game would be shocked to get a lunch invitation. Yet still, through the gloom, he made more runs than anyone else in England in the 1935 season (2,616 runs) and at an average of nearly 50. He also took 60 wickets and 54 catches.

Despite being more withdrawn than ever, he had his eye on the main trophy left for him to attain: the captaincy of England. Apart from making and keeping the right contacts at the MCC, he had to lift his Test ratings to make it clear to all that he still had the power to dominate at the top level.

In the Tests against South Africa he improved his performance with scores of 28, 27, 27, 63, 87 not out, 29, 63 not out and 65. At Lord's in the Second Test he bowled a bit, taking 2 for 8, and 1 for 26. Bob Wyatt cajoled him to the bowling crease in the Third Test at Headingley, where he removed Mitchell (who had won the Lord's Test for the tourists with 164 not out) for 8 and 58, and then again cheaply in the Fourth Test at Old Trafford. England went down 0:1 with four Tests drawn.

In 1936, Hammond finally faced the knife and had those troublesome tonsils removed, which caused him to miss the First Test against the visiting Indians. He played in the Second at Old Trafford and regained the international form that had evaded him for years. He came in at 1 for 12 and hammered a century in as many minutes, going on to 167 out of 261 in 183 minutes. Writers went into raptures about the return of the 'old Hammond', meaning the youthful, more carefree player of a decade earlier. He went on to The Oval for the Fourth Test and hit 217, the first-ever double century against India by an Englishman. It took him 290 murderous minutes and he hit 30 fours.

In this mood, he was unstoppable. In August he scored a record 1,281 runs, capped off with a stunning 317 against Nottingham. That humming Hammond off-drive, which scorched the grass, was only matched by cover slashes off the back foot. He couldn't have been in finer shape for the next stanza of his career, a third trip to Australia. It may not have been a new challenge, but it was one that brought a hint of a smile to his lips.

Allen's Challenge

His excitement and anticipation were justified the moment he left the gangplank at Perth in early December 1936. He hit four successive centuries in the preparation for the First Test, which concluded a fine sequence of scores since his 167 in Manchester totalling 2,106 in 23 completed innings at an average of 91. He was fit and ready to take on Bradman, the new Australian skipper, and his men, who to every England batsman's pleasant surprise did not include Clarrie Grimmett.

'They (Australia's selectors) must be mad,' Gubby Allen remarked to Hammond.

'And wonderful,' Hammond replied, showing a rare glimpse of his well-hidden sense of humour. The only world-class bowler in the opposition line-up was now O'Reilly.

However, fortunes in cricket can be fickle. Hammond faced a lively Ernie McCormick, who had him caught for a duck at short leg. In the second innings, he was out (hit wicket) to spinner Frank Ward for 25. Bradman fared no better, making 38, and then on a rotten sticky after torrential rain, was out for a duck. The weather did the most to win the game for England by 322 runs. In the Second Test at Sydney, Hammond recovered his form of the previous half-year with a thumping 231, his fourth double century against Australia. It took him a workmanlike 458 minutes and he belted 27 fours. It was a more subdued effort than before, yet one required in a tight Ashes contest.

The rain came down again and Bradman was caught out on a sticky again for a duck. He batted better in the second innings for 82, but the damage had been done by Hammond's mighty innings, which led to England's second successive win. Hammond's scores at Sydney in Tests to date were 251, 112, 101, 75 not out and now 231 not out for an aggregate of 770 at 256.66. Wally the wonderful had conquered Sydney, which had to be one of his favourite arenas. Certainly none other had been as productive at this level for him.

Hammond and the rest of the touring squad enjoyed the furore surrounding Bradman as many observers called for his sacking as captain, but they did not relax. They had all chased too much leather from the little champion over the past decade to become complacent. Bad weather marred the Third Test at Melbourne and Bradman failed again, deceived by Verity for 13 in Australia's score of 200. England batted on an awful glue-pot with Hammond at his very best, scoring 32 from 9 for 76 declared. Hammond himself ranked this cameo as his finest innings, better than any double century he ever hit.

Bradman sent in his rabbits, O'Reilly and Fleetwood-Smith, to open the Australian second innings and kept himself down the order to avoid the dirty wicket for as long as possible. He came in at 5 for 97 and went on to make 270, thus evening up his performances with Hammond—who was bowled by Sievers for 51 in the second innings—for the series so far. When Bradman performed like this, Australia usually won; this time it was by 365 runs.

This left the series in the balance with England ahead 2:1 and two games left to play. The weather had given England the edge in its two wins, and Australia in the other. At the business end of the series it was up to Hammond or Bradman to take control. As the sides' top jousting knights, one would probably be knocked off his horse and one would stay on. Then again, the series outcome could well depend on something much more prosaic, such as the weather once again.

Australia batted first and Bradman was dismissed by Allen for 26 in Australia's 288. Hammond also couldn't get going in England's innings and was removed by his nemesis, O'Reilly, for 20. Australia began their second innings, which was Bradman's last chance to keep his team in the hunt to retain the Ashes, 42 runs in arrears. As ever, he rose to the occasion with another big score. Hammond, who had taken 2 for 30 in the first innings, was called on to make an even bigger effort as Bradman built his score. In the end, Hammond caught and bowled Bradman—for 212. It was a minor consolation and, in Hammond's mind, came 200 runs too late. Nevertheless, he snared an impressive 5 (including Fingleton) for 57 and forestalled serious embarrassment for his country in containing Australia at 433. That left England with the huge task of scoring 390 to win. It was up to Hammond to deliver another double hundred. At 39, he received one of the best-ever deliveries in Test cricket from the left-arm wrong'un bowler, Fleetwood-Smith. It drew Hammond forward. The ball swerved away from him in the air, then spun back between bat and pad and disturbed his timber. England crumbled at 243. The series was level and 2:2.

The Fifth and deciding Test at Melbourne was played in front of huge crowds. Australia batted first and reached 604, Bradman again dominant with 169 and well supported by McCabe with 112 and Badcock with 118. England was fatigued and succumbed to the venom and guile of O'Reilly. Hammond, the key to his team's chances, was out for 14, and England was all out for 239. Bradman enforced the follow on.

In England's second innings, Hammond looked his best, making an attractive 56 in 95 minutes. O'Reilly then deceived him and Hammond drove it straight to Bradman for a simple enough catch. It was clear that Hammond had not come to terms with O'Reilly's nagging habit of bowling steadily on his leg stump. Sooner or later, he had to hit out. After Hammond's demise, England capitulated and surrendered the Ashes again. Hammond's stupendous beginning to the season had ended disappointingly for him and his legion of followers. Yet England, losing 2:3, and Hammond with 468 runs for the series at 58.50, were not disgraced. He had batted to his capacities yet was troubled by spin from O'Reilly and Fleetwood-Smith, who, while no Grimmett, was the next best thing.

Hammond frowned, sighed at the what-might-have-beens and moved on to another satisfying county season in 1937, topping the averages at 65.04 from 3,252 runs for the fourth time, and swatting 140 in the first of three Tests against New Zealand. His other Test scores—33, 0, and 31—were disappointing, but as England won the series 1:0, he was more challenged by Gloucester's battles for the county championship. He took 48 wickets at 22.79 and held 38 catches.

Captain Hammond

In 1938 Hammond turned amateur so he could captain England for the first time against Bradman's touring Australians. Like generals leading two marauding armies, these two champions stroked their way across England for the first big clash, the Trent Bridge Test. En route, Hammond belted 4 centuries and scored 951, while Bradman reached 1,000 and also hit 4 centuries. Once more, Hammond's build-up to the series was formidable and he looked set for a fine contribution, but he had to contend with O'Reilly, who bowled him for 26 in the first innings of the First Test at Nottingham. It was of little consequence except as a psychological battle between the bowler and the batsman. England rumbled on with centuries from Bennett (126), Hutton (100), Paynter (216) and Compton (102) to finish the innings on 8 declared for 658.

Hammond, perhaps frustrated about being deprived of time at the crease, confronted the young Compton after he was caught out on 102 sweeping in a cavalier fashion.

'You don't do that against Australia,' Hammond said. 'I thought I told you to get 200.'

Compton, thrilled at having scored his first Ashes century, was chastened. Their exchange did not endear him to Hammond the captain, or the man. Compton later said he never received praise from Hammond.

Bradman scored 51 and 144 not out and took the honours between the two champions, while McCabe stole the man of the match, with 232, his finest Test innings. The match was drawn.

Hammond turned the tables at Lord's with a smashing 210 on the opening day, scoring 70 before lunch, another 70 between lunch and tea and a third one in the final session. Hammond loved the easy batting pitch, while O'Reilly hated it. England ended the day on 5 for 409. Hammond pulled countless balls during his superb performance and was still there at stumps with every intention of going on to a world record. McCormick spoiled his plans by bowling him with a prodigious inswinger after he reached 240. Bradman for once couldn't match him and was out for 18. McCabe dismissed Hammond in the second innings for just 2, while Bradman saved Australia with a rearguard 102 not out in his second knock. This game was also drawn.

The series remained locked after a washout at Manchester. In the Fourth Test at Headingley Hammond won the toss and batted. He looked positive when he came in and was set at 76 when O'Reilly, wily as ever, gave him an off-break and bowled him. England sank for 223. Australia replied with 242, Bradman hitting 103, his third hundred in as many Tests. England replied and O'Reilly and Fleetwood-Smith immediately spun the ball. Hammond arrived at the crease aware that O'Reilly was spinning his leg-break more than normal. Anticipating that Hammond would be looking for a big leg-spinner, O'Reilly delivered a wrong'un and bowled him for a duck. England collapsed for 123. Australia struggled but polished off the runs with 5 wickets to spare. England was drawn 0:1.

The historic Fifth Test at The Oval saw England grind its way to 7 for 903, with Hutton, not Hammond, hitting a world record 364. Hammond was this time trapped LBW by Fleetwood-Smith for 59. Bradman injured an ankle and did not bat. Australia collapsed without him and was given the biggest thrashing in Ashes history. This left the series unresolved at 1:1, and Australia went home with the Ashes in its keeping for the third successive series.

Hammond was relieved that he did not lose his first series as skipper but was dissatisfied with his own efforts, though his figures were good: 344 at an average of 66.8. It was in his nature to brood on his failures, whereas Bradman always put them behind him and moved on. Both were perfectionists, one intent on righting wrongs, the other more relaxed and focused on matters that he could influence.

Hammond had fewer worries on a tour of South Africa in 1938-39. He achieved his best Test figures since his 1928-29 season in Australia, with scores of 24, 58, 181, 120, 1, 61 not out, 24 and 140 for a total of 609 at an average of 87. Just as pleasing for him was his meeting with a Durban beauty queen, Sybil Ness-Harvey. They began an affair, and Hammond returned to England a happy and successful skipper with a 1:0 Test win and a new, secret relationship.

War Stops Play

Hammond was appointed captain of Gloucester and lifted his county to third place in 1939. The experienced old campaigners on the circuit predicted war before the year was out, as conflict widened in Europe. Nevertheless, Test cricket carried on, this time a three-game series against the West Indies. Hammond was again content with a 1:0 win, but unhappy with his own efforts of 14, 30 not out, 22, 32, 43, and a little salvation with 138 in the final innings at The Oval. Less than a month later, England was at war and Hammond's cricket career was over for the time being. At 36, with still plenty left in him, a successful period for a powerful young England line-up under his leadership was cut short.

Hammond joined the Royal Air Force in October 1939 and was immediately commissioned. An England skipper with no experience of the military was never going to be rushed to any front line. Hammond was given public relations work, and played a bit of cricket. He had a stint as an instructor, the idea being that as captain of England and Gloucester he might know a bit about gaining new recruits' attention. This he did a little overbearingly, taking his role seriously and humourlessly.

He was initially stationed in Sussex and Devon but at the end of 1940 he was posted to the RAF's Middle East headquarters in Cairo, from where he managed to wangle trips to South Africa for assignations with the stunning Sybil. Fibrositis struck him in this period, coincidentally about the same time as it struck Bradman in Australia. Hammond was sent back to England at the beginning of 1944 and discharged from the RAF in 1945. He played in the so-called Victory Tests against the Australian RAF in 1945, scoring a century in each innings in one fine game against the Dominions. Only a dashing young

Australian airman named Keith Miller upstaged him with a fabulous 185.

Decline and Fall of a Champion

With hostilities over, Hammond returned in 1946 to play for Gloucester and England in a three-Test series against India. Just to show that at the age of 42 he had lost very little, if nothing, he began the season with 5 innings of 132, 134, 59 not out, 143 and 104. In the Tests he led England to another 1:0 series win. His own performances in the Tests were undistinguished with scores of 33, 69, 8 and 9 not out, but his season for Gloucester was as strong as ever as he compiled in all first-class games 1,783 at 84.90 with 7 centuries and 9 fifties. His bowling days were over though. He sent down just 6 overs for 1 wicket at 14 runs, and took just 19 catches. Regardless, his batting alone was easily enough to persuade England selectors that in 1946-47 he could lead the national side downunder on his fourth tour.

Hammond's team was strong on paper and began hopefully against the Australian states. His own form was mediocre and spinners in the final game against Queensland troubled him, but he was unconcerned. Grimmett and O'Reilly had retired. He had heard that Ray Lindwall was quick, but speedsters from Australia had come and gone with little impact. Certainly the country had produced no-one of note since McDonald and Gregory in the 1920s. Miller was fast enough, but he had not concerned Hammond in the Victory Tests and the Dominion match.

No, Hammond's main worry was not Australia's bowlers. It was Bradman. He had experienced a long, debilitating fibrositis episode but, with the same quiet determination that had marked his cricket over two decades, had nursed himself back to fitness and some sort of form, although every honest observer said he was just a shadow of his former self.

Bradman's batting in the First Test at Brisbane confirmed their doubts. He seemed unsure, stiff and cautious early in Australia's first innings. At 28 he chopped down on a ball, attempting a late cut off paceman Bill Voce. Ikin took the ball at second slips. Hammond moved delightedly forward to congratulate the bowler but Bradman seemed unconcerned. There was a belated appeal, after which the umpire called not out. He and the square leg umpire saw the incident clearly, as did Lindsay Hassett batting with Bradman. All three plus Bradman were not in the slightest doubt that it had been a bump ball. Ikin, Hammond and other English fielders were certain it had been a catch.

'I had a clear view of it,' Hassett said later, 'and I was surprised at the fielders' reaction. Don played it hard into the ground and it slid out to Ikin. It was a bump ball.'

'Fine way to start a bloody series,' a bitterly disappointed Hammond remarked to Bradman, who remained his impassive self. The English press sent bleating 'we wuz robbed' reports back to England, blowing the incident out of proportion. Bradman went on to 187, regaining form and confidence, and with Hassett (128) lifted Australia's score to 645. England was then caught on a sticky and dismissed for 141 and 172, Hammond falling LBW and bowled to left-arm medium-pacer Ernie Toshack for 32 and 23.

The series had started badly for England and there were grumbles of discontent in the team. Alec Bedser would have liked an encouraging word or two, and some advice on how to bowl to Bradman. The skipper remained uninspiring and uncommunicative, preferring the company of friends, away from the team hotel.

Hammond's demeanour did not improve in the Second Test at Sydney when Colin McCool had him caught behind for 1. England could only manage 255. Australia replied with 659,

Bradman and Sid Barnes both hitting 234. This compounded the pressure on Hammond, whom McCool again removed, this time for 37, as England went under by more than an innings.

Bitterness had crept into the England camp, and Hammond, realising that his great powers were declining, now regretted the trip. His age had caught up with him and he was feeling it more due to his and the team's failures. Bradman, as fiercely competitive as ever, would give no quarter after the Third Test at Melbourne was drawn. Hammond, now feeling like a bunny at a shooting gallery, succumbed cheaply in this game to two more bowlers, Bruce Dooland and Ray Lindwall for 9 and 26. Toshack caused his undoing, dismissing him twice for 18 and 22 in the Fourth Test at Adelaide, which was also drawn. Hammond had had enough. He decided not to play in the final Test at Sydney, and Norman Yardley took his place at the helm. He led a losing side.

Hammond's 33 appearances against the old enemy had netted him 2,852 runs at 51.85. He had scored 9 centuries, including 4 doubles, as well as a further 7 fifties. His complete Test record saw him score 7,249 runs at an average of 58.45. He hit 22 centuries, 7 doubles, a triple and a further 24 fifties. Bradman acknowledged him then as England's greatest batsman of that era. Hammond took 83 wickets at 37.80 and held 110 catches. His 85 Tests represented the finest all-round England career to that point. It was a magnificent record.

After divorcing first wife Dorothy in 1945, he was free to marry Sybil on his return from Australia in April 1947. Roger, the first of their three children, was born in 1948, then came Carolyn in 1950 and Valerie in 1952. Hammond played some club cricket and a farewell game for Gloucester in 1951, at the age of 48. He'd had no practice and made just 7. Thus officially ended his phenomenal first-class career, which saw him make 50,551 runs at 56.11, including 167 centuries. From 1933 he had headed the national batting averages for a record eight summers in succession. He hit more than 1,000 runs in a season 17 times in England and five times overseas. He got beyond 2,000 in a dozen seasons and 3,000 in three. He hit 167 centuries, 36 times reaching a double century and four times topping 300 in 1,005 first-class matches. (Only Bradman, with 37 doubles and six triples from 338 innings, did better.)

From the late 1940s, he absorbed himself in business, wrote on cricket for an evening newspaper and compiled three books on cricket with the help of ghostwriters. In the early 1950s, Sybil persuaded him to leave England and live in South Africa, where he coached cricket for a time. Barry Richards came under his tutelage. Hammond became general manager of Denham Motors in Durban and when the firm went under he became a sports administrator at Natal University. In 1959 he survived a serious car crash from which he took some time to recover.

Bradman spoke with admiration for Hammond the cricketer and competitor. He didn't feel he was a natural leader (Bradman didn't think he was himself), but as a conventional type of captain. In the little they had to do with each other off the field, Bradman always found Hammond cordial and modest, if reserved. Bradman liked reserve and modesty. Bradman was relaxed enough to tell him the odd joke, yet it appeared that Hammond didn't share Bradman's propensity towards humour. Bradman didn't find him a poor communicator, just laconic.

'I always found him polite, very English. He was always courteous,' said Bradman.

Of their rivalry, Bradman was circumspect.

'I think it was overplayed,' he said. 'After all, neither of us could do much to influence the efforts of the other. He rarely bowled to me, and I was never going to threaten him with the ball. I think there was much more direct competition between Wally and Bill O'Reilly.'

Bradman thought Hammond 'an excellent all-rounder, who could have taken many more Test wickets if he had been of a mind to bowl more'. 'He was also a top-class slipper,' he said.

Whether these old sporting foes would have become friends in their later years will never be known. Hammond died of a heart attack in 1965, aged 62.

Bradman paid Wally Hammond, his greatest long-term international rival, the ultimate compliment by naming him in his best-ever world team.

Index

Photo Credits